SUNDERLAND AFC

SUNDERLAND AFC
The Definitive History

ROB MASON

ICON

Published in 2024, this book gives some records as up to 2023, 2024 or even 2025. This varies depending on whether a record could be broken or not within twelve months of publication.

Published in the UK in 2024 by
Icon Books Ltd, Omnibus Business Centre,
39–41 North Road, London N7 9DP
email: info@iconbooks.com
www.iconbooks.com

ISBN: 978-183773-016-2
eBook: 978-183773-017-9

Text copyright © 2024 Rob Mason

The author has asserted his moral rights.

No part of this book may be reproduced in any form, or by any means, without prior permission in writing from the publisher.

Typeset by SJmagic DESIGN SERVICES, India

Printed and bound in the UK

CONTENTS

1. Beginnings — 9
2. The Team of All The Talents — 61
3. The Greatest Season — 86
4. Almost Roaring Twenties — 106
5. Raich and the Thirties — 116
6. The Bank of England Club — 132
7. Browned Off — 147
8. Stokoe's Stars — 165
9. Murray's Vision — 199
10. Niall's Taxis — 241
11. Short Changed — 261
12. *Sunderland 'Til I Die* & Beyond — 281

Bibliography — 303
Acknowledgements — 307
About the Author — 309
Index — 310

I

BEGINNINGS

How James Allan brought the round-ball game to Wearside 1857–90

On 9 October 1857, fifteen days before the creation of the world's oldest association football team, Sheffield FC, James Allan was born 259 miles away in Green Street in Ayr, on the west coast of Scotland. Allan would one day bring the game of association football to Sunderland, ultimately leading to the creation of Sunderland AFC. Yet this founding father would later fall out with the club he had created to such an extent that he formed the rival Sunderland Albion, and at one point was assaulted when representing Albion back at Sunderland AFC. This drama and intrigue are emblematic of the story of Sunderland AFC, as we shall see.

SAFC became an early giant of the game and has remained so ever since, even if for long periods it has been more accurately described as a 'sleeping giant'. The history of the club intertwined with the passion of its vast support have allowed Sunderland to maintain this status despite the relative lack of recent success compared to its early years in the Football League.

Renowned throughout the football world, Sunderland's support stems from a mixture of the industrial heritage of the city (Sunderland was awarded city status in 1992, a year in which the club played in the FA Cup final) and the enormous early success of the football club, which was bankrolled by some of Sunderland's shipyard owners. This success saw Sunderland proclaimed 'World Champions' in 1895, a year in which they were Football League champions for the third time in four years, providing the base for Sunderland to always be included in any conversation about historically significant clubs. As the Second World War began in 1939, no club had been English champions more than Sunderland. With the relegation of founder Football League members Aston Villa and Blackburn Rovers in 1936 (a year in which Sunderland were champions for the sixth time), for over two more decades, until 1958, only Sunderland could proudly claim to have never played at anything other than the top level. Until Queen Elizabeth II passed away in 2022, only Sunderland could claim to have won a major honour during the reign of every monarch from Queen Victoria to the present day.

When James Allan was an Ayrshire baby, Sunderland was enjoying a fairly prosperous time, explains Marie Gardiner, author of *Sunderland, Industrial Giant*:

> With shipbuilding booming; at the start of the decade the *Sunderland Herald* had dubbed the town *the greatest shipbuilding port in the world*. Its residents were benefitting from the newly opened Mowbray Park, and with new sewers being built and two cholera epidemics now behind them, things were starting to look a little healthier too! Those wanting to cross the river might have found themselves inconvenienced by maintenance going on to repair the Wearmouth Bridge by engineer Robert Stephenson, who added the motto, Nil Desperandum Auspice Deo.

This Latin motto, meaning 'When God is on our side there is no cause for despair', had been adopted by the town of Sunderland eight years earlier. Of course, whenever the football team has a run of games without scoring the *Nil Desperandum* part of the motto can seem only too apt – not

Beginnings

least in 1976–77, when the team incredibly went ten league games without scoring a goal.

In May of the year of Allan's birth in 1857, the town's premier park – Mowbray Park – had been opened by John Candlish, the Liberal MP for Sunderland whose statue now stands in that park. The *Sunderland Daily Echo and Shipping Gazette* did not begin life until 1873, but on the day of Allan's birth, a Friday, on Wearside the weekly issue of the *Sunderland and Durham County Herald* newspaper was published. Amidst much news of the Indian Mutiny – a rebellion against British rule that had begun that year – and reports concerning Sunderland-born Henry Havelock (who has statues in Mowbray Park and London's Trafalgar Square), there were lots of domestic advertisements and snippets that give a flavour of life in the place James Allan would eventually call home.

You could travel from Sunderland by ship to Hamburg for 15 shillings (75p), while a typical advert offered treatment for deafness. Headed 'Deafness and noises in the head', the advert ran:

> Mr. Smith, Aurist in Sunderland from five to eight o'clock every evening at Borough road, opposite Smyrna Chapel. A son of Mr. J. Anderson of Smyrna Place who had been deaf eight years has been perfectly cured by Mr. Smith. Also a daughter of Mr. Atkinson, Station Master, Tynemouth, deaf from infancy and Mr. Spence, 6 Middle Street Tynemouth, deaf five years. N.B. Mr. Smith attends at his usual hours ten to three daily: Sundays to one at 4 Albion Street, Newcastle.

Oddly enough, the Smyrna Chapel was only a goal-kick or so away from what in 2024 is known as the Norfolk Hotel, which in 1879 was a place known to be visited by James Allan after his arrival in Sunderland and which played a key role in the earliest meetings of what would become Sunderland AFC.

James Allan was educated at Glasgow Training College before spending a year studying medicine at university in Glasgow. He then took the decision to become a teacher rather than a doctor. Allan was an early student of the game of association football. Busby, Oxford, East Kilbride and the 3rd Lanark Rifle Volunteers FC were among the clubs he played for in the Glasgow area. The latter of these – which became better known simply as Third Lanark from 1903 – were one of Scotland's highest-rated clubs at the time. The future founding father of Sunderland reached their second XI.

At this time in Sunderland, rugby and cricket were the pre-eminent sports. The Sunderland Rugby Club began in 1873, the first game taking place at the home of the local cricket club, which was then in Holmeside. Association football in the town had not yet started, but Sunderland had already made a significant contribution to the game. The world's oldest association football competition, the FA Cup, had started in November 1871, with the final in March 1872. The competition was the brainchild of Charles William Alcock. He was not only born in Bishopwearmouth on 2 December 1842, but in the very same street – Norfolk Street – as the aforementioned Norfolk Hotel. On 14 April 1841, his brother John Forster Alcock had also been born in Sunderland. Like his younger brother, John Alcock was a leading light of early football. In 1863 he represented the Forest club at meetings that led to the formation of the Football Association. Forest went on to become known as Wanderers – the first winners of the FA Cup.

The creation of the FA Cup was just one of the younger Alcock brother's achievements: he also came up with the idea of international football and Test cricket. Charles Alcock was educated at Harrow School after leaving Sunderland as a boy, having had a spell living at 17 John Street as well as in Norfolk Street. The Alcock family moved south between the 1851 and 1861 census, with Charles Alcock enjoying a privileged education. An obituary of C.W. Alcock in the *Yorkshire Post* on 27 February 1907 pointed out that while it was his brother, rather than Charles, who was at the inaugural meeting of the FA, Charles 'did more than any other individual ... to establish it [the game of association football] firmly'.

Beginnings

Charles Alcock captained the first ever FA Cup winners in 1872 and even had a 'goal' disallowed in the final, in which his Wanderers team beat Royal Engineers 1–0. Alcock went on to referee the cup finals of 1875 and 1879 in a glittering career that saw him hold a series of significant administrative posts within both football and cricket. He also captained England against Scotland in his one official international football appearance in 1875, getting on the scoresheet in the process. Five years earlier he had also captained an England side against Scotland in what was the first unofficial international football match in history. In the first ever official international football match each country named an umpire to assist the referee, with Alcock being his country's umpire for a match with Scotland, which ended goalless. Alcock played in all five games between England and Scotland before the first officially recognised international. The first five games are classed as unofficial because the players representing Scotland in those games were all based in England.

This stellar contribution by a son of Sunderland to what has become the planet's most popular sport was almost entirely unknown and unheralded in Charles Alcock's birthplace as the sport grew. It would be James Allan rather than Alcock to whom Sunderland owes its footballing origins.

The ninth of thirteen children born to William Allan (a shoe-maker) and Helen Ronald, James Allan grew up in Tarbolton in South Ayrshire, a place that was also once home to the Scottish bard Robert Burns. Indeed, Burns's 1780 poem 'The Ronalds of the Bennals' is about the family of James Allan's mother, Burns having once been romantically linked to Anne, a member of the Ronald family from two generations earlier. Burns's brother Gilbert was also linked with Jean Ronald, who apparently rejected him due to his poverty. Both Jean and Anna Ronald are referred to in Burns' poem, and Bennals was the name of the Ronalds' 200-acre farm.

From 1 April 1879, Jimmy Allan became second assistant master at Hendon Board School at a salary of £60, rising to

£90 per annum. Having enthusiastically played association football for several teams in Glasgow, Allan was evidently disappointed to find that the dribbling game – rather than the handling game – had yet to arrive in Sunderland.

Allan arrived in a town that was still on the up, as it had been when he was born. 'A new museum, art gallery, and winter gardens was opened in 1879, after the foundation stone was laid two years prior, watched over by former US president Ulysses S. Grant,' Marie Gardiner wrote. 'The Elephant Tea Warehouse and Grocers – or the Elephant Tea Rooms as it would later become – designed by architect Frank Caws, had recently been finished, and so the town was starting to take shape in a way we can recognise today. Horse-drawn tramways were an exciting new way to get around, running from Monkwearmouth to Roker by the Sunderland Tramways Company.'

James Allan did show some interest in rugby as a spectator member with Sunderland Rovers. They played at the Blue House Field in Hendon, which would become the first home of soccer in Sunderland. However, rugby was never going to satisfy the sporting demands of the young teacher.

Bringing a round football back to Wearside with him after his first trip home to Scotland, Allan began to introduce the game to his teaching colleagues and friends. Among those believed to be involved with Allan in learning about the game were Walter Chappel, who was assistant master at Hendon Board School around this time, William Elliot, a teacher at Thomas Street Board Boys' School in Monkwearmouth, Robert Singleton, headmaster at Gray School and John Coates of Rectory Park School, as well as John Sewell, who taught at Herrington Wesleyan School. Sadly, Sewell would pass away on 28 October 1888 as a result of a swimming accident in Gatton, a town in Queensland, Australia, where he had emigrated in 1886. Sewell had studied at Westminster Training College in 1877–78 and was one of the early players likely to have had some experience of the round ball game while at teacher-training colleges or public schools in the south of England.

Beginnings

Some debate exists concerning the earliest days of what we now know as Sunderland AFC. A case has been made for the club to be dated from 25 September 1880 instead of the long-accepted date of October 1879. This is a matter of defining the difference between the words 'formed' or 'founded'.

What is certain is that its existence was formally announced to the wider world on 25 September 1880. On that date there was a meeting of the Sunderland and District Teachers' Association, which was not called for the purposes of announcing a football club, but James Allan and his associates took advantage of the chance to announce that they had formed a football team.

This was reported in the *Sunderland Echo* on 27 September 1880. However, was this the very start of what we now know as Sunderland AFC? Does a relationship begin when it is announced to the world in the formal setting of a marriage or even an engagement – or does it commence when the couple meet, are attracted to each other or go on a first date? What preceded the announcement of the football club to the world in September 1880? Clearly the people making the announcement did not do so on a whim at that moment. Where had this desire come from?

Having brought a round ball to Wearside, Allan began to introduce friends and colleagues to the sport of association football. As with any new sport, this took some time as players developed new skills and learned new rules. It certainly wasn't as if one day a team started and soon after they played a proper game. Clearly they would not be anywhere near ready for that, and in any case it was not as if the area was teeming with other clubs looking for fixtures. To begin with, the early life of what grew into the club we know today involved kickabouts with a group of teaching colleagues. Imagine a modern-day pre-season where players train and get fit before even thinking of playing a friendly, let alone a competitive match. In comparison, this period can be seen as a giant pre-season, but in terms of preparation for the future development of the team and the game.

One of Allan's colleagues was John Grayston. Born in Halifax on 21 March 1862, he arrived in Sunderland in 1877 as a pupil-teacher at Hendon Board School. Only since 1870 had children aged between five and ten had to go to school, and as records of school meetings show – when they weren't discussing football – attendance was often very poor. Most teachers in these day schools were unmarried women, which is why even to this day female teachers are almost invariably addressed as Miss, regardless of their marital status. It also meant James Allan didn't have an awful lot of male teachers to call upon for football. As a pupil-teacher, Grayston was teaching younger pupils as well as continuing his own education.

Grayston not only had an aptitude for learning, but also for recording the history of the club, and while some of his later memories are known to be chronologically inaccurate, were it not for many of Grayston's articles even less would be known about the club's earliest years.

Writing in the *Sunderland Weekly News* in 1931, by which time he was approaching seventy and remembering things from when he was seventeen, Grayston recalled experiences at Hendon Board School yard: 'This is the actual and spiritual home of Sunderland Association Football.' Acknowledging his own fallibility of detail, he added, 'and though all the memories of later and more scintillating years may come between, my clearest memory is of my first game in the play yard'. Accepting Grayston's hazy memory as an old man, his 'clearest memory' of the 'spiritual home' nonetheless seems key to the earliest origins of the club.

It is likely, although not definite, that James Allan was one of seven new members admitted to the Sunderland and District Teachers' Association at their quarterly meeting recorded on 13 September 1879. This would have given Allan the opportunity to sound out any interest in playing association football. An obituary of Walter Chappel in 1898 stated that Chappel, a fellow teacher at Hendon Board School, was the first gentleman approached on this subject.

As interest in the game developed, along with the proficiency of those playing in Sunderland, the possibility grew of staging games against other teams. This was not a simple task. As Grayston noted they 'found difficulty in getting fixtures, many of our Saturdays being spent in practises.' Not that it seems Allan's troops were ready for stern opposition. 'I must confess that we needed these Saturday practises very much, but we were very conscientious in our training.'

However, an advert published in the *Athletic News* on 22 September 1880 made clear when they were ready. This pointed out that the closing date for entries to the first season of the Northumberland and Durham Cup was on the 25th of the following month. Three days later, at the Rectory Park Schools meeting, came the announcement that Sunderland had a team with elected officials.

This is a significant date in the history of the club, but not necessarily the beginning of the club. The *Sunderland Echo* of 9 October 1880 records the 'first practice match of the season' rather than the 'first practice match' or 'first practice match ever.' This match at the Blue House Field in Hendon was staged between a captain's XI and a vice-captain's XI, with the vice-captain's side handsomely winning 5–0.

There is no record of Sunderland playing a game against another club until 13 November 1880 against Ferryhill, but that is not to say football was not being played. It is possible but unlikely that a formal full-sized game was played against any other club prior to that Ferryhill game. Even in practice matches there were unlikely to be sufficient players to make eleven-a-side games possible. If any did take place, they are likely to have been the exception rather than the rule.

On Monday, 8 November 1880 it was reported that the draw had been made for the first round of the inaugural Northumberland and Durham Football Association Challenge Cup. Ferryhill were drawn against Darlington Grammar School, only for the latter to withdraw and therefore hand Ferryhill a bye into round two. Now without a fixture for 13 November, Ferryhill arranged a friendly with Sunderland at the Blue House Field for what was Sunderland's first known match, which was 40 minutes each way. Losing the toss, Sunderland faced a strong wind in the first half but soon scored their first ever goal, or 'point', as it was recorded – only to have it disallowed. Given that in years to come the club would be docked the first ever points they won in the Football League, this disallowed 'goal' would seem to be a prelude for many a disappointment, at least in the modern era.

Sunderland's line-up in this match was: Robert (Bob) Singleton in goal (captain), John Thomas Taylor and Adam Shearlaw as backs, Joseph Lake Gibbons and John Anderson as half-backs and a six-strong forward line of Edward Guy Watson, Matthew Barron, Peter Dove, Frank Woodward, Walter Chappel and James (Jimmy) Allan. All except Dove, a merchant's office clerk, were teachers by profession. For the record the Ferryhill side was: W.J. Kitching, E. Latheron, J. Hodgson (captain), J. Soulsby, J. Barry, T. Field, J. Mann, F. Devine, J. Oliver, J. McCutcheon and M. Carney.

Match reports in both the *Sunderland Echo* and the *Newcastle Journal* fail to mention that the Ferryhill match was Sunderland's first ever game, but both do state that Sunderland were without their five best men. Quite possibly the reporters had been fed this information by a club official, but if this was a first ever game how would anyone know who the five best men were? A report in the *Athletic News* does state that Sunderland staged its first match, but this is not completely clear as to whether it is a first match ever, a first match of the season or most likely a first match against a different club. Notably, no fewer than four of the members present at the September 1880 announcement – Grayston, Sewell, Elliott and Coates – were not in attendance for this game, and if it was a very first match would it not be more likely that, having put so much effort into getting a team up and running, they would be there and eager to play?

It was Ferryhill that scored the solitary legitimate goal of the match. Although the scorer is not recorded, Geoff Wall, a local historian from Ferryhill, speculates that it may have been J. McCutcheon, one of Ferryhill's six-man attack, who two years later would play regularly for Sunderland. Wall also suggests that the game with Ferryhill might have come about through Sunderland player Adam Shearlaw.

'Ferryhill at that time were in what they called the Palatine League,' says Wall. 'There were two players who played for Sunderland at the time who were prominent names in Ferryhill, so that may have been the connection for the game to have been arranged in the first place. The oldest house in Ferryhill was owned by a family who came from the Sunderland area. One of the players was a guy called Adam Shearlaw. He was a teacher at an orphanage in Ferryhill which was where his house, the Manor House, was, and he might have been the connection with the teachers' team at Sunderland. I can't be 100 per cent about this but it is feasible. There had to be a connection somewhere and especially in terms of arranging a game in those years, because we're not talking about just jumping in your car to get there, are we?'

Adam Shearlaw and John Anderson both hailed from the same Berwickshire village and had moved to Sunderland to be teachers. Anderson appears to have been a lodger with James Jardine, a Scot who was a *Sunderland Echo* reporter and who played a couple of games for Sunderland in the first two seasons. Perhaps this connection is how some of the club's early games are well documented in the *Echo*?

Despite many mentions in the press over the following couple of decades, when the formation would have been fresh in the minds of so many, the original date of 1879 was not questioned. For instance, following the death of Councillor Robert Singleton, the club's first captain and treasurer, in 1895, an article in the *Sunderland Echo* stated of Singleton:

> He presided over the first meeting held for the purpose of forming a club, the other gentlemen present being Messrs J. Allan, W.C. Chappel, E. Watson and W. Elliott. The meeting took place at the British School, Norfolk Street in October 1879. A club was then formed under the title of, 'The Sunderland Teachers' Association Football Club'.

It would appear from this that the October 1879 meeting was 'the first meeting held for the purpose of forming a club'. Quite possibly further meetings were held, perhaps informally to discuss the progress being made with playing the new game, until the stage was reached in September 1880 when they were ready to take part in organised competitions. *The Rise of the Leaguers* by the editor of the *Athletic News*, James Catton, published in 1897 states that 'a number of schoolmasters and pupil teachers resident in Sunderland formed a team for their own amusement'.

While it is believed the original name of the club was in fact the Sunderland and District Teachers' Association Football Club, the date of the initial meeting stated in the *Echo* article does not appear to have been challenged at the time. Nor was it challenged a decade later in a book by Alfred Gibson and William Pickford called *Association Football and the Men Who Made It* – published in 1905. The opening sentence on Sunderland says: 'It was in the year 1879 that "The Sunderland School Teachers' Association Football Club" was formed with no more serious purpose than to provide amusement for the members who were drawn from the schools in the town.'

A report in the *Sunderland Echo* of 25 May 1879 indicated that the four districts of the Sunderland School Board consisted of: A – East and West End of Sunderland; B – South Bishopwearmouth; C – North Bishopwearmouth; and D – Monkwearmouth.

Gibson and Pickford's explanation that the initial purpose of the club was simply to provide amusement for the town's teachers backs up John Grayston's recollections from 1931. It would seem that as interest in the sport developed, it was decided to take this interest further.

Even before James Allan brought a round football from Scotland to Sunderland, there was a team playing in Sunderland by the name of Bishopwearmouth Mutual Improvement Association Football Club. They took on Sunderland Rovers rugby team in March 1879, the very team of which James Allan would later become a spectator member. However, a report of the game in the *Sunderland Echo* of 24 March 1879 lists fifteen players in the Rovers team, indicating a game of rugby rather than soccer, with the report noting that Rovers scored three touches down. Previous *Echo* reports of the Bishopwearmouth Mutual Improvement Association Football Club cement the belief that the club were indeed playing rugby. A report of a game against Fulwell in the *Echo* of 11 March 1878 clearly uses rugby terminology, and Bishopwearmouth Mutual Improvement Association Football Club were undoubtedly a rugby club rather than a soccer outfit.

As association football took its first tentative steps there was plenty of confusion over its rules, blurred as they were with those of rugby football. Remember that in the game of football that we cherish, the early days of the sport were very different to the game we know now. Even now, in the twenty-first century, the game is constantly changing. Think of the recent introduction of VAR, goal-line technology and constant alterations of the offside rule, for instance. Until 1912 goalkeepers could handle the ball anywhere in their own half, and until two years earlier wore the same unnumbered shirts as outfield players. In the first three seasons of the Football League, which commenced in 1888–89, there were no goal nets or penalties, and when penalties were introduced they could be taken anywhere from along a twelve yard line that stretched across a pitch with very different markings to those we are familiar with in the modern game.

Within the developing game of association football there were differences in rules that needed resolving. These were described in a letter from J.F. Hall, the treasurer of the Sheffield Football Association in the Field, dated 3 March 1877:

> For many years past Mr. Alcock on the part of the London Association and Mr. Dix and myself on the part of the Sheffield Association, have been trying to assimilate the two codes of rules, which only vary in two points. The one is that London play three men 'offside' and we only one. The other is that London throw in the ball from touch in a straight line, and we kick it in any direction.

Hall goes on to say that C.W. Alcock 'has perhaps done more for Association football than any other man in the kingdom' and bemoans the fact that Alcock, Hall himself and others including 'the Scotch Association' had been outvoted on key matters by people representing far fewer players, before he concludes: 'but of this I am certain, that before many years are over most of those gentlemen of the opposition will regret that such a good opportunity for bringing about one code of Association rules was lost'.

While this has to remain conjecture, it is perhaps possible that embryonic attempts at the new game of association football did take place prior to Allan's arrival in Sunderland. In the *Sunderland Echo* of 25 March 1878, a report headed 'Football' stated: 'SUNDERLAND V WESTOE – A match between those teams was played on the Chester-road ground on Saturday, when Sunderland were victorious by four goals to none.' This was undoubtedly rugby, but it is worth noting that immediately underneath in an article headed 'INTERNATIONAL FOOTBALL MATCH' the report says: 'A match between the selected teams of Scotland and Wales was played at Glasgow on Saturday. The Welshmen were completely overpowered, Scotland winning by nine goals to nothing.'

On 23 March 1878, Scotland did indeed beat Wales 9–0 at association football at the first Hampden Park. Scotland were certainly the leaders in 'soccer' at this time, due to their ability to play as a passing team rather than as a set of individuals. The previous month on the same ground they had thrashed England 7–2 with a completely different Scottish line-up to that which featured in the Wales fixture.

Completing a trio of stories under the generic heading of 'Football', the article continues with 'RECTORY PARK SCHOOLS V MONKWEARMOUTH COLLIERY SCHOOLS', and says: 'An interesting match between the teachers and scholars of these schools took place on Saturday morning in the field of the Mutual Improvement Association, Chester-road, and resulted in a victory to the former of four goals to one.

Beginnings

The team from the Colliery Schools, though inferior in weight to their opponents, played very bravely.' It is absolutely not provable that this schools game was a soccer game rather than a rugby match, although a score of 4–0 with no references to touchdowns would suggest that it could have been a game under association rather than rugby rules, albeit at this stage there was considerable bafflement over the rules or laws of the new game. The reference to one team being 'inferior in weight' perhaps points to the game in question being rugby.

At the time goals applied to both codes. In rugby a touchdown led to a 'try' at kicking the ball over the posts and making it into a goal. The historian of Ashbrooke Rugby Club, Keith Gregson, says: 'In the very early days I think only goals counted in the rugby code, so you could have, say, five touchdowns/tries unconverted to none and it would still be considered a draw.'

Another example of the game developing but not being played in a way we would recognise now occurred on 20 September 1884, when a combined Sunderland and Bedes XI lost to Castle Eden at Monkwearmouth by a score of two goals and three posters to one. Mike Huggins, the president of the European Congress of Sports Historians, explains:

> Before the centralised organisations like the FA gained much influence and standardisation emerged, lads in a town starting a team would draw on the multiple rules they learned at schools or where they grew up. Quite often even within a team there would be lads arguing about whose rules they should follow, and when they wanted to actually play someone else they'd have to negotiate with the other team, who had their own ideas. So sometimes first half one rule, second half another.

Mysteriously, and quite possibly erroneously, there is also a mention in the *Sunderland Echo* of 14 August 1939 of a Hendon Teachers' Football Club, which 'was started before the Town club'. The 'Town club' would seem to be Sunderland. Perhaps there was a previous attempt by Allan to set up this team? The 1939 article claims this club became defunct during the war 'when the field was dug up for trenches'. Presumably this was the First World War. It is known – and reported in the *Sunderland Echo* – that in 1916 trenches were dug in Fulwell Dene, but whether trenches were dug in the Hendon area in that period is not known. If there was a Hendon Teachers' Football Club 'started before the Town club', the chances are high that this would be Allan trying to get the sport off the ground, but if it continued until the war surely more would have been known of the club? Nonetheless, this fleeting mention raises another fascinating lead into the origins of football in Sunderland.

As to 1879 being the start date of the club, it is worth considering the recollections of William Thwaites Wallace, the club secretary in the 1880s. In 1929 he began a series of highly informative and entertaining columns in the *Sunderland Football Echo*. In his 'Peeps from the Past' of 14 September 1929 he stated:

> I must again place on record the extent to which lovers of the game are indebted to Jimmy Allan and James McMillan. These two players were really the founders of Association Football on Wearside, and the former, by virtue of his profession as a schoolmaster was in a unique position for training the 'young idea' of these days in the rudiments of the game. It was in 1879 that James Allan, a native of Ayr and a student of Glasgow University, came to Sunderland to take over the position of second master at Hendon School and afterwards was transferred to Thomas Street School where he remained till 1888 when he was appointed head master of Hylton Road Schools, a position he held until his death in 1911 ... Shortly after his arrival he gathered a few friends around him with the intention of forming a football club for the teachers. As a result of his enthusiasm the Sunderland Teachers' Association Football club came into being in 1879.

Beginnings

From its beginnings following the arrival of James Allan on Wearside, through the embryonic stages of Allan introducing local schoolteachers to the game throughout 1879 and 1880, up to the formal announcement of the club on 25 September 1880, the early days of the club are a fascinating if hazy period. Whether you see the start of the club as being dated from 1879 or 1880 is down to your own interpretation. The view of the club, the descendants of club founder James Allan and myself as club historian is that the club started in 1879 before officially announcing itself to the world in 1880. Regardless of which year you choose to see as the start, once we start to examine the period when games were played against other teams and duly recorded, we can trace more accurately how the club grew.

Like so many new organisations, sporting or otherwise, the early years of the club were fraught with financial difficulties. In his *Football Echo* column of 14 September 1929, W.T. Wallace tells us:

> To start a new type of sport is always difficult and the new club had many ups and downs in its early years. Funds were always low and the duties of the treasurer were practically non-existent. In fact it is on record that on one occasion the exchequer was so empty that one of the members offered a green canary as the prize in a raffle and in this way the sum of seventeen shillings and sixpence was realised.

This would be between 87 and 88p in today's money, the equivalent of about £140 in 2024. Two weeks earlier, in his 'Peeps into the Past' column in the same publication, Wallace had explained that in the club's very early days, players paid subs to play and provided their own 'jersey, boots and other gear', with some players having to pay their subs by instalments if they could not meet their full subscription outright. It would be 1884 before any entrance money was taken at a Sunderland match.

We do know from a report in the *Sunderland Echo* on 27 September 1880 that when the club announced its officers,

Robert Singleton was appointed as captain and treasurer, with James Allan as vice-captain. The likelihood is that Singleton was captain ahead of Allan due to his being a headmaster, holding a post at Gray School from May 1877 to December 1884, when he was appointed Superintendent of the George Hudson Charity. On 14 August 1879, Singleton had been initiated as a Freemason into the Palatine Lodge in Sunderland, becoming an auditor of the lodge just four months later. Two years later he was appointed as the Worshipful Master of the Lodge, and three years after that became Director of Ceremonies. This was a position he held until 1894, a year before his death at the age of only 42 due to – according to the doctor at an inquest into his death – alcohol poisoning. Both Singleton and his wife were believed to be heavy drinkers. Their son, Robert Clifton Singleton, also met an early end. Seven when his father died, he spent some time in Sunderland Orphan Asylum and later emigrated to Canada, but was killed in the First World War at the beginning of June 1916 in Ypres.

Both of James Allan's sons would also be killed in the world wars: Walter Allan aboard the SS *Halifax* in December 1917 and Wallace Allan on the SS *Kirkdale* in February 1940. Walter's son Arthur was also a victim of the Second World War, losing his life with the sinking of the SS *Deptford* in December 1939.

A goalkeeper or back who played in all of the known line-ups in Sunderland's matches between 1880 and 1882, Bob Singleton was a Lancastrian from Garstang, where he was born in July 1852. In Sunderland he lived at 12 Peel Street in Hendon, a house that still stands to this day and is within walking distance of both Norfolk Street and the Blue House Field.

In addition to Singleton and Allan, the club's committee at the September 1880 meeting was listed as Messrs Gibbons, Chappel, Coates and Sewell, while the secretary was Mr Elliott of 4 Rudland Terrace. By the time of the 1881 census, Elliott, a 23-year-old teacher, was lodging with Singleton. Rather like Sunderland's team of 2024, Sunderland's committee of 1880 was a very young affair. Joseph Lake Gibbons had just turned eighteen. Born in June 1862 in Sunderland, he was a pupil-teacher at Rectory Park School late in 1880 before becoming a student at Carmarthen training college in April 1881. As mentioned earlier, Walter Chappel was assistant master at Hendon Board School and was 26 at the time, 23-year-old John Coates was a master at Rectory Park School, while John Sewell was a 22-year-old teacher at Herrington St Wesleyan School.

Shortly after deciding to enter the new cup competition, the schoolteachers, who had been practising among themselves for over a year, decided to open up the club to people from outside the teaching profession and to change their name to reflect this. In a meeting after a practice game on 16 October 1880 it was agreed to drop 'and District Teachers' from the club's name, thereafter being called simply Sunderland Association Football Club. Subsequently, in the *Sunderland Echo* from 5 to 11 November of the same year, a series of advertisements appeared appealing for new players:

SUNDERLAND ASSOCIATION F.B.C, – WANTED, YOUNG GENTLEMEN to join the above. Grounds Blue House Field, Hendon. Address to honorary secretary Mr. Wm Elliott, 4 Rudland-terrace.

Having reached the stage where they felt able to take on other teams, Sunderland's matches against other clubs began to be reported. A fortnight after playing Ferryhill, they entertained Ovingham on 27 November 1880. Secretary Elliott scored Sunderland's first ever known goal against opponents, something he may well have had pleasure in recording as Sunderland won 4–0, with James (Jimmy) Allan getting two of the goals and Ted Watson the other. Two weeks later Burnopfield held Sunderland to a 2–2 draw at the Blue House Field in the Northumberland and Durham Cup.

The Blue House Field was not so much a ground as just a pitch to play on when Sunderland called it home. It wasn't an enclosed venue, so admission money could not be taken, and in any case who would want to pay to see a team taking its first steps in a new sport? While the club's first headquarters in Norman Street are long since demolished, there is still a football pitch where the Blue House Field was: it's now Valley Road Academy School's pitch.

In 2010 I took it upon myself to organise blue plaques to mark all of the grounds Sunderland called home prior to the 1997 move to the Stadium of Light. I enlisted the support of then chairman Niall Quinn and the city council, financial support from the Sunderland Supporters' Association led by George Forster, and then I had to approach the owners of the properties that occupied the sites, some public and some private. In the case of the Blue House Field I enjoyed great support from the school's deputy head of the time, a Mr George Stobart, who already knew that when they played, his school team were following in the footsteps of Sunderland's first footballers.

Those footballers wore blue rather than red and white. Perhaps selected as club colours due to the first home pitch being at the Blue House Field, blue remained the colour until 1884, at which point Sunderland switched to red and white, although stripes took another three years to emerge.

Having drawn in the cup with Burnopfield in 1880, Sunderland travelled for a replay, which was won 2–0 a week before Christmas. The next round of the competition on 12 February 1881 took Sunderland to St James' Park in Newcastle, meaning that they played at this venue long before Newcastle United, who didn't come into being until 1892 through a merger between Newcastle East End and Newcastle West End.

Sunderland's first match at St James' brought a heavy 5–0 defeat at the hands of Newcastle team the Rangers and, of course, elimination from the cup. A week earlier Allan, Singleton and Roberts (one of the first non-teachers to play for the club, who had learned to play football in Bangor, Wales) had gained representative honours at Middlesbrough, playing for the Northumberland and Durham FA, but were on the receiving end of a 10–0 thrashing by the Cleveland FA. The same trio had been chosen for another Durham game a week earlier, along with teammates John Sewell and John Coates, only for the game to be postponed.

The season ended with a return friendly at Ferryhill at the beginning of April, which finished goalless. Given that there was a seven-week gap between the end of the cup campaign and the friendly at Ferryhill, it seems possible that other games might have been played in between only to go unreported. The sport within the North East was still in its very early stages of development and not yet attracting huge public interest, so there would be no great need for local newspapers to report on games. The local paper was first and foremost a shipping gazette, and if something more newsworthy was taking place, particularly at sea, sports reports would be squeezed out of the newspapers, sometimes never to be published.

On the other hand, a group of educated men looking to develop their club might well have ensured any games played did receive some publicity. As it is, we know of the trio of cup games and the Ferryhill and Ovingham friendlies in 1880–81, and these may have been the only games played, with perhaps plenty of in-house practices taking up the rest of their time, as they had from 1879.

In the following season thirteen games are known to have been played, again featuring an early home fixture against Ferryhill, this time eliciting a 1–0 win at the start of October. Interest in the Northumberland and Durham Challenge Cup was ended at the first hurdle with a 4–0 loss at Sedgefield later the same month. Seven of the thirteen games were defeats, with one draw and five victories, one of which came at Whitburn Cricket Club, where North Eastern were beaten 2–0 in February.

Life for Sunderland as an up-and-coming football team was fraught with difficulty in those early years. Money being tight was just one of the issues, with another being the search for a new place to play, not least because rent for use of the Blue House Field was ten pounds per year. Numerous fields were turned into pitches, one such playing field near to the Cedars and off Villette Road in Grangetown being used and included in the Blue Plaques trail. This pitch was only around half a mile from the Blue House Field. Evidently, at times they were also struggling for players. In October and November 1882, three of the first four games of the season were played with just ten men. The team were evidently getting better, though, as draws were managed in two of these games despite the numerical disadvantage, with the only defeat coming away to the Rangers of Newcastle, who also had just ten players.

At the beginning of November in 1882, a 2–1 win over North Eastern became the first game played at the new home of Groves Field, which is part of the Ashbrooke home of cricket and rugby in Sunderland, though the match was abandoned due to disputes. Groves Field only staged five Sunderland soccer matches, but its claim to club history was assured by one of these being the club's record win in a competitive fixture: a 12–1 win over Stanley Star in the Northumberland and Durham Challenge Cup on 20 January 1883. This started a sequence of five successive victories in a season where one of just three defeats from eleven games played came in the club's first cup final, a 1–0 defeat to Tyne at Brandling Park, Newcastle, on the last day of March.

That summer Sunderland not only moved home again, but left the south side of the River Wear, where they had originated, to move to the north side. The club have never returned to the south of the Wear after this 1883 move from Groves Field to Roker, although, as we shall see, James Allan would later set up another club there. When Sunderland were leaving Roker Park in the late 1990s there was a move to Ryhope (south of the river) briefly mooted, but it was never a likely prospect.

The new Roker home in 1883, however, was not Roker Park. The arrival there was another decade and a half away, and there would be three north side home venues before Roker Park became home to SAFC. The new home in 1883 would be known variously as the Dolly Field, the Clay-Dolly Field, Cooper Street or Horatio Street. It was through this initial move to the area that Sunderland's nickname of the Black Cats was born.

Beginnings

The story originates from almost three-quarters of a century before football started in Sunderland. Joshua Dunn was at work in the year 1805. At the time there were fears that the French navy might attack Britain, and Dunn was stationed at a gun battery on the sea front at Roker, where he was on the look-out for enemy ships. One night, as Dunn was on duty, he thought he heard a baby crying. When he went to investigate he found that the noise he had heard was not from a baby, but a big black cat. Maybe before going on duty Joshua had been drinking. He was so scared of the cat he thought it was the devil. Dunn was teased about this for the rest of his life, until he died in 1850 – so much so that the area where it happened became known as the Black Cat Battery.

Once Sunderland played near the river the nickname the Black Cats began to be associated with the team – although the Black Cats has only been the club's official nickname since the year 2000 (ironically after the move away from Roker Park to the Stadium of Light). As long ago as 1905 there was a cartoon drawn of a black cat with Sunderland chairman F.W. Taylor, while when Sunderland first played in the FA Cup final in 1913 many supporters wore black cat badges. A black cat has always been the emblem of the Sunderland Supporters' Association, since it was set up in 1965. In the 1930s Sunderland's match programme had a black cat on the cover. These days, Sunderland's mascots Samson and Delilah are black cats, while the Stadium of Light has black cats on its walls and the club's administration building is called Black Cat House.

The new ground in 1883 was situated near a brickworks and claypit. The pitch at the Dolly Field was regularly heavy to play on. Nearby stood the Wolseley pub, which was used for getting changed. The pub still stands and is a regular stopping-off point for occasional guided tours of Sunderland's former homes. Long-since built over, the site of the Dolly Field is now occupied by Givens Street and Appley Terrace.

Sunderland Rugby Club historian Keith Gregson offers some thoughtful speculation as to why Sunderland Association

Football Club moved across the river from south to north, and also why the club first incorporated the word association into their name: 'I have references back to December 1873 and January 1874 in other local papers to Sunderland Football Club (which is still the rugby club) and its formation at that point. Post-move to Ashbrooke in 1887 all printed material had Sunderland CC and FC stamped on it (CC is the Cricket Club and FC the Football – rugby – Club). At some point someone stuck an R in (possibly late-twentieth century) so it became Sunderland RFC, but I checked recently with Twickenham and its records still have the rugby club as Sunderland Football Club. I have often mused as to whether SAFC had to put in the A more frequently than other association clubs because there was already an established Sunderland Football Club. Moving on to the 1880s, there were a number of rugby clubs south of the river, of which Sunderland was the most successful (and on the national stage). Ashbrooke was a very middle/upper-middle class area, so perhaps the association side's move across the river might have been due to the dominance of rugby in the south of the city?'

Gregson's suggestion sounds entirely feasible, although we cannot be certain. Nonetheless, having crossed the Wear, the club only stayed at the Dolly Field for a year. Just as Groves Field staged what in 2023 remains Sunderland's biggest competitive victory, the Dolly Field was Sunderland's home when they won their first trophy – although the Dolly Field did not stage the final and, in fact, there was no trophy! The cup in question was the new Durham Challenge Cup, but the Durham FA did not have sufficient money to pay for a trophy initially, so Sunderland subsequently received it eight months after actually winning it.

The separation of the Northumberland and Durham FAs was significant in that Sunderland have always seen themselves as County Durham's club. Notwithstanding that in years to come Durham City and Darlington would play in the Football League and that clubs such as Bishop Auckland and Crook Town would go on to have magnificent records in amateur football, it is Sunderland who have always represented the apex of association football in the county. Sunderland was part of County Durham until the creation of Tyne and Wear in 1974, and regardless of that new metropolitan county, Sunderland have continued to play in the Durham Challenge Cup. To 2024, Sunderland's 22 wins in the competition are more than any other club, although in many years Sunderland have not entered. Nineteen of those wins came before 1930, with most achieved by Sunderland's second team, most recently in 2020, when the Under 23s shared the trophy with Spennymoor. The fourth of these Durham Challenge Cup triumphs in 1890 would be the last time the trophy was won by the first team, as by that time they were about to enter the Football League.

The opening Sunderland game at the Dolly Field was an 8–1 win over Castle Eden in a friendly on 29 September 1883. Newly acquired supporters at the club's new home quickly got used to success, as the first ten home games were won and there were triumphs in not one, but two competitions in this season. Fifty-five goals were scored and just six conceded in those first ten home fixtures. These included 7–2, 5–2 and 3–1 wins in the Durham Challenge Cup against Milkwell Burn, Jarrow and Hamsterley Rangers, before a tempestuous climax to the competition away from home.

The semi-final with Hobson Wanderers took place at Whitburn, as did a 6–0 replay victory after an initial goalless draw. However, it was the final that showed that, even in these early days, the passion of the Wearside public for their football team was already strongly in evidence. The match with Darlington was staged in Sunderland, but not at the club's home ground. Hosted at the Monkwearmouth Cricket Ground on Newcastle Road, the match was won 4–3 by the Wearsiders, with John Grayston one of the scorers, only for the Durham FA to order a replay to be held at Birtley after complaints were upheld about supporters' behaviour. An estimated crowd of between one and two thousand represented the first time an attendance figure had been reported for a Sunderland match.

Determined to win the trophy, not least after having won it on the pitch already, Sunderland rested four key players, including captain James McMillan, in the one game played before the replayed final. This resulted in a first home defeat at the Dolly Field, but the move paid off when Darlington were beaten again in the replayed final, this time 2–0, with two of the rested quartet, Joyce and McDonald, getting the goals on a pitch that had a cinder track running across its centre, a considerable danger to the players.

Credited by W.T. Wallace as being one of two players – along with Jimmy Allan – who were 'really the founders of Association Football on Wearside', James McMillan was born at 22 Howick Street in Alnwick on 28 April 1863, making him just sixteen when association football started in Sunderland, where his family had moved to when he was three. The son of a stonemason, McMillan captained the club as well as serving it administratively. In late January 1884 the *Sunderland Echo* reported that he had been elected as honorary secretary of a new Sunderland Lacrosse Club, which was being formed 'under the auspices of Sunderland Association Football Club'. As a player he started as a right-back and played for the club during the years they frequently moved grounds, until retiring from playing in 1887. He would have only been in his mid-twenties then, but, as we shall see, at that time Sunderland's standards stepped up and Scottish players began to be imported and paid.

McMillan's influence at the club only increased at this point, though. Having captained the team and represented the county, he did as much as anyone to promote the club in its early years, becoming treasurer, secretary and then succeeding James Marr as chairman – all this while running the master stonemason's business he had inherited from his father on Hudson Road in Hendon. Both McMillan and Marr were also involved with Sunderland Cricket and Rugby Club too, making significant contributions across the generations, mainly as players. Two of McMillan's sons played rugby for the club, while James Marr was the father of John Lynn Marr, who played rugby well into the twentieth century.

Summer football is seen as a modern-day aspect of the game, but in 1884 Sunderland played four games on their way to winning another competition in June. This was a North of England Temperance Festival tournament held on Newcastle's Town Moor. After winning three games, including two that took extra-time, Sunderland met Newcastle East End in the final on 25 June. A first meeting of Sunderland and East End had taken place at Heaton Cricket Field on 3 November 1883, when Jock McDonald was the scourge of the Tynesiders with two of the goals in a 3–0 win.

In winning two trophies in a highly successful season, Sunderland won the vast majority of games they played and scored over 100 goals. There are records of two other games in December and one in April, which were advertised in the local press but without any reports being published, as far as is known. This highlights the earlier point regarding other prior games that may have been played but of which there is no record – who knows, this could even include one or more before the first known meeting with Ferryhill in November 1880.

Although Sunderland were already dominating games in their own region, they came a cropper when, for the first time, they ventured outside of the North East. Proposed fixtures against Blackburn Rovers and Blackburn Olympic failed to materialise, but they did play a game against Great Lever from the Woodside area of Bolton on Monday, 25 February 1884. The Blackburn clubs were early giants of the game. Olympic were the English (FA) Cup holders, while Rovers would replace them as cup winners in 1883–84 and retain the trophy for the next two years, having been finalists in 1882. Sunderland met Great Lever in a match that had been arranged by Reverend Robinson Hindle, who had a brother who ran a hotel in Accrington. In years to come Reverend Hindle would play a leading role in helping Sunderland to join the Football League. A curate in Monkwearmouth at the Venerable Bede Church, and later vicar at Eppleton, he was very interested in sport and, like many young clergy at the time, encouraged his parishioners to share this passion. Hindle became involved in the club, playing when he could, for instance turning out in a match in Dumfries in April 1885. He would also sometimes officiate at games, and he became an important figure behind the scenes, often being seen as a trustworthy figure when writing to officialdom on behalf of the club. When he later left the area for professional reasons, Reverend Hindle was presented with a framed photograph of the team.

The match in Lancashire was an education for Sunderland after they were smashed 11–0 by Great Lever. They were a leading side of the time who, at the start of the season, had brought in so many quality players that, rather like the elite clubs of today who have such strong squads, they could virtually have a 'league team' and a 'cup team'. Great Lever had a side they used for local games, and another, stronger team they fielded in friendlies, or challenge matches, as they were more accurately described. Funded by local mill owners, Great Lever's side included future England captain John Goodall, who scored five times, and Thurston 'Tot' Rostron, who played twice for England as a seventeen-year-old. They also fielded Jimmy Trainer, who went on to play for Wales (and, like Goodall, became a member of the great Preston North End team later in the decade), as well as Jack Switherby, who scored twice and became the first man to captain the USA. He moved there to play for a mill owner who was investing vast fortunes in the mill business and setting up football and cricket teams in and around Newark in New Jersey.

No doubt embarrassed by the margin of the defeat, Sunderland tried to brush this loss under the carpet. Despite this season bringing about the club's first annual general meeting, neither the trip nor the trouncing were mentioned. In Lancashire, match reports referred to Great Lever hammering Durham rather than Sunderland. Were it not for Alfred Grundy, the chairman of the Durham FA, making it clear in the *Athletic* newspaper a week later that it was Sunderland and not his Durham side that had been beaten 11–0, perhaps the defeat might have been kept secret. Clearly, Sunderland still had a long way to go to be able to compete with the best, despite the silverware already on show.

Looking to grow, and having witnessed the standard of Great Lever, Sunderland moved home again for the 1884–85 season. Significantly, the move to Abbs Field in Fulwell – where they had agreed to share the pitch with St Bede's FC – enabled them to play in a completely enclosed ground for the first time. This meant that admission could be charged to see games, boosting the finances of the club as the sport's popularity increased.

Abbs Field was near where the Blue Bell pub now stands in Fulwell, the furthest north of all the places Sunderland have called home. As with all the club's former homes, it is marked with a blue plaque, in this case situated on Prengarth Avenue. The first match the club staged at Abbs Field was a showpiece game against a District XI who were defeated 5–2 on 13 September 1884, with Birtley being the first visiting club a fortnight later when Jock McDonald and John Grayston got the goals in a 2–1 win. At this time Sunderland had not completely cut ties with their original home of the Blue House Field; throughout the 1884–85 season it was still used for second-team games as well as practice matches between married and single players.

Clearly the ground-sharers at Abbs Field were on good terms, as occasionally St Bede's players would appear for Sunderland when the club could not muster eleven men, while on the Saturday between the games against the District XI and Birtley, a combined Sunderland and St Bede's XI took on a Castle Eden team. Evidently the crossover of rules between association football and rugby was still hazy, as Castle Eden were reported to have beaten the combined opposition by two goals and three posters to one!

This 1884–85 season was of great importance to the development of SAFC. Alongside the introduction of admission charges for matches, it was the first time they entered a national competition – the FA Cup, or English Cup, as it was known – and the club changed their colours from the original blue to the red and white they have become synonymous with today. Football was really taking off in the Wearside area. In the

Sunderland Echo of 18 September 1884, R. Hobourn announced that his shop had received full ranges of all the colours (shirts) for Sunderland and District clubs.

The first English Cup appearance came five weeks before the switch to red and white, and took place away to Redcar, where a crowd of approximately a thousand saw Sunderland's first ever game in national competition refereed by a Mr G. Bastard of the Cleveland FA. He oversaw a 3–1 defeat for Sunderland, with Redcar being knocked out the following month at the hands of Grimsby Town.

Defeat in the cup was the only one of the first fifteen games of the season that Sunderland did not win. Locally, they were far too good for the opposition, with 9–0, 8–1 and 8–2 victories the highlights before an astonishing 23–0 win over Castletown five days before Christmas. This remains Sunderland's biggest win in any game, with James (Jimmy) Allan incredibly scoring twelve of the goals. The half-time score was 16–0 – two goals for each of the eight players Castletown had turned up with. Three of Sunderland's second-team players had brought Castletown's side up to a full complement in a game that was played as a friendly instead of the scheduled Durham County Cup fixture, from which the visitors had withdrawn due to their inability to raise a team.

A week before the slaughter of Castletown, Castle Eden had been beaten 8–1 in a game that was significant for Sunderland wearing red and white for the first time. At this stage the shirts were not striped, but instead halved in the style of Blackburn Rovers, the pre-eminent team of the day who were in the middle of a three-year run of being English Cup winners. Sunderland's strips were described in the *Sunderland Echo* of 11 December 1884 as quartered rather than halved, but this took into account the back as well as the front of the shirt.

Following the 8–1 and 23–0 wins over Castle Eden and Castletown, three more games were won by modest scorelines, but without conceding a goal, before a big and, to that point, probably record crowd of around 1,500 turned up at Abbs

Field on 3 January 1885. The attraction was the first club from outside the North East to play on Wearside, Port Glasgow Athletic.

The Scots matched Great Lever's goal tally of the previous season, slaughtering Sunderland 11–1. With a goalkeeper called Blackadder, the visitors hatched a cunning plan of passing the ball to each other. Whereas in England at this time football teams tended to chase the ball in packs – another remnant of the crossover from rugby – in Scotland a more superior passing game had developed. At the time of Port Glasgow Athletic's visit to Wearside, Scotland had won all of their last five meetings with England (although England would draw with them in London two months later). Port Glasgow Athletic were a good side, but only good enough to reach the second round of the Scottish Cup that season. Although Sunderland were by now a force locally, their first two attempts to play teams from outside the North East had seen them concede eleven goals each time.

Determined to learn from their experiences, Sunderland continued to make progress. Later in the season, home and away meetings with the 5th Kirkcudbright Rifle Volunteers of Maxwelltown both brought hard-earned draws (the away game took place at Palmerston Park, now developed as the home of Queen of the South in Dumfries), as did a home meeting with Sheffield, while in the Durham Challenge Cup, Sunderland again reached the final.

The final against Darlington at Feethams brought great controversy. Sunderland were so aggrieved at the way their complaint over the game's officiating was dismissed, they refused to enter the competition the following year. Remembering that a year earlier Sunderland had been forced to replay the final against the same opposition after Darlington's protest, Sunderland were mightily miffed when their claims that the Quakers' first goal had not crossed the line and that the second (in a 3–0 defeat) had been offside were rebuffed. As well as fury at Middlesbrough referee Fred Hardisty, the officials of SAFC were livid with one of the umpires.

Having turned down the potential revenue from another run in the Durham Challenge Cup in 1885–86, Sunderland were dealt a blow at the start of their second season at Abbs Field when their landlords increased the rent by 500 per cent. Having seen the increasing crowds being pulled in by big games and with the prospect of more lucrative challenge matches against opposition from afar, the asking price for Sunderland's renting of Abbs Field went from £2.10 shillings (£2.50) to £15.

Consequently, Sunderland started the 1885–86 season searching once again for a new home, which didn't come about until the spring of 1886, when Sunderland signed off from Abbs Field with a 6–0 win over St John's of Middlesbrough on 13 March 1886. Home fans had been treated with that victory to the twelfth win in fifteen home games in the season so far. Newcastle East End had creditably taken a draw, but the two defeats had shown more than anything how Sunderland were narrowing the gap on teams from outside the region. The first two days of 1886 brought visits from Port Glasgow and Linthouse (of Govan, which at that time was not yet officially part of Glasgow). Whereas a year earlier Port Glasgow Athletic had inflicted a humiliating 11–1 defeat, this time both games brought narrow 2–1 losses. There had also been a proposed game against (Glasgow) Rangers, only for this fixture not to materialise.

At the end of the following month Sunderland travelled to Edinburgh to take on Heart of Midlothian, where again they were defeated 2–1, but they travelled home with pride intact. This game took place two months before Hearts hosted their first game at the Tynecastle ground, which has been their home ever since, Bolton Wanderers being the first visitors.

By then Sunderland had a new ground themselves, having moved to the Newcastle Road venue that would become the club's home for a dozen years, considerably longer than the life of the club so far. Newcastle Road was where the club was able to put down roots. With a pitch reported by James Allan to be about 120 yards long by 75 yards wide, it was a large arena that would require players of stamina. It was here where the club would enter the Football League, win three league titles and host an England international.

No doubt with an eye on a bumper crowd in light of the previous season's Durham Challenge Cup final, Darlington were invited to be the first visitors to Newcastle Road since the ground became Sunderland's home venue. The Quakers were beaten 3–1 on 3 April 1886, despite injury to Joe Smart reducing Sunderland to ten men for the second half, in which Jimmy Allan and Harry Jones joined James Hunter on the scoresheet. Hunter had become Sunderland's first semi-professional player fourteen months earlier when joining from Queen of the South Wanderers, with a job at J.L. Thompson's shipyard alongside being paid for playing. Edinburgh University and Sheffield were early visitors to Newcastle Road, Edinburgh being beaten 1–0 and Sheffield edging a 4–3 win. A second attempt at the English Cup brought a sense of déjà-vu, as once again they were drawn away to Redcar in the autumn, this time losing 3–0.

Sunderland again entered the summer Temperance Festival Cup at the Town Moor in Newcastle, losing the final 1–0 to Shankhouse Black Watch on the final day of June. This was not the only final Sunderland players were involved in this season. Although the club had refused to enter the Durham Challenge Cup, several Sunderland players appeared in that year's competition for other clubs, among them the trio of Jameses – Allan, McMillan and Hunter – who all played in the final for Birtley as they lost to Bishop Auckland at Feethams.

By 1886–87, Sunderland were not only ready to start their first full season at the Newcastle Road ground, but they did so in the knowledge that they were the team to beat in the North East. Sunderland had the finances to pay £15 per year for the rent of the ground. This was the same as they had been asked to pay at Abbs Field, but the ground at Newcastle Road offered much more potential, although evidently things were still pretty basic, as tents were initially used for changing rooms, while the summer of 1886 saw the ground rented out for grazing.

The club was undoubtedly progressing. What had started out as a pastime for schoolteachers – and several of the team, including James Allan, were continuing their careers in education – was expanding into something more serious. Up to this point Thomas Street School, where Allan was headmaster, had been used as a base for club meetings, but around the same time that Newcastle Road became Sunderland's new ground, Whitburn Street Workmen's Hall in Monkwearmouth became the new headquarters. Money-wise there was also a welcome boost for the club when the owners of the Newcastle Road Ground, the Thompson sisters, unexpectedly refunded £3.15 shillings (£3.75) of the £15 annual rent as a mark of appreciation of how well the premises had been cared for.

As the success of the team brought increasingly large crowds, who paid for the privilege of watching the team, before long a grandstand and a press gallery were added, the latter itself evidence of the rising interest in the town's major football club. This 1886–87 season saw the Durham Challenge Cup return to Sunderland, who again beat Darlington in the final, as they had in 1884. A medal won by Jacob Spain in this final is the oldest medal on display at the Stadium of Light.

A week after the final, Sunderland, as winners of the Durham Challenge Cup, entertained the winners of the Northumberland Challenge Cup, Shankhouse Black Watch on 2 April 1887. The honours were shared after a goalless draw, although the following October Sunderland won a replay 3–1 at Shankhouse.

There was also an increasing number of money-spinning friendlies against teams from further afield. These included a first meeting with (Glasgow) Rangers, who were beaten 1–0 on Wearside on New Year's Day in 1887. At that time teams from Scotland and Ireland as well as Wales entered the English Cup, with Rangers going on to reach the semi-final that season, where they lost to eventual winners Aston Villa. There were still some heavy defeats against more established clubs, though, with the last five games of the campaign all lost at home, including

5–0, 7–0 and 3–1 losses at the hands of Edinburgh St Bernard's, Nottingham Rangers and Accrington, the first fully professional team that Sunderland played against, with admission doubled in price to 6d.

Sunderland entered the English Cup for the third time, their first match against Newcastle West End. But, having boycotted the Durham Challenge Cup the previous season over the handling of their protest concerning the 1885 final, and being made to replay the 1884 final following complaints from Darlington, Sunderland were given more cause to be aggrieved by the authorities.

The tie with Newcastle West End was played at Newcastle Road on 30 October. Despite going behind early on, Sunderland – backed by an extraordinary crowd of 4–6,000 – fought back to win 2–1 after extra-time, thanks to two goals from Jack Lord, only for West End to complain that the match had been completed in near darkness. Upholding the complaint, the FA ruled the first English Cup game ever staged in Sunderland to be void and ordered a replay on Tyneside.

Played a fortnight later, the game was level at half-time, but by then Sunderland were a man short, as defender William Oliver had broken his collarbone ten minutes before. West End went on to win 1–0 with a Jack Angus goal fifteen minutes from time. Two weeks later West End returned to Newcastle Road for a benefit match in aid of Oliver, a crowd at least as big as that for the cup tie seeing Reuben Smith secure a 1–0 win for the home team.

With crowds mushrooming and the sport forging its own identity separate to rugby, it wasn't just the football team that was prospering – the town itself was. Between 1886 and 1890 a grand new town hall was being constructed in Fawcett Street in Sunderland, while around this time two million tons of coal was annually passing through the docks at the mouth of the Wear. While there was a lot of poverty and hardship in the town, there was also a lot of money being made, and increasingly wealthy backers wanted to get involved with the football club. As the club grew, the changing power structure was moving from the original schoolteachers to the money men of the shipyards.

The season began with a new club president and chairman in the shape of shipbuilders Robert Thompson and James Marr.

September 1887 saw Sunderland don a new kit. Ditching the red and white halves and mainly blue shorts – or knickerbockers – they had worn since December 1884, a new red and white striped shirt with white knickerbockers was worn for the first time in the third match of the season, a 1–0 win over Darlington St Augustine's on 24 September 1887. Arnie Davison wrote his name into the history of the club by scoring the first goal in the kit with which Sunderland would become synonymous. By 2024 Sunderland had won more major trophies than all the other English teams who wear red and white stripes put together.

Trophies were not in short supply in 1887–88. The Durham Challenge Cup was won once again, with the Northumberland Challenge Cup winners also defeated in the annual challenge match: Bishop Auckland Church Institute and Newcastle West End being the victims of the red and whites. Not only that, but Sunderland were becoming more and more competitive against the best teams in England and Scotland. While there were still defeats, such as 2–0 to Blackburn Rovers, 3–1 to Blackburn Olympic and 4–2 to both Partick Thistle and Renton, as well as a record-equalling 11–0 home new year loss to Cambuslang, there were also some big wins against renowned opposition from beyond the region.

By the time Renton visited Sunderland in April they were Scottish Cup holders, having thrashed Cambuslang 6–1 in the cup final the month after Cambuslang's huge win on Wearside. Renton's trip to Newcastle Road brought a first visit from a man who would become one of the heroes of 'The Team of All The Talents' at Sunderland in the following decade, one of the game's greatest goal-scorers and still fifth in the all-time list of Sunderland scorers: Johnny Campbell.

In a season in which association football on Wearside attracted its first five-figure crowds, Sunderland did not always struggle against strong sides from outside the region, and there was, for the first time, legitimate and approved progress in the English

Beginnings

Cup. Notts Mellors, Derby Junction and Sheffield Park Grange had all lost heavily on Wearside before a notable trio of triumphs on an Easter weekend that truly was a red and white rising.

Firstly, 1883 English Cup winners Blackburn Olympic were trounced 4–1 on Easter Saturday. By this stage Olympic were in decline, having been usurped by their local rivals Rovers, but this was nonetheless a considerable scalp for Sunderland. Buoyed by this result, 48 hours later Sheffield were beaten 4–0, and then Edinburgh St Bernard's were smashed 5–1 the following day. These games all pulled in healthy crowds mustering a combined total of between 20 and 25,000, and while admission prices were clearly cheap, the totals evidently added up as the club raked in the cash.

Increasing money pouring into the club aided the ambition of those who were enjoying the fact that Sunderland were now a team capable of taking on and sometimes beating good teams from around England and Scotland.

Newcastle West End had also been beaten earlier in the season in the English Cup. This was Sunderland's first official home win ever in the competition, and a second legitimate victory in the competition for the club, having already won 3–2 at Morpeth Harriers in the first round. That tie had to be won twice, as Morpeth had been awarded a replay after Sunderland initially beat them 4–2, only for the Harriers to grumble that a Sunderland player (Peter Ford) had not been registered in time.

Sunderland actually won in the third round too, beating Middlesbrough 4–2 after a 2–2 draw, only to fall foul of the lawmakers once again. Middlesbrough protested that three of Sunderland's side – Andrew Hastings, Joe Richardson and one of the scorers, George Monaghan (who had all played in earlier rounds) – were all Scottish professionals. Contemporary regulations stated that to play as a professional you needed to have lived locally for two years, and the Teessiders successfully argued that the Scots trio had only been with Sunderland since the start of the season and that, moreover, Sunderland had paid their train fares from Dumfries, so the players had profited financially and were therefore professional. All of these players had jobs outside of football. In Monaghan's case he had been employed in the construction of Sunderland's new town hall.

A commission of inquiry heard the case two days after Christmas in Darlington, with Sunderland subsequently found guilty. Perhaps Sunderland knew they were on dodgy ground with their Scots players. Two seasons earlier Monaghan appears to have played for Sunderland in the English Cup tie at Redcar under an assumed and false name of D. Logan.

Writing in his 'Peeps into the Past' column in the *Football Echo* in 1929, W.T. Wallace admitted:

> At the beginning of each season it was my duty as secretary to send to Mr. J. Glover, the Secretary of the Durham Football Association, a list of all the players – the usual registration – and like all good secretaries at that time a few names (fictitious of course) were added so that if any new player presented himself for membership he was given one of these names and accordingly played under the same. This action however would have a very poor chance of succeeding at the present time owing to the great publicity and greater interest and knowledge of the spectators generally, but I suppose it was a case of 'other times other methods'.

The increasing affluence and ambition of the club had seen them casting their net for players much wider than before. Until recently the team had primarily consisted of players who lived and worked locally. Sunderland were well aware that Scottish footballers were generally of a more accomplished standard and had begun to acquire Scots, a tradition that would serve the club exceptionally well over the decades.

But following the furore over the expulsion from the English Cup, disputes within the club over its future direction ultimately led to the acrimonious departure of club founder James Allan, who wanted Sunderland to continue playing more local players. He had always enjoyed playing as part of the pleasure of running the club. Perhaps he was injured, but having played against Morpeth Harriers in the first round of the cup, he had been missing from the line-ups in the subsequent matches with Newcastle West End and Middlesbrough. Obviously, if the club wanted to bring in more players from outside the area some of the long-standing and mainly local players were going to have to make way. Indeed, in January 1888 there was an attempt to form a club called Sunderland Rovers just for local players, but this proved to be a short-lived venture.

Clearly unhappy with the way things were going at the club he had strived to bring into being almost a decade earlier, Jimmy Allan not only left Sunderland, but just 101 days after the ill-fated Middlesbrough match, on 13 March, Allan hosted a meeting at the Empress Hotel on Union Street in Sunderland to form a rival football club called Sunderland Albion. Yet at the time Allan was still officially the treasurer of Sunderland, and remained so at the club's annual general meeting held at the Monkwearmouth Workmen's Hall a month and a half later.

As the founder of Sunderland AFC, but having lost control, Allan's creation of the rival club could have led to the demise of the original club. For a while Albion threatened to become serious rivals of Sunderland, and had they been more successful, perhaps the Sunderland AFC we know today would have been short-lived and instead Sunderland Albion would be the town's premier team.

Seven players and former Sunderland president Alderman Potts jumped ship to join Allan at Albion. One of these players was the aforementioned Scottish 'professional' George Monaghan, who played in Albion's first game against Shankhouse Black Watch on 5 May 1888, just two days after Sunderland's AGM. This was staged at a pitch known as the Ashville Ground, only a few goal-kicks away from Sunderland's Newcastle Road home, before Albion took up residence at Sunderland's first home at the Blue House Field.

In the case of Sunderland, following the expulsion from the English Cup, the 1887–88 season continued successfully, with the Durham Challenge Cup being won once again. Only seven of the total of thirty-nine games (including the expunged one at Morpeth in the English Cup) were lost, and seven Sunderland players played for Durham County at Newcastle Road in a highly prestigious friendly with Corinthians, who beat the County XI 4–2. Corinthians were a famous amateur club, the only one ever to provide all eleven players for an England international. Sunderland later played them in the Sheriff of London Shield (a forerunner of the Community Shield) in 1903, while the renowned modern-day Brazilian club of the same name are named after them.

With Allan gone and focusing on his new team, the original Sunderland club continued to broaden its horizons and kicked off 1888–89 as a professional club. The opening two games illustrated how much Sunderland were improving.

The Football League – the world's first – kicked off on 8 September 1888 without Sunderland, in the league of twelve teams all from the North West or the Midlands. The previous Saturday one of the founder members of the league, Blackburn Rovers, English Cup winners in 1884, 1885 and 1886, were beaten 4–3 at Newcastle Road. And as the first league fixtures kicked off, Sunderland again took on Cambuslang, and improved on the previous season's 11–0 humiliation by holding the Scots to a 1–1 draw.

Preston North End's Invincibles strode to the first league title. Unbeaten in a 22-game season with two points for a win, they finished eleven points clear of runners-up Aston Villa. Preston, however, were not so invincible when they came to Wearside that season, as Sunderland thrashed them 4–1. Fielding seven of the eleven players who had also played in the English Cup final victory a month earlier, Preston were outplayed. Clearly at this time relations between Sunderland and Sunderland Albion were not as frosty as they were later known to be, as three of Sunderland's goals were scored by Bob Brand, an Albion player appearing as a 'guest player'.

During the first season of the Football League, Sunderland were unbeaten in eight home friendlies against Football League clubs, winning six of those games to provide a record much better than almost all of the dozen clubs in the league. However, their one away game against a Football League club brought a sobering 10–1 December defeat at Bolton Wanderers – the Trotters being beaten later in the campaign on Wearside. There was also a home draw with the Corinthians and 12–0 Boxing Day win over Druids, along with some encouraging results against Scottish clubs.

In the same season as the inaugural Football League, another league, known as the Combination, took place, but lasted for just a single campaign. This consisted of twenty clubs, none of whom were from the North East. These clubs had all failed in their bids to become founder members of the Football League. Each of them played between five and twenty-five games, with the table topped by Notts Rangers.

Sunderland and Sunderland Albion were among nine clubs who applied for election to the Football League for its second season. None were successful, as the four clubs who had finished in the last four places in the inaugural league table were all re-elected. Of the other aspirants, only Birmingham St George's and the Wednesday attracted more than the two votes received by Sunderland, with Sunderland Albion being one of four teams to receive no support.

During this 1888–89 season, Sunderland progressed through the opening hurdles of the English Cup only to then withdraw from the competition. The reason was that the next round paired them with James Allan's Sunderland Albion, who had already knocked out Shankhouse, Newcastle West End and Birtley. Sunderland had also withdrawn from the Durham Challenge Cup having been paired with Sunderland Albion. The simple reason for these withdrawals was that Sunderland wanted to snuff out James Allan's breakaway club. A share of what would have been a massive attendance from a cup game between the two clubs would have given Albion a financial boost, and the original club wished to deny them this.

Nonetheless, Allan's new club were attracting financial support, especially from the Monkwearmouth-based Wear Glass Works, owned by the Hartley brothers, James and John. Indeed, James would carry out much of the correspondence between Albion and SAFC.

Despite Sunderland's cup withdrawals, the clubs did meet on 1 December 1888, the date for what would have been the Durham Challenge Cup fixture. Sunderland agreed to the match on the condition that, other than expenses, the proceeds would go to charity. Indicative of the lack of trust between the clubs, Allan wrote to W.T. Wallace on 'Albion' headed notepaper asking:

> Dear Sir, I will feel obliged if you will inform me if the members of the Albion will be admitted free on production of membership card. What time will the gates be opened. What system you have of taking gate. If by sale of tickets, are the tickets collected? Where you intend to count gate. I leave other matters in your hands. Yours truly, James Allan.

The gate money from a record Newcastle Road crowd estimated at between 14 and 15,000 came to £154, which ended up being shared between the clubs after all. On the pitch, despite some hard pressing by an Albion side that included five players who at one time had played for Sunderland, first-half goals from Arnie Davison and John Breconridge gave Sunderland a 2–0 victory.

Local pressure for a rematch brought another Sunderland derby on 12 January 1889. This time the proceeds from a crowd of 9,374 were split between the Eye Infirmary, Children's Hospital, Royal Infirmary and the Monkwearmouth Dispensary. Despite Albion's attempts to have the rematch staged at Ashbrooke, the game once again took place at Newcastle Road, with pre-match publicity claiming that Albion were going to bring in a guest centre-forward, probably at great expense. Albion did include two 'guest' players from Accrington in Bob Brand and Alex Barbour, but still lost the match 3–2. Brand had played for Albion earlier in the year, as well as appearing as a 'guest' for Sunderland.

Albion took a 2–0 half-time lead against their great rivals. With the Peacock brothers prevalent (Andrew and Willie – or

Wallie as he was known in Scotland – who were also big figures in the early history of Rangers), however, Sunderland fought back to win in highly controversial circumstances. After Will Gibson and Andrew Peacock had made it 2–2, a late effort by John Breconridge was ruled by Sheffield referee Stacey to be a valid Sunderland winner, despite the protests by Albion. This was not a dispute about whether the ball had crossed the goal line, rather if it had gone under the crossbar, a common source of conflict in the days before nets. The lack of nets would haunt Sunderland in the FA Cup semi-final of 1891 and its replay, as we shall see, but on this occasion the decision went in their favour.

All hell broke loose, with eight of the Albion players storming off the pitch and refusing to continue, despite the cajoling of James Allan who was acting as Albion's umpire (each side provided an umpire – or linesman). The arguments continued, and it was another hour and a half before the referee ended the game.

Sunderland supporters have always been passionate in backing their team, but passion does not excuse violent or threatening behaviour, and this was not the first occasion that supporters had got out of hand. Stones were thrown when the visiting team left in their horse-drawn carriage, known as a brake. Several Albion players were hit, as was James Allan – the very man whose love of the game had created both clubs and who by now was headmaster at Hylton Road School, a position he had taken up at the start of both the football season and academic year. Having received not so much as a word of thanks from Sunderland when he left the club, Allan now had to be treated by a doctor for the injury he had sustained from supporters of the club he set up. Sunderland, on the other hand, received a trophy for winning the game, a silver cup presented to them that evening at the Queen's Hotel on Fawcett Street.

In the aftermath of the match, supporters of both clubs vented their views in the local press. There was a hostile exchange of letters between the clubs, Sunderland secretary W.T. Wallace forcibly declining a proposal from the Albion committee for a third meeting on a neutral ground for the prize of a £20 silver cup. Wallace's comments were summed up by his line: 'We decline to make any arrangements with people we cannot trust to keep them.'

Allan retorted in the press in a long reply which included the following:

> Now I come to some charges in Mr. Wallace's letter of which I demand proof, viz, that I have during the last few months done my best to break up the Sunderland club. I must give this statement an emphatic denial. If assisting to get together a strong club in another part of the town will break up the SAFC then I must plead guilty; but beyond this I have taken no steps, either directly or indirectly, against the SAFC. My action has only tended, as I hoped it would, to cause the SAFC committee to exert themselves to get talent to raise the game in the North of England. Since I came to Sunderland my endeavours have been to raise the tone of football, and I have taken no step to my knowledge to hinder the progress of the game. This much I might tell Mr. Wallace and his committee: that for the very existence of the club they are indebted to myself.

The continuing bitterness in the relationship between the two clubs saw Albion complain to the Football Association. Thomas Jobling had taken over from James Allan as Albion's secretary, and wrote:

> I beg to lodge a formal complaint as to the brutal conduct of the Sunderland supporters on January 12th in the match Sunderland v Albion. One player was openly threatened in the field as was also our umpire and during the latter period of the game mud was thrown at our players and umpire. Mr. Stacey the referee was hooted and howled at by the crowd at any decision he gave in favour of the Albion and after the match the brake conveying our players from the field was stoned and several of our players including our umpire injured. I am only giving you the head of our objection but can support further details by witnesses if necessary.

This led to an inquiry on the last day of January at the Grand Hotel on Bridge Street, presided over by the president of the Durham FA, Alf Grundy of Whitburn. The complaints in 1889 centred around claims that the Sunderland crowd had influenced the referee, that James Allan and others from Albion had been pelted with mud and that the Albion brake had been stoned when departing after the match. Further worsening the tarnished relationship between James Allan and the original club, it emerged during the inquiry – which lasted well over four hours – that Allan had threatened to strike some of the supporters with his stick. On the court documents 'The Case for the Sunderland Club' the words, 'Case dismissed without costs by the English Football Ass' are handwritten in red. Among the lengthy handwritten contents are extensive quotes listing rules 21 and 28 of the FA, attributed to none other than C.W. Alcock Esq.

This is followed by a list of called witnesses, starting with William Thwaites Wallace and committee witnesses James McMillan, James Marr, John Cook, R. Fenton and Sam Tyzack. Following these leading lights of Sunderland's early history were a number of police witnesses, including Inspector Best, Jas Towie, umpire of the Sunderland club, and the Sunderland players who played on the left flank: William Gibson and the Peacock brothers. Then came five spectators from the 'third side', starting with John Heaton of 44 Devonshire Street, and ten witnesses from the grandstand. These included Councillor Roger Errington, John Alcock, Captain Butchart and Mr Gales of the *Daily Leader*.

James Allan's testimony read:

> In the second half the mud commenced. I was struck with it. I turned [unreadable word, presumably towards] Mr. McMillan Wallace [Presumably Mr. McMillan and Mr. Wallace]. I did not complain to anyone except the man who threw it. I said, 'If the mud throwing continued I would leave'. I went to the club house. One of the Sunderland members threatened after the game. I never saw

the Sunderland officials. We all proceeded to gather. I was struck by one Stephenson. Don't know who stoned me on any occasion.

George Monaghan also spoke – yes, one of the players whose inclusion in the Sunderland side had seen them thrown out of the English Cup the previous season. He was in the Albion team on 12 January. He claimed: 'Whittle attempted to strike me.'

The Reverend Robinson Hindle was unable to attend the inquiry, but in the presence of George Towers, clerk to solicitor J. Tindell Green, his written evidence read:

> I am unable to attend the Inquiry this evening as I am engaged at a lecture at Dalton le Dale. I was present at and witnessed the match between Sunderland and Albion on January 12th and occupied a position on the Grand Stand under the Reporters' Box. Having been present at several football matches in this and other districts. I consider that the excitement was much less than may have been expected considering the local rivalry of the two clubs. There was certainly nothing done which I saw to interfere with the play of any individual member of either team. The decisions of the referee as invariably happens were at times questioned by the partisans of the two clubs and were received with hooting by the spectators. This applys [applies] to decisions in favour of Sunderland as well as the Albion. I know nothing of the umpires and the referee being threatened and did not see any mud thrown on the field. Owing to the Albion team leaving the field before the completion of the game great excitement was created and I went as usual to the dressing room where I found several of the Albion players, three of whom had already left the field. I advised them to stay within the tent until the crowd had left the field but one of the Albion players after a short interval said: 'Let's go. What is there to be afraid of?' and with the rest left the field and were accompanied by myself in conversation with Brand. They were not in any

way molested and got into the brake safely. I consider the arrangements made by the Sunderland Committee for this and other matches were much in advance of other clubs.

Allegations had also been made that the referee had called into Albion's Waverley Hotel headquarters on his way home to express regret if he had made a mistake in awarding the winning goal. Replying to a telegram from W.T. Wallace from his home address in Sheffield on 16 January, referee Stacey wrote:

> I am much surprised and hurt at the contents of your letter ... I hasten to reply to your queries. You say the paper says, 'that I expressed my regret at what occurred'. You also ask me to kindly tell you now, if I still aver that it was a goal. In the first place I never said that, 'I expressed my regret at what occurred'.

Underlining some words, Stacey continued:

> I had nothing to regret and the only regrettable part was the Albion team leaving the field before time. I still aver as I have all the time, that Sunderland obtained a goal just before time, making the game Sunderland 3 goals Albion 2 ... Surely the tension between your clubs is 'too tight' when it prevents you meeting the Referee either personally or by deputy for fear of offence to another Club ... I never had such questions put to me before and hope never to have again. Yours faithfully, W.H. Stacey.

After the inquiry ruled in Sunderland's favour, the outcome was that the relationship between Sunderland AFC and its founder had reached a low that seems not to have been healed in Allan's lifetime. Allan continued to be a success in his teaching career and he was with Albion until their demise in 1892. In 1899 he followed Robert Singleton in becoming a Freemason, although at the Williamson Lodge No 949 in Sunderland rather than the Palatine Lodge.

James Allan passed away at the age of just 54 on 18 October 1911, by which time the Sunderland club he had started in 1879 had established themselves among football's elite, having been champions of England four times. There is no known record of Allan reconciling his differences with SAFC, and following the demise of Albion any continued interest he had in football appears to have been very low profile. More than a century had passed since the alleged assault on Allan back at Sunderland before a rapprochement began with his descendants.

This came about in 2009 when, as the editor of the club's official magazine *Legion of Light*, I wrote an article about James Allan. A few days later I received a phone call in my office at the club from the great grandson of Allan, Ray O'Donnell. Now a Sunderland supporter and resident in Lytham St Annes, the long-term home of the Football League, Ray O'Donnell had seen the article after a friend had passed it on to him. Having re-established contact with the family of the man who gave birth to football in Sunderland, I invited Ray, his son Brendan and daughter Julia to a match at the Stadium of Light in 2009, as the 130th anniversary of Allan bringing football to Wearside was marked. Chairman at the time Niall Quinn made a presentation on the pitch to Allan's descendants, and since then Brendan in particular (now a staunch Sunderland fan, having transferred his allegiance from Manchester United) has become a strong friend of the club, often helping out with various initiatives and kindly sharing his knowledge of his famous footballing ancestor. At last a happy ending to what was an awful way for the club founder to be treated.

Coming back to the 1888–89 season, two days after the inquiry into Albion's complaint about SAFC, Albion suffered another defeat. They went out of the first round proper of the English Cup away to Grimsby Town, qualifying rounds having been introduced, with Football League clubs able to enter after those qualifying games.

In Sunderland's case, having seen off Albion in two matches and despite the inquiry, the season carried on with some high-scoring matches, 59 goals being scored in a sequence of 8 games, all of which were won, with 43 goals in their favour and 16 against. These victories included wins over Football League clubs Bolton Wanderers and Everton. Beating Bolton was some revenge for the 10–1 defeat there before Christmas, when Bolton became the last English club to beat Sunderland all season, the club's only other reverses coming to Scottish sides.

The third of June 1889 saw Sunderland appoint their first manager – and what a manager he turned out to be. At the time of writing he remains the most successful manager in the history of North East football. He won the league title three times with Sunderland, and after leaving his native North East, the Byker-born boss went on to manage Liverpool's first ever top-flight winning team. This was the great Tom Watson. Just eighteen months younger than James Allan, Watson came to the club on the recommendation of John Grayston. One of the people involved with the club at its birth, Grayston remained loyal when others followed Allan to Albion. In recommending Watson – who had previously managed both Newcastle West End and Newcastle East End – Grayston was responsible for one of the finest pieces of recruitment in SAFC's history.

Accepting a salary of 35 shillings (£1.75) per week and a house to live in, Watson's recruitment was outstanding. With treasurer Sam Tyzack, Watson made numerous scouting trips to Scotland to secure some of the players who would make Sunderland great.

The opening match of the 1889–90 season, with Watson in charge, saw Blackburn Rovers beaten. Sunderland were going places. Two games later the previous season's double winners Preston were held to a 1–1 draw, thanks to a late equaliser from John Harvie (he preferred his surname to be spelled Harvey), who had been signed from the powerful Scottish club Renton within three weeks of Watson taking over. Sunderland would win half of their fourteen games against Football League clubs during the season and lose just four, winning one of their three away games in the process. Most notably they thrashed Aston Villa 7–2 – with a hat-trick from James Gillespie and a couple from Johnny Campbell – on Easter Saturday. Attending the game was Aston Villa director and future chairman William McGregor. A Scot, McGregor had been the instigator of the Football League, and he was the first chairman of the League Management Committee. Villa had beaten Blackburn Rovers 3–0 in their final league game of the season a few days earlier but were no match for Sunderland. In their two seasons as a Football League club the only time Villa had conceded as many goals was in a match at Everton, where they had been a man short from half-time after a player called Archie Hunter (who had complained to the referee about the turn-of-year conditions before kick-off) had collapsed and never played again.

There were no such extenuating circumstances when Villa were trounced at Newcastle Road where, after the match, McGregor remarked: 'They have a talented man in every position.' It was from this statement that Sunderland became known as The Team of All The Talents. It was a moniker that would be well deserved in the coming decade, as Sunderland and Villa contested the right to be called the best team in the country, or indeed the world, at that time. On the day they received McGregor's accolade, England drew 1–1 away to Scotland. One of Sunderland's best players, John 'Dowk' Oliver had been selected as a reserve by England for that game. It would be almost another year until Tom Porteous became the first player to be capped while with Sunderland, but evidently Sunderland's pre-league players were already being noticed at international level.

In what was to be Sunderland's last season before being elected to the Football League, their attempts to illustrate their credentials through a good cup run faltered at the first hurdle. Drawn away to Blackburn Rovers – who won more games and scored more goals at home than any other club in the league that season – Sunderland drew 2–2 after 90 minutes. Although there were replays between Accrington and West Bromwich Albion, and Notts County and Birmingham St George's in the same round of the cup, Sunderland's match at Blackburn went straight to extra-time, and Rovers emerged as 4–2 victors. Sunderland's conquerors went on to win the trophy (and retain it the following season). Only in the final, when (Sheffield) Wednesday got a consolation goal in a 6–1 defeat, did anyone else score against Blackburn in the competition. Sunderland had shown they were a force to be reckoned with. Had Blackburn come to Newcastle Road for a replay, perhaps Sunderland might have defeated them as they had done in a friendly at the beginning of the season.

Sunderland's hammering of Villa was well timed. Less than a month later, at the AGM of the Football League in the Douglas Hotel in Manchester, Sunderland were among the clubs stating their case for admission to the league. As in the inaugural 1888–89 season, the clubs at the bottom of the Football League had to apply for re-election. It was supposed to be the bottom four who had to re-apply, but fourth-from-bottom Bolton Wanderers were excused this, as they had finished level on points with fifth-from-bottom Villa. Notts County and Burnley were duly accepted back into the fold, but wooden spoonists Stoke were replaced by Sunderland, who became the first club after the founder members to join and the first from outside the North West and Midlands to participate.

Represented by chairman James Marr and the Reverend Hindle, Sunderland evidently had a strong case due to their results on the field and the sizeable crowds they had shown themselves able to attract. The club's biggest disadvantage was that, geographically, they were even more out on a limb than they are now, given the ways of travelling in 1890 and the long distance each existing league club would have to agree to travel to fulfil a league fixture on Wearside. In order to help overcome this obstacle, SAFC's representatives offered to: 'Make some allowance for the travelling expenses of the visitors for the first season.' So Sunderland, delighted to be the first club to be admitted to the new elite, had to assist with the travelling expenses of all of their opponents, despite the prospect of having to make a lengthy journey themselves to every away game, not just one per season.

Who knows how James Allan felt when the club he had created achieved their place in the Football League. His Sunderland Albion were one of four other clubs (Including Newton Heath, who became Manchester United) to have unsuccessfully applied to join. Albion had had a good season, averaging over 3,000 supporters at home games, slightly more than the outgoing Stoke, and finishing as runners-up to FA Cup finalists Wednesday in the Football Alliance. Wednesday had withdrawn their own application shortly before the meeting.

James Allan, James McMillan, John Grayston, Robert Singleton, Sam Tyzack, James Marr, the Reverend Robinson Hindle and latterly Tom Watson had been among those who had played their part in building a club. It had begun as a group of school teachers learning a new sport in 1879, and progressed to a club that had been elected to the Football League. At the same meeting that saw Sunderland elected into the league, the members decided to spend 50 guineas on a splendid league championship trophy. Sunderland would not have to wait long to win it.

2

THE TEAM OF ALL THE TALENTS

Victorian dominance from the world champions (1890–97)
Sunderland won the league in only their second season, retained the title a year later and after two more years became the first club to be champions three times, being proclaimed 'World Champions' for good measure. This truly was The Team of All The Talents. For all of Sunderland's achievements since, including the near-double side of 1912–13 and the fabulous Raich Carter-inspired era of the 1930s, it is this period in the early 1890s that remains Sunderland's greatest and most successful period. It is the time that established Sunderland in the national consciousness as being at the top of the footballing tree. Regardless of the failings in any of the poor periods since, particularly in the post-Second World War years, this was the team of greats who did not just put Sunderland on the footballing map, but made an indelible impression that means when the giant clubs of football are discussed, Sunderland must be part of that debate.

Sunderland's support is second to none. Would any other club average over 30,000 fans in a fourth successive season in the third tier of the national league system, almost half a century on from winning their only major trophy in over eight decades, as Sunderland did in 2021–22? That unstinting support brought to worldwide attention in the Netflix series *Sunderland 'Til I Die* in 2018, 2020 and 2024 comes from the fact that right from the very early days of the Football League in the century before last, Sunderland's team brought pride to what was then still a town. That fierce pride in Sunderland and the wider North East has never diminished. It has been built on and renewed by other great teams, such as the FA Cup winners of 1973 and the record-breaking 105-point promotion team of 1998–99, but its origins lie in the 1890s side that featured greats such as Ted Doig, Johnny Campbell, Jamie Millar, Johnny Auld and Hughie Wilson. These players, and others among them, are legends on Wearside.

Preparations for the club's first foray into league football, in the 1890–91 season, commenced with a game against Scottish powerhouses Renton, themselves preparing to kick off the first ever Scottish League season. A year earlier Sunderland had signed goal-machine Johnny Campbell from Renton. (In 2024 Campbell was still fifth in the list of Sunderland's all-time top scorers, having hit 154 goals for the club.) In an era when the unofficial 'World Championship' was contested by clubs from Scotland and England – who were the only countries playing the game to any notable standard at the time – Campbell was the only player to become a world champion with clubs from both sides of the border, Renton in 1888 and Sunderland in 1895. As Scottish Cup winners, Renton had beaten English Cup holders West Bromwich Albion in 1888. But Renton had lost some of their best players to English clubs when the Football League commenced. These included the Harry Campbell – no relation to Johnny – who would win the English Cup in 1890 with Blackburn Rovers, having played against Sunderland and his old namesake teammate during that cup run.

Johnny Campbell was one of the scorers as Sunderland showed they meant business, taming Renton 5–1 at Newcastle Road. In five warm-up games only Middlesbrough held the Lads, earning a goalless draw on Teesside, but the big sign of what was to come was the hosting of Preston North End, the team who had won the only two league seasons so far played. Preston had been beaten in only four of the forty-four league games they had ever played, but were trounced 6–3 by Sunderland.

Having scored eleven goals in their two home warm-up matches, there was optimism in the air ahead of Sunderland's first ever league fixture on 13 September 1890. The visitors were Burnley, a club who had finished second from bottom of the table the previous season and had had to apply for re-election in both years of the league. The league season had actually kicked off the week before Sunderland's first game, Burnley drawing 1–1 at Accrington.

There was a shock in store for the 8,000 crowd at Newcastle Road on Sunderland's big day, as the home side fell behind as early as the eighth minute. Alec Stewart put Burnley ahead with the first ever goal in a Sunderland league fixture, the Scot scoring his first ever league goal. By the half-hour mark Sunderland had asserted themselves and led 2–1, Campbell nudging them ahead after John Spence had claimed the Wearsiders' first league strike. Spence had arrived the previous season from his hometown club Airdrieonians. Disappointment was to follow as Burnley swept ahead with a couple of goals in the next few minutes, through Claude Lambie and Alexander McLardie, and the visitors ran out 3–2 victors.

Just two days later Sunderland had the chance to make amends when they entertained Wolverhampton Wanderers. Forty-eight hours earlier, Wolves had been hammered 5–0 by Everton at Anfield, which was then the Toffees' home ground. Wolves had already defeated Aston Villa prior to that, and they made the trip to Sunderland looking to bounce back. Such hopes for the Midlanders seemed forlorn, as with over an hour gone they trailed 3–0. Calamity was to strike, however, as Sunderland astonishingly went on to lose 3–4, the dispiriting winner coming a couple of minutes from time from England international Harry Wood, who denied Sunderland what would have been their first point.

Football is a brutal and ruthless business. For all the talk about astronomical sums of money ruining modern-day football, the fact is that this is nothing new. All that really changes is the number of noughts on the end of transfer fees and salaries. Even in 1905, Alf Common's transfer from Sunderland to Middlesbrough for the game's first £1,000 fee led to questions in Parliament. Money was dominating the sport and, as we have seen, controversy over players being paid as professionals had already caused problems for Sunderland, as well as the wider sport.

After just two league matches ruthlessness reared its head at Sunderland. Monkwearmouth-born goalkeeper Bill Kirkley had been a stalwart of the club's early years. He had been at the club since 1885 and had played in all but the first of Sunderland's pre-league English Cup ties, as well as the opening two league games. Nonetheless, he was instantly dropped, never to play again, despite reports that he had been ill during the Wolves game when he made mistakes that led to the defeat. He would go on to play for Sunderland Albion.

There was clearly no room for sentiment at Sunderland, but at least Kirkley's replacement was someone who would become a giant of the club. Two days after the Wolves defeat Sunderland swooped to sign Ted Doig. Commonly known as Ned elsewhere, Doig's eventual 457 appearances for Sunderland remains the third highest in the club's history as of 2024, and is likely to remain so for many years to come. Only Len Ashurst, with one more appearance than Doig (including six outings as a substitute), and Jim Montgomery have ever played more.

Ted Doig's grandson Eric carried out immense research into his grandfather and claims that, in total, Doig played more games for the club than even record appearance holder Montgomery's 627, pointing out that in Doig's day the so-called 'friendly' matches that made up much of the season were usually lucrative and prestigious challenge matches that were keenly contested, unlike friendlies of modern times. What is certain is that Doig was a key figure in the success of Sunderland in the 1890s and beyond, when he became one of only two players to win four league title medals with SAFC. To 2024 he also

The Team of All The Talents

remains the man to have played the most top-flight games for Sunderland – 417.

Doig kept a clean sheet on his Sunderland debut as the club's third league match brought a handsome 4–0 win at West Bromwich Albion's Stoney Lane. Albion were the only other club without a point at this stage, but despite their victory Sunderland were not rewarded with the points. Remember that Sunderland's first ever English Cup win in 1887 against Morpeth Harriers had to be replayed, as a player had not been registered in time. Once again, Sunderland's administrators had slipped up.

Doig had not been correctly registered, so not only were the club docked their first points, but they were fined too: £25 for the incorrect registration, caused by a slow postal delivery to the League headquarters, and £5 for a technical rule breach following a protest by Doig's former league club Blackburn Rovers for not having their written consent for him to play. Welcome to the league!

Having been capped twice by Scotland while with Arbroath – still by the end of the 2023–24 season the only man to win a full international cap with the club – Doig had played one game in the English league before coming to Sunderland. In November 1889 he had appeared for Blackburn Rovers in a 9–1 win over Notts County. Doig had signed for them after the game, accepted a £30 signing-on fee, but then changed his mind and returned to Scotland. Feelings were obviously high, as Rovers served a court summons against Doig on 14 December 1889 for 'stealing the sum of £30', only to settle out of court for the repayment of the amount less £4 travel expenses. When he played for Sunderland he had not been registered with the club for seven days, so technically he was considered to be still on Blackburn's books.

Regardless of this initial difficulty, Doig was a superb keeper who would earn Sunderland many points in future, 147 clean sheets in competitive games being an indication of that. The first opportunity home fans had to see Doig in action was a 3–1 friendly win over Cambuslang, but before then there had been three games on the road. A friendly defeat at Stoke (with Potts rather than Doig or Kirkley in goal against Stoke, who were now in the Football Alliance, having been replaced in the Football League by the Wearsiders) and a 2–2 draw at Glasgow Celtic in challenge matches, and in between Sunderland succeeded in winning their first ever league point. This came at Burnley on 27 September in a 3–3 draw. Doig was beaten in the first minute by Alexander McLardie, who had scored at Newcastle Road and would score twice here, but goals from John Harvie, Jock Scott and John Spence earned Sunderland a point on a day that Scotland international John Murray made his debut.

Welcome though the point was, there would be another defeat and another draw before a first legitimate victory. A four-goal blast from Campbell, plus one from Jamie Millar saw the red and whites roar back from being two James Brogan goals down to win 5–2 away to Bolton Wanderers at their Pike's Lane home.

Campbell and Millar were Sunderland's Victorian hotshots. They would score a total of 281 competitive goals between them for the club. A week after the taming of the Trotters, the same combination did for Blackburn, who lost 3–1 at Newcastle Road, Millar's late strike putting the icing on the cake of Campbell's earlier brace just a few days before Sunderland's impressive new town hall was opened. Sunderland had been bottom of the league before the win at Bolton. Now 'The Talents' were on their way.

There was another hiccup before they really began to climb the table. Only one point was gleaned from the next four league games, as Sunderland dropped back to the foot of the table. Five days before Christmas, league leaders Everton came to Newcastle Road and lost 1–0. The Toffees were in the middle of a run of seven wins out of eight games and had just won 6–2 away to Derby County. A goal from Davy Hannah midway through the second half upset the form book and set Sunderland off onto an excellent run, in which they would win seven, draw two and lose only one of their final ten league fixtures. This sequence included 5–1 home wins over Aston Villa and Derby, plus a 3–0 Newcastle Road triumph over Preston North End. Losing to Sunderland in what was their final fixture (after being held by Sunderland at home the previous month) thwarted Preston's hopes of retaining their grip on the title and handed the championship to Everton (who lost their last game that day at Burnley) for the first time.

In between the two meetings with Preston, Sunderland's rising status in the game had been recognised by the staging of a full England international at Newcastle Road. The England team stayed at the Grand Hotel in Bridge Street, just the other side of the river from the ground but within walking distance of it. What's more, Sunderland full-back Tom Porteous played in the 4–1 British Championship win against Wales to become the club's first international player. Porteous had a good game, made some telling clearances and even had a goal disallowed as his long distance indirect free-kick went in without touching anyone else, but after his late miskick led to Wales's consolation goal he never earned another cap.

Sunderland finished their first season in a creditable seventh place, out of twelve. But for their points deduction they would have been fifth, just two points off the runners-up spot and four behind the champions. Given the way Sunderland had ended the season there was plenty of room for optimism for the following year.

Less than a month after champions-elect Everton were beaten on Wearside, they returned for Sunderland's first English Cup tie as a league club and were beaten by the same 1–0 scoreline on 17 January 1891. Further victories at Darwen and at home to Nottingham Forest saw Sunderland reach the semi-final without their goal being breached. Defeating Forest prevented an all-Nottingham semi-final, as Sunderland were drawn to face Notts County. There might have been an all-Wearside quarter-final but for Forest knocking out Sunderland Albion in a tie that took two replays to settle.

At this point James Allan's Albion were doing well. They were second to Stoke in the Football Alliance, and while the Potters held a commanding eight-point lead, Albion had five games in hand and had been beaten in the league only once all season. Sunderland, though, had amply demonstrated that they were the dominant club in the town as members of the Football League and English Cup semi-finalists to boot.

Stoke's Victoria Ground staged the other semi-final, where Blackburn Rovers beat West Bromwich Albion to reach the final. But they had to wait to find out who their opponents in that game would be, as Sunderland and Notts County shared six goals at Sheffield United's Bramall Lane. Under a month earlier Notts had lost 4–0 to Sunderland in the North East, but this time Sunderland were minus skipper Johnny Auld through injury and also Jamie Millar. He had notched a hat-trick in the recent league victory over the semi-final opponents, but was absent on compassionate leave following the sudden death of his father.

Sunderland's semi-final was controversial to say the least. In the 2020s technology in football debates surrounds Video Assistant Referees and the idea of technologically decided offside decisions. In 1891 the debate about technology in football concerned goal nets – there weren't any – as we had seen in the controversy over one of the goals in Sunderland's win over local rivals Albion in 1889. None of the goals described thus far have used the term 'netted'. Had nets been in use at the time, Sunderland's first season as a Football League club would quite possibly have seen them also become English Cup finalists. Given their form in the second half of the season, they might even have won it.

The semi-final saw an estimated 10,000 supporters travel from Sunderland to Sheffield, including those on eight special trains, no doubt the highest number of Wearsiders ever to move outside the North East en masse. They saw Sheffield referee Mr Clegg award Notts County two debateable goals in a 3–3 draw. Sometimes in modern football people complain about referees not keeping up with play. In 1891 the referee was permanently positioned on the sidelines at the halfway line! There was an umpire for each half, but they were only asked

The Team of All The Talents

to adjudicate if a player made an appeal. When the umpires disagreed on a decision the final say went to the referee. As with the introduction of goal nets, referees taking control of matches commenced in 1891–92.

The first of Notts' questionable goals was certainly preventable. Doig made no attempt to stop Andrew McGregor's shot, as he was certain he was well offside. Sunderland's Johnny Campbell had already had a goal ruled out for the same reason. Obviously, Doig should have done what generations of footballers since have been advised to do – play to the whistle. However, the greatest controversy came when the match officials ruled that a shot from Notts' Jimmy Oswald had gone in off the crossbar, when the Sunderland players were adamant it had gone over the bar. This goal regained the lead for the Nottinghamshire side. Sunderland had gone 2–1 ahead thanks to an own goal and one from John Harvie, only for Tom McInnes to have made it all square at the break, but Campbell duly levelled for Sunderland to earn a replay, only for that match to produce yet more controversy.

Back at Sheffield United eleven days later, Sunderland went down 2–0, once again with questions around whether one of the goals had gone in. This time it was argued that McGregor's shot had gone wide, but after much debate a goal was awarded. Ironically, nets had first been used in 1882 – at Bramall Lane. These were not nets for the goals, though, but long nets at each end of the pitch designed to stop the ball going a long way out of play. Goal nets were made compulsory by the FA and Football League from the 1891–92 season, partially as a result of Sunderland's semi-final controversy. There had also been similar debates over goals in international matches, while Merseysider John Alexander Brodie, who came up with the idea of goal nets, did so after a disallowed goal in an 1889 match between Everton and Accrington.

After the league and cup season was completed on 21 March, Sunderland embarked on no fewer than thirteen 'friendlies' that took them up to the end of April. Newcastle West End held

Sunderland to a draw at St James' Park, but the other twelve games were all won with an aggregate score of forty-seven goals to seven. This sequence included a rematch with Notts County, fresh from losing the cup final, who were thrashed 6–0.

Sunderland's second season as a league club saw them firmly establish themselves among the game's elite. They strode to the league title with a 100 per cent home record that to the end of 2023–24 has never been equalled. For good measure they again reached the semi-final of the cup.

The Football League was extended to fourteen clubs, with the addition of Stoke and fellow Alliance club Darwen, and the season consisted of twenty-six games, with the pair of newcomers propping up the final table. In addition to winning all thirteen of their home fixtures, Tom Watson's side won eight of their thirteen away games, but lost the other five, not drawing at all in the league. They finished five points clear of runners-up Preston North End, who continued their proud record of never finishing lower than the top two in the four seasons of league football played so far. North End would maintain that record the following season, when they were once again second to Sunderland's Team of All The Talents.

Three of Sunderland's five away losses came in the first three away games. Alarmingly, a dozen goals were conceded in those three games, three-quarters of them in the first half of matches. This meant that despite beating Wolverhampton Wanderers 5–2 on the opening day of the season at Newcastle Road, the Wearsiders were bottom of the table as September closed.

The team hastily got into its stride. Fifteen goals in the next four fixtures brought maximum points, and after a hiccup of a defeat at Blackburn Rovers, Sunderland set off on what (to the summer of 2024) remains a club record: thirteen consecutive league victories, a sequence that included a handsome 4–1 win over Preston. But Sunderland didn't actually top the table until the penultimate victory of this thirteen-game sequence.

A surprise 1–0 loss at Notts County ended the run but set things up for a home game with Blackburn Rovers. They were the FA Cup holders and had won five of the previous eight FA (or English) Cup finals. Rovers had also been the only team to beat Sunderland earlier in the season during a run where the red and whites won seventeen out of eighteen league games. On a day when closest rivals Preston lost at Aston Villa, Sunderland tore Blackburn apart, beating them 6–1 as the club's first ever league title was sealed.

As the club's all-time top-scorer Bobby Gurney would do on the day the title was won in 1936, and as SAFC's top post-Second World War scorer Kevin Phillips would do on the day promotion was sealed in 1999, goal-machine Johnny Campbell scored four times in this game. The Scot opened the scoring after just eight minutes, with his partner Jamie Millar instantly restoring the lead after the visitors' Coombe Hall levelled. Some contemporary reports attribute one of Campbell's goals to David Hannah, but it was the unrelated Jimmy Hannah who joined Campbell and Millar on the scoresheet.

The title was secured with two games to spare. Both of these were won on the road, the first of them bringing another Campbell hat-trick in a 7–1 win at Darwen. The league newcomers had been beaten 7–0 earlier in the season at Sunderland. Campbell's 31 goals in 24 league appearances made him the country's top scorer, a feat he would repeat in both of the seasons in the coming three years when his goals again fired Sunderland to the title.

As in their previous season, Sunderland reached the semi-final of the English Cup. Adding to their 100 per cent home league record, convincing victories were produced in both home games in the cup run, which once again ended at Sheffield United's Bramall Lane. This time Aston Villa were the opponents. Villa finished fourth in the league and had given Sunderland two tough games. They had been one of the clubs to inflict an early away defeat – to the tune of 5–3. Late in the season they had narrowly been beaten 2–1 on Wearside in the only one of Sunderland's home games from December onwards that was not won by at least three goals.

In front of a huge – for the time – crowd of 28,000, Sunderland were surprisingly well beaten in the semi-final. Having led through an early Campbell goal, Sunderland were pegged back on the stroke of half-time by Jack Devey, with Villa going on to win 4–1, although they would lose the final to neighbours West Bromwich Albion.

On top of league and cup encounters, a further 26 friendly or benefit matches took place during this 1891–92 season. Many of these produced big wins, notably an 11–0 hammering of Glasgow Thistle. Adding these extra games to Sunderland's competitive fixtures, the Lads scored an incredible 217 goals across the campaign.

The most significant of these extra matches came in the closing weeks of the season. Whereas only a year or two earlier there had been fierce competition from Sunderland Albion for dominance of the town, by now James Allan's Albion were melting in the heat of Sunderland's success. The first club Allan established in the town were proving themselves to be not just the best in the town, but in the country.

Albion had left the Football Alliance just as Sunderland became Football League champions. By now Albion were members of the Northern League, and unable to finish in the top half of it. Two days after Sunderland became champions, a bigger crowd than had seen the Blackburn game returned to Newcastle Road for the Wearside derby; Albion were spanked 6–1, just as Blackburn had been. Under a fortnight later Sunderland paid a return visit to Albion at the Blue House Field. Once again, Campbell was torturer in chief with a hat-trick as Albion were pulverised 8–0. The battle for the town was well and truly over. Sunderland would not be like Sheffield, Nottingham or Bristol, for example, came to be. There would be only one major club in Sunderland, and they were not only the league champions, but would retain that title twelve months on.

A meeting attended by Tom Watson at Manchester's Royal Hotel decided that a League Division Two was to be created.

The Team of All The Talents

Following this, the AGM of the Football League was held at the Queen's Hotel in Sunderland on 13 May 1892. Consequently, it was in Sunderland that Darwen, Ardwick, Bootle, Burslem Port Vale, Burton Swifts, Crewe Alexandra, Grimsby, Lincoln City, Northwich Victoria, Sheffield United, Small Heath Alliance and Walsall Town Swifts were all made members of that new league. More importantly, from SAFC's point of view, it was at this same meeting that the championship trophy was handed over to the Wearsiders.

Teams often talk about making their home ground a fortress. Newcastle Road was undoubtedly this for Sunderland during this period of dominance. After the loss of the first ever two home league games in September 1890, Sunderland were unbeaten in 49 home league and cup matches until falling 2–3 to Blackburn Rovers in December 1893. The response to this would be to remain undefeated in the following 43 competitive home matches, until the start of the 1896–97 season – a single loss in 93 home games, the vast majority of which were won, in a six-year spell.

The 1892–93 season saw Sunderland set off on the defence of their title by dropping just a single point from their first eight games. Incredibly, at this stage Sunderland were not top. They were a point behind Preston, although they did have a game in hand and a goal average better than twice anyone else's after the eighth game brought an 8–1 demolition of West Bromwich Albion. The season had kicked off with a 6–0 win at Accrington, complete with the almost obligatory Campbell hat-trick. Soon afterwards a first ever win at Aston Villa's Perry Barr saw another six-goal haul, Campbell getting two. Villa were later punished 6–0 on Wearside.

Between those first two big away wins Notts County pulled off a surprise 2–2 draw on Wearside, where the only other team to take a point all season were Bolton. Wanderers looked like they were breaking hearts on Valentine's Day when they astonishingly led 3–0 with little over quarter of an hour to go, only for Sunderland to fight back to 3–3.

Unlike the previous seasons as a league outfit, SAFC did not reach the semi-final of the FA Cup. After a 6–0 victory over Royal Arsenal in the FA Cup, in which Campbell scored twice, they went out in the third round at Blackburn Rovers four days after that home fight-back against Bolton.

Having briefly gone top on Christmas Eve, Sunderland took over more permanently at the top of the table at the turn of the year. Only one of the final fourteen league games were lost, at Bolton. Confirmation that Sunderland had retained the league title came at the beginning of April on a day the Wearsiders weren't playing. Preston's failure to beat Accrington at home confirmed that no one could catch Watson's men, who still had three games to go. The players still had ambition though. Not content with being the first team to win the two-tier Football League, having been the last of only three clubs to win the single-tier league, they wanted another feather in their cap. With three games to go they needed to score 10 more goals to become the first side to register 100 league goals in a season.

Six of those goals were plundered at home to Newton Heath. The club that would become Manchester United had already been defeated 5–0 on their own patch, and to 2023 they have never suffered a higher aggregate league loss. A one-all draw at Derby left Sunderland needing three goals at Burnley. They did this with three in six minutes just past the half-hour mark, eventually winning 3–2, with Harvie bagging two and Wilson the other as cartwheels marked the celebration of becoming the first side to ever score 100 league goals in a season. Remarkably, this had been achieved in a mere 30 games. No team would match this century of goals until the league season was extended to 42 games after the First World War.

Pulling in the cash from being the most talked-about team in the country, a further half-dozen friendlies were played at the end of the season. After losing the first two, the remaining four were won with nineteen goals scored, including six in a big win against Rangers in Glasgow. Campbell scored a brace at the old Ibrox. He had been top scorer with 34 league and cup goals from 30 competitive appearances, and 22 of those goals had come from his first 14 games, in which he scored in every match. Phenomenal!

Lucrative friendlies continued to be highly prized by the board of directors as Sunderland lost the league title in 1893–94. Aston Villa were the other great team of the decade, and not only deposed the Wearsiders as champions, but also knocked them out of the cup. Sunderland could not get the better of Villa in any of six league, cup and friendly meetings during that season. This was Villa's first league title, and they would be champions another three times during the decade, as well as twice winning the FA Cup. The 1896–97 season was the pinnacle of Villa's success, when they achieved the magnificent double of league and cup. This feat was not managed by any team again until Tottenham Hotspur in 1960–61.

Villa were undertaking regular extra matches in 1893–94, but perhaps Sunderland greedily took on too many. More friendlies were played throughout the campaign than league and cup games. The club often made more from their guaranteed payment as esteemed and attractive visitors than they would from their share of gate receipts from league matches. Seven years earlier a total spend for the season of under £29 for travelling expenses had been criticised, but by now this had risen to something approaching £1,000! There was a plan for even more travelling, as Sunderland had received permission to tour the USA, which would have made Sunderland the first English team to play there. Proposed in May 1894, the cross-Atlantic excursion was to take place from mid-April to June the following year, but it never happened. A tour of France was also being contemplated by Tom Watson around this time.

Nonetheless, in the first week of the season, after an opening day away game, two midweek friendlies, in Glasgow and Newcastle, were fitted in before a key home game with Villa, which was drawn. The season saw over half the league games immediately preceded by at least one friendly. One of the extra games at the end of the season saw Sunderland lose 3–0 to a

Scottish League XI at Celtic Park. Celtic's Sandy McMahon, who got two of the goals, had scored for Scotland against England on the same ground earlier in the month.

The success Sunderland were having not just on the pitch but on the balance sheet was attracting envious glances from Sunderland Rugby Football Club at Ashbrooke on the south side of the Wear. Sunderland had squashed in crowds of up to 23,000 during the season and regularly attracted big gates. According to club historian Keith Gregson, around this time the rugby club considered swapping codes and taking up association football due to the vast attendances now being attracted to soccer games. The rugby devotees ultimately decided to stick to their own sport and celebrated their 150th anniversary in 2023–24. In the coming decades Sunderland chairmen F.W. Taylor, W.H. Bell and Colonel Turnbull were closely associated with Ashbrooke, while Robyn Auld, the grandson of The Team of All The Talents' first captain Johnny Auld became president of Ashbrooke (then Sunderland Cricket and Football – rugby – Club between 1980 and 1989). In 2019 Robyn accepted his grandfather's induction into the SAFC Hall of Fame. Although historically inaccurate, given that Sunderland AFC wore blue rather than red and white when they used Ashbrooke as a home ground, the modern-day soccer club returned to the venue in 2017 to launch their new playing kit for the following season.

Unhappy at being deposed as champions, Sunderland redoubled their efforts for the 1894–95 season. It would be a year imprinted into even modern consciousness thanks to a painting by Thomas Marie Madawaska Hemy – *Madawaska* being the name of the ship on which the artist was born. Hemy's painting, which is believed to be the world's biggest and possibly oldest oil painting of a football match, shows the scene at the Newcastle Road ground on 2 January 1895 when arch-rivals Sunderland and Aston Villa played out a 4–4 draw.

In the 1920s this painting took pride of place in the Bells Restaurant, Grill and Lounge, in Bridge Street in Sunderland. The proprietors of this establishment were Jas. Henderson and sons. The painting came to Roker Park shortly after a new main stand was opened in 1929, once the club had a space big enough to house it. When the Stadium of Light was constructed just over a century after the painting was produced, the picture was afforded pride of place in the entrance hall to the stadium. As every player and official enters through the main entrance, Hemy's painting illustrates that they are coming to a club steeped in history and tradition.

Three of the players in the Hemy painting are Andrew McCreadie, Harry Johnston and Bob McNeil, who were all signed to bolster the team after the failure to win the league for a third successive season in 1894. Scotland international McCreadie came from Rangers, where he had just won the Scottish Cup, playing in the final against Celtic alongside his brother Hugh, who scored. Johnston and McNeill arrived from Clyde. The trio would all be regulars as the title was regained, with McNeill (whose brother Alexander, another Clyde player, had a trial at Sunderland in 1895) going on to captain the club later in the decade.

Learning from the previous season, the number of friendlies and benefit games was halved, just eighteen being played, with three of those after the last league game. An early marker was put down when Villa were beaten at Perry Barr in the third match, despite the champions taking an early lead. This maintained Sunderland's 100 per cent record, the opening game having produced an 8–0 thrashing of a Derby County side that included the legendary Steve Bloomer. Sunderland actually scored eleven against Derby that day. The referee had been delayed, so a local referee started the game and Sunderland were 3–0 up at 'half-time' when the real referee, Mr Kirkham from Darwen, turned up and insisted that the game be restarted.

Eleven were scored for real later in the season, in the first round of the cup against Lancashire League leaders Fairfield. Thirteen goals had been scored in the three previous games, all away from home, including a 4–1 friendly win over Newcastle United at St James' Park. Astonishingly, Johnny Campbell did not score in the rout against Fairfield – but with Sunderland already 6–0 up at half-time he did play the second half as centre-half, having swapped positions with Andrew McCreadie. In those days centre-half was more what we would call a midfielder in modern terminology.

McCreadie duly scored the first goal of the second half, in which Jimmy Hannah completed a hat-trick, but the day was about Jamie Millar. In scoring five goals he became the first Sunderland player to do so in a national competition, and to 2023 he remains one of only four men to do so, Charlie Buchan, Bobby Gurney and Nick Sharkey being the only men to emulate him. The nephew of Sunderland teammate Billy Dunlop, Millar became the only outfield Sunderland player to win four league-title medals. In between his third in 1895 and fourth in 1902, he won two Scottish League medals and two Scottish Cups with Rangers. He scored twice in the 1897 Scottish Cup final, with his former Sunderland teammate Tommy Hyslop also on the scoresheet and another SAFC old boy Andrew McCreadie in the side. One of Sunderland's all-time greats, Millar (who had various spellings of both of his names) passed away shortly before what would have been his 36th birthday due to tuberculosis.

The second round of the cup gave league leaders Sunderland a difficult tie away to Preston North End, where Campbell contributed both goals in a 2–0 victory. After Bolton were beaten in the quarter-final, courtesy of a brace from Hughie Wilson, the draw for the semi-final featured Sunderland, West Bromwich Albion, Aston Villa and The Wednesday of Sheffield. Sunderland were drawn against Villa in a match played at Blackburn's Ewood Park. Having taken three of the available four points from Villa already in the league, there was cause for optimism that the Lads could surmount this most difficult of obstacles and reach the final for the first time, but it wasn't to be.

Despite Jimmy Hannah giving Sunderland an early lead in a game which, unusually for the time, did not kick off until four o'clock, it was the Midlanders who triumphed, thanks to two second-half goals from Steve Smith, a winger who would, the following month, mark what proved to be his only international with a goal for England against Scotland. Villa would be Sunderland's most troublesome cup opponents. They came out on top against the Lads on the first seven occasions they were drawn together, including the 1913 final and two semi-finals. When Sunderland did finally knock Villa out of the cup for the only time in 1933, the following season Villa inflicted what remains Sunderland's heaviest FA Cup defeat, 7–2.

As Sunderland returned home from the disappointment of cup elimination in 1895, there were four league games remaining. All of these were won. Victory at Burnley in the penultimate fixture all but wrapped up the league, as the only viable challengers, Everton, lost at home on the same day to Derby. Sunderland made mathematically certain of their third league title in four years on the same afternoon that Villa were lifting the cup, having beaten their near neighbours West Bromwich Albion at Crystal Palace. At Newcastle Road Everton had to win and then win their one remaining fixture while turning over a substantial goal-average deficit to pip Sunderland at the post. Unsurprisingly, it was a closely fought and tense match. A draw would have been sufficient for Sunderland, but that man Campbell popped up with the championship-winning goal a quarter of an hour from time, and in the final analysis Sunderland finished five points clear of the Toffees.

Seven days after securing the league, Sunderland were in Edinburgh to face new Scottish champions Heart of Midlothian at Tynecastle. Like Sunderland, Hearts had won their league by five points and reached their domestic cup semi-final. At the time Scotland and England were the only countries staging league football of any decent standard, so the match between the two champions was proclaimed to be the 'World Championship' of football. The cup winners of Scotland and England had met before, but this was the first time the countries had pitted their league champions against each other in such a match.

The Team of All The Talents had served Sunderland marvellously. They had put the town on the footballing map, and this was their zenith. Contemporary reports vary as to the goal-scorers (nothing unusual in that), but what is clear is that Sunderland emerged as 5-3 winners, and were therefore able to describe themselves as the best team in the world. Like Hearts, Sunderland fielded an entirely Scottish XI in a game where fortunes swung wildly. To their credit the home side overturned a two-goal deficit to lead 3-2 after an hour, but the Wearsiders roared back to win 5-3.

No team dominates football unendingly, no matter how impregnable their reign seems at the time. Arsenal in the 1930s, Liverpool in the 1980s and Manchester United in the 1990s and early 2000s spring to mind. So it was that for all their success, The Team of All The Talents had a 'best before' date, and after the high of 1894-95 they were in decline. Although they once again remained unbeaten at home, the following season saw them slump to fifth place, level on points with fourth-placed Bolton but eight adrift of new champions Villa. Most significantly, the season marked the end of Tom Watson's time as manager.

During his time at the club Watson had owned a tobacconists opposite Monkwearmouth Station from 1894 and had lived on Warwick Street, just around the corner from the Newcastle Road ground. He remains the most successful manager in the history of North East football, having led Sunderland to three league titles as well as that unofficial world championship. Never shy about paying out top money for players in this period, Sunderland probably should have matched or bettered the offer of £300 per year that Liverpool lured Watson away with on 25 July 1896. Watson led the Merseysiders to their first two league titles in 1901 and 1906, but passed away in May 1915, a month after his 56th birthday. Sadly, he lay in an unmarked grave in Anfield Cemetery between Liverpool's ground and Everton's Goodison Park for a century (a penalty area's distance from his SAFC and LFC goalkeeper Ted Doig).

Having worked with Liverpool's club historian Stephen Done and Doig's grandson Eric, I was delighted to accompany former Sunderland keeper Jim Montgomery to join with representatives of Liverpool, including former player Alan Kennedy (Sunderland-born and a former Sunderland player too), as we finally marked Watson's grave on the centenary of his death with a headstone showing the club crests of both of his great clubs. Tracking down the descendants of the club's early greats is something I have undertaken over the years as club historian. One of Watson's descendants is Gerald Jensen. Born in Detroit USA, Gerald is a guitarist who toured for many years with the Four Tops and has accompanied artists ranging from Andy Williams to Snoop Dogg on TV. He makes occasional visits to the UK and is always keen to see both Sunderland and Liverpool in action.

Watson's departure came in the same month that Sunderland AFC was wound up with a limited liability company formed in its place. This meeting took place on 9 July 1896 at the Assembly Rooms on Fawcett Street. SAFC Limited began with £5,000 worth of authorised capital in £1 shares. The qualification to become a director was 50 shares. Robert Thompson became president, with John Potts Henderson becoming chairman. Henderson had been involved with the club for four years at this point, having initially become a guarantor of funds. A councillor for the Bridge Ward in the town, he had previously been vice chairman and took over from Thompson as president. The new share capital saw Henderson's brother James join the board of directors, along with Robert and Charles Edward Thompson, James Taylor Calvert and Samuel Wilson (Wilson would become chairman between 1913 and 1921). Like the club's longest-serving chairman, Sir Bob Murray CBE, a century later, J.P. Henderson could see that the club needed a new home.

There had been incredible success at Newcastle Road, but it was not sufficient in size for the biggest crowds Sunderland could attract. The new limited company's prospectus stated that Newcastle Road could hold 18,000 spectators with ease – although more had previously been squeezed in. The rent for the ground had by now increased to £100 per annum. Henderson set about exploring the possibilities of a new purpose-built stadium ready for the forthcoming century. Possibly such ambitions got in the way of rebuilding the team that, while truly great, had passed their peak and needed strengthening. Maybe Watson also knew it was time for a new challenge as his team began to decline.

Watson's replacement as Sunderland manager for the new limited company was Johnny Campbell's stepbrother Robert. He stepped up from running the second team, or 'A' team as they were called. After Sunderland had won the Durham Challenge Cup four times between 1884 and 1890, the 'A' team had lifted the trophy in 1894 (and would win it in six years out of seven between 1901 and 1907). For many years Robert and Johnny Campbell were believed to be brothers, but more recent research has discovered that Johnny was born John Middleton and added the name Campbell after being adopted, the theory being that John may have been the illegitimate child of Robert's father. Robert had come to Wearside in December 1889, not long after his stepbrother came to play.

Robert could have done with Johnny remaining prolific in front of goal. While the younger Campbell had managed a still commendable goal per 2 games from his 32 appearances in Tom Watson's final campaign, he scored just 4 in 35 games in his last and his stepbrother's first season. Previously, Johnny had scored 150 times in 180 competitive games. At the end of Robert Campbell's first season, at the age of 28, Johnny moved on to Newcastle United in a double deal with John Harvie. Campbell subsequently helped the Magpies to their first ever promotion to the top flight, having netted a dozen goals in 29 appearances. He played in Newcastle's first two top-flight fixtures before being sacked for becoming the manager of a pub called the Darnell on Barrack Road. He later returned to Wearside to run the Turf

Hotel. One of the all-time greats, Johnny Campbell died suddenly in 1906, aged only 37. He had fallen on such hard times that his old Sunderland skipper John Auld (by now a Newcastle United director) paid for his funeral. To 2024 Campbell remains joint fourth (behind Jimmy Greaves, Steve Bloomer and Thierry Henry) as the player who was the highest scorer in the top flight most often.

Robert Campbell's first season in charge of Sunderland saw the club struggle for the first time since joining the Football League. They would survive at the top level for over six more decades, but came perilously close to losing that record in 1896–97. They were unable to taste victory until the ninth game of the season, when the ageing Talents roused themselves to beat the returning Tom Watson's Liverpool 4–3. Only seven of thirty league games were won, although one of these was a 4–2 victory over old rivals Villa, who went on to do the double.

The final table showed Sunderland, the club that had scared others to death earlier in the decade, as second bottom. Thankfully this did not result in relegation, but it obligated Sunderland to participate in what were known as 'Test Matches' – a Victorian equivalent of play-offs. Test Matches were introduced at the end of Division Two's inaugural season in 1892–93. They involved the bottom teams in the top tier meeting the top teams from the second tier to determine which two clubs would play in the following season's Division One. The year before Sunderland took part, the format of these Test Matches became a mini-league, whereby the bottom two of the First Division took on the top two from the Second Division on a home and away basis, but teams did not face opponents from the same division. At the conclusion of each club's four games, the top two would be the sides who played in the top flight the following season.

So it was that Sunderland and bottom of the table Burnley had to face off against Notts County and Newton Heath. Things began disastrously, as Sunderland failed to win any of their opening three fixtures. Starting with a trip to Trent Bridge to face Division Two champions Notts County, who had scored 60 goals in their 15 home games, Sunderland went down 1–0 to a side including Will Gibson. He had played in two of Sunderland's title-winning sides and moved to Notts at the start of the season. A couple of days later Sunderland again failed to score in the return against Notts, but at least took a point from a goalless draw.

Next stop was a trip to Newton Heath. The club who would take up the name Manchester United five years later had two points at this stage, as did Burnley, as each team had won their home Test Match 2–0. With a single point Sunderland propped up the four-team table in which they simply had to finish in the top two. Defeat would have meant curtains for Sunderland, but after falling behind to a goal from former Sunderland Albion player Henry Boyd (who had once broken a leg playing against Sunderland for Woolwich Arsenal), the Wearsiders equalised thanks to Hugh Morgan, who would a few years later sign for Newton Heath.

Never has the term 'must-win game' been more significant than it was for Sunderland on 26 April 1897. Anything but victory in the final Test Match at home to Newton Heath would have seen Sunderland relegated just two years after being declared world champions. In fact, victory alone might not have been enough for Robert Campbell's team. Beating Newton Heath would give Sunderland four points to Newton Heath's three, but Notts County already had five points, and if Burnley could beat them in Nottinghamshire they would also have four points, and it could come down to goal average, as indicated by an article in the 1896 *Athletic News Annual*.

The Team of All The Talents had played many important games, and this was their last hurrah. James Gillespie, Donald Gow, Jimmy Hannah, John Harvie and the celebrated Johnny Campbell were making their farewell appearances for the club. A trumpeter welcomed the teams onto the pitch by playing Robert Burns's 'The Campbells are Coming'. One of the lines of this poem reads, 'Their loyal faith and truth to show'. The departing Talents certainly lived up to that, as they won 2–0, Gillespie the hero with both goals, the second ten minutes from time after he'd opened the scoring in the fifteenth minute. This invaluable brace took Gillespie to double figures for the season, making him top scorer. A former Sunderland Albion player, he had been part of the title-winning teams of 1893 and 1895, but never did he play a more important game. Thankfully, Burnley could only manage a draw at Notts County, so victory for Sunderland was sufficient to stay up.

Sunderland's first great era was over. The league championships and world title were consigned to the history books, Tom Watson and many of the Talents had moved on, and now the club had to look forward to a new chapter. There would be just one further season at Newcastle Road as chairman J.P. Henderson looked for a new home that would enable the club to enjoy new successes.

3

THE GREATEST SEASON

The near double of 1912–13 (1897–1913)

With one great era having come to an end, Sunderland started to look to reinvent and reinvigorate themselves. All great teams at all great clubs have a natural lifespan and need to be replaced eventually, no matter how special a chapter they have created in a club's story. So it was that as The Team of All The Talents came to an end, the club looked to rebuild and regain success.

A new start for the club included a new ground. As the final season at Newcastle Road was underway, plans were being realised to move a quarter of a mile back to Roker, this time to the newly constructed Roker Park rather than the old Dolly Field. Chairman J.P. Henderson had earmarked an area of farmland that would be developed into a football ground with surrounding streets. A century on, it would be being hemmed in on three sides by houses that contributed to the club eventually building the Stadium of Light rather than looking to stay and develop the ground with which Sunderland had become synonymous.

The new home needed solid foundations, and that was also the basis upon which manager Robert Campbell assembled his new-look team. Sunderland would have the meanest defence in the country and finish as runners-up, regardless of failing to score more goals than any team outside the bottom six. One of the Talents who had remained was Ted Doig, who was ever present and as imperious as ever in goal. In April 1896 he had added to the caps he won with Arbroath when he became the first player ever to be capped by Scotland while with Sunderland, helping the Scots to a 2–1 win over England at Celtic Park.

Just as five players signed off with final league appearances in the last fixture of 1896–97, five new faces were in the line-up for the opening match of the new season. Among these were Jimmy Chalmers, Jimmy Leslie and Phil Bach. Chalmers would score the last goal at Newcastle Road, Leslie would claim the first at Roker Park and, sounding remarkably like his position, full-back Bach would go on to become Sunderland's second England international. Once again this would be in a match staged on Wearside, but at Roker Park.

Winning the first two matches of 1897–98 signalled that after the struggles of the previous season, the team would fare better this time round, but by the time of a Christmas Day defeat at Blackburn the Lads were a worrying twelfth out of sixteen clubs. It was a visit to Tom Watson's Liverpool that proved to be the catalyst for a vast improvement in form as 1897 turned into 1898. A 2–0 win was the first of seven successive league victories that lifted Campbell's side from twelfth to second – another of these wins being the return with the Merseysiders.

The slow start prevented Sunderland from mounting a sustained title challenge, although they did have a serious chance late in the campaign. They eventually finished five points shy of Sheffield United in what remains the Yorkshire outfit's solitary season as league champions. However, on a day in early March when Blades' Monkwearmouth-born Thomas Morren was absent – debuting, and scoring, for England – Sunderland took advantage by beating the league leaders 3–1 at Newcastle Road to move within three points of the top, with a game in hand. So many supporters squeezed into the ground that day that the visitors' dressing room was accidently wrecked after people clambered on top of it, straining for a view of the pitch. At a Football League Management Committee meeting six days later Sheffield's protest that the excessive and uncontrolled crowd should mean the result was annulled was rejected, with Sunderland getting a warning not to allow spectators inside the boundary rails again. After beating Blackburn next time out, the return with Sheffield United proved crucial.

Having seen a seven-point lead whittled down to one, Sheffield were nervous. Only one point had been taken from their previous four games, with the only goal scored being in the defeat at Newcastle Road. As the sides took to the Bramall Lane pitch in early April they knew a win for the Wearsiders would see them leapfrog United and go top of the table, with Sunderland still having three games to play to United's two. Even if Sunderland had managed a draw at the Lane they would have been guaranteed to win the league if they took maximum points from their final three fixtures, regardless of what Sheffield United managed.

Once again international call-ups had an influence. With England playing Scotland at Celtic Park on the same afternoon, Sheffield were without England half-back Ernest Needham. He played as England won 3–1, with Scotland's goal coming from Jamie Millar – then of Rangers between two spells with Sunderland. Ted Doig and Hugh Wilson had been selected to play for Scotland. Both declined their caps in order to play for Sunderland, but the Lads lost anyway, going down 1–0 to a goal from Harry Johnson, whose son of the same name would go on to score more goals against Sunderland than any other player (19) and become the all-time top scorer for both Sheffield United and Mansfield Town.

The Blades deservedly wrapped up the title by winning their last two games, inflicting what was only Bolton Wanderers' third home defeat of the season and beating West Bromwich Albion, who had been third at the time of the showdown with Sunderland. Dispirited after losing at the Lane, Sunderland meanwhile lost their next two games on the road and finished well behind in second place.

Had it not been for that late-season drop off, the 4–0 home win over Nottingham Forest on the final day of the season could have seen the last home game at Newcastle Road correspond with the regaining of the league title that had come to the club three times at the venue. Sunderland would equal this at Roker Park, but would play there for almost nine times as long (excluding the war years).

Moving to a new ground was a sign of progress in the rapidly developing landscape of the late nineteenth century. Sunderland's visit to Sheffield to play The Wednesday during the final season at Newcastle Road had seen Sunderland filmed for the first time. Footage from the 1–0 win on the opening day of the season had been screened at the Albert Hall in Sheffield the following Saturday.

Like the summer of 1997, when Sunderland moved from Roker Park to the newly built Stadium of Light, the summer of 1898 was a very significant one for SAFC as they moved to their new ground. Roker Park would host many great games, some fabulous footballers and be a home from home for generations of supporters. People could go there in its later years knowing that they were watching the Lads play at the same place that their ancestors had decades upon decades earlier. People loved Roker Park, and it was that sense of history, both family and footballing, that made it so special to so many. The league title would come to Roker Park in 1902, 1913 and 1936, with the FA Cup secured in 1937 and 1973. Additionally, the stadium would stage an FA Cup semi-final and a host of internationals, including a quarter-final and three group games at the 1966 FIFA World Cup.

The opening event at Sunderland's new home was not, however, a football match. Instead, just under a month before the first home league game, the club staged a self-styled 'Olympic Games' day watched by just under 20,000 spectators. The Olympic spirit did not extend to taking part just for the sporting challenge, as cash prizes were offered for the various events. With more on offer for winning the 110 yards than the dribbling contest, perhaps this was an early indicator that in years to come football would begin to value athleticism over artistry.

Originally rented from a Mr Tennant, before being purchased by the club in May 1908, the new ground had a grandstand able to seat between two and three thousand, with the ends originally named North and South, just as they would be when the Stadium of Light opened. With a pitch made up of the finest Irish turf, the ground was opened by the Marquis of Londonderry, an eminent coal-mine owner and politician who had become the club's new president. In a sign of things to come, the *Sunderland Echo* in mid-August asked for agents to contact Robert Campbell to bid for advertising space on the new stands and hoardings.

Starting the season with a friendly draw at Newcastle United and a league win at Preston, a record crowd of 27,000 filled the new ground for the visit of Liverpool, who were still managed by the old Talents supremo Tom Watson. He had an early viewing of the progress made by the club he had brought immense success to before departing for Merseyside. Jim Leslie claimed the first ever goal at Roker Park in a 1–0 win. Ninety-nine years later Liverpool would be invited back for the Farewell to Roker game, this time a goal from John Mullin ensuring symmetry in the scorelines of the first and last games, albeit the latter occasion being a friendly.

In a division expanded to eighteen teams in 1898–99, Sunderland accrued just one point fewer than the previous season, but this time it was only good enough to secure seventh place, albeit three more points would have seen Robert Campbell's team finish third. Although they conceded eleven goals more than the previous year (from four extra games), the defence was still the side's strong point. Only the top two leaked fewer, but in an attacking sense Sunderland were still blunt, with just the bottom two scoring fewer.

The season brought the first league meetings with Newcastle United. The Magpies had been promoted despite finishing third in the Test Matches, from which only two teams were meant to go up. However, after controversy over the final game, when Stoke and Burnley 'manufactured' a goalless draw that ensured they finished as the top two in what became infamously known as 'the match without a shot at goal', the football authorities decided to expand the league.

Newcastle won the first league derby at Roker, with Sunderland winning the return fixture. Away wins would become the norm in early league derbies between the clubs. The first year at Roker Park also brought a thrilling 4–2 Easter home win over old rivals Villa. They would win the league, clinching the title on the final day with a home win over Watson's Liverpool, who would have pipped Villa had they been able to procure a victory.

The first season at Roker Park saw the new ground stage an England international. Sunderland's Phil Bach won his only cap as Ireland were trounced 13–2, before a crowd of 13,000 who paid £558 in gate receipts.

Come the end of the season, Robert Campbell left to manage Bristol City, a club he had agreed to join in March. Happy with progress under him, the board attempted to retain the Scot's services but, insisting his agreement was only verbal with no written contract, Campbell joined the Southern League club, taking them into the Football League after two seasons. Less than a fortnight after Campbell moved to Bristol, so did stalwart Hughie Wilson. He joined Bedminster, who would merge with Bristol City in 1900. Wilson was 30 by the time of his move and may have felt that his days as a regular at Roker were coming to an end, although the absence of a maximum wage in the Southern League probably played a part in the departure of one of the last remaining members of The Team of All The Talents.

During the summer, administrative matters were looked after by schoolteacher and secretary Alexander Watson (a man who would die in the vestry of St Andrew's Church, near Roker Park, in 1931) until a new manager was appointed in August 1899. This was Alex Mackie, someone whose career would become clouded in controversy. On the pitch, however, Mackie led the club to considerable success. In the first four of his six seasons Sunderland finished in the top three, taking the title in 1902.

Losing at home to champions Villa in Mackie's first match did not stop the side quickly getting into its stride. Just one point was dropped from the next seven games, the run starting with victory at Watson's Liverpool. Although they were second for much of the autumn, the team could not make a real impression on the title race and finished third, nine points behind table-toppers Villa. This was not the case the following season, 1900–01, when the title could so easily have come back to Wearside for the first time since the days of the Talents.

Defeat at (Sheffield) Wednesday in the penultimate fixture of the season effectively cost Mackie's men the title. After a modest start to the campaign, the team broke into the top three at the turn of the year, and after going second in early January were never out of the top two thereafter. An eleven-game unbeaten league run came to a costly end when they were defeated at home by Liverpool, who had lost their previous three games. Victory at Sunderland became the first of a twelve-match unbeaten run to the end of the season, and Liverpool topped the table for the first time on the final day – which is when it matters!

However, when Sunderland travelled to Hillsborough, they were top with two games to go. The two Nottingham teams were just behind but couldn't catch SAFC if the Lads took maximum points from their last two games. The danger came from Liverpool, who were four points behind but with two games in hand. Even if they drew level (two points for a win), Sunderland possessed a significantly superior goal average.

Five days before entertaining Sunderland, Wednesday had thrashed third-placed Forest, and they proceeded to defeat the Rokermen 1–0. Although Newcastle were beaten at St James' in Sunderland's final fixture, Liverpool secured their first ever title as Watson became the first manager to win the league title with two different clubs.

While Watson's side fell away into the bottom half of the table in the following 1901–02 season, Mackie enjoyed his greatest campaign by bringing the title to Sunderland for a fourth time. Unlike the prolific goal-scorers of previous title-winning teams, Mackie's champions were based on defence. In his first three seasons in charge, 102 league games were played and only 96 goals conceded. No team had previously won the title with as few as the 50 goals Sunderland scored in 1901–02, exactly half the number of the 1892–93 champions, who played four fewer fixtures.

In taking the title Sunderland were a model of consistency. Unlike in 1891–92 – or in 1912–13 – they did not give rivals a head start by being poor early in the season. Winning six and drawing one of the first eight games had them top of the table by mid-October. Other than a spell in November and December when they were second (and third for a few days at the turn of the year), they remained top until the end. In addition, crowds were also increasing, with the Easter Monday visit of Newcastle United drawing a record crowd for Roker Park of 34,819. This was the first Sunderland game to generate receipts of over £1,000.

Of Sunderland's six league titles, this was the only one sealed at Roker Park. For goalkeeper Ted Doig and forward Jamie Millar, it was their fourth league-title medal with the club. Millar had returned in 1900, and on the day the title was sealed against Bury in mid-April he hadn't scored in the league since November. When it mattered, though, the old maestro of the Talents conjured up his magic to score his second hat-trick of the season to wrap up a 3–0 win and with it the trophy. Having played in that game, 26-year-old skipper Matthew Ferguson missed the last couple of league fixtures, but did play and score in a 5–1 British Cup defeat at Celtic in the very last match of the season. Forty-three days later he was dead, a victim of pleuropneumonia. A benefit match for Ferguson's widow and family was held at the end of the following season against a Wearside League XI.

More than 120 years on, into the 2020s, when people talk about the most important games ever between Wearside and Tyneside, they often point to the 1990 play-off, the 1956 FA Cup quarter-final or the 1913 FA Cup quarter-final second replay, all won by Sunderland at St James'. However, what is surely the most important game between the clubs resulted in a 1–0 win for Newcastle at St James' on the last day of the 1902–03 season. Lowly Newcastle had nothing but pride to play for, but for defending champions Sunderland victory would see them retain the league championship.

Sunderland had actually won at St James' seven days earlier – but against Middlesbrough rather than Newcastle. Sunderland were using St James' for a home game, as Roker Park had been closed by the authorities as a punishment for the crowd throwing stones at the match officials and visiting team after a 1–0 home defeat by title rivals Wednesday in mid-March. Sunderland had three goals disallowed in that game by referee Tom Armitt, who was pelted with oranges during the match by a greatly disgruntled crowd.

With two games for the price of one – on the same day St James' staged the final of the Northumberland Senior Cup between Morpeth Harriers and Dudley Wanderers – more people saw the Wear–Tees derby on Tyneside than had attended any of Newcastle's home matches so far that season. With the addition of some 500 Wednesday fans rooting for Newcastle, that gate was slightly exceeded for the Tyne–Wear derby. This was attended by representatives of the FA, there to see that there was no skulduggery on the part of Newcastle by allowing Sunderland to win. As if! When the game kicked off Wednesday had completed their fixtures and were top of the table. They were powerless to stop Sunderland overtaking them if the Lads could win at St James' again. Sunderland had won all four of their previous league games away to Newcastle and would also win the following two. On this crucial occasion, though, they lost. It would seem stupid now that in between the two consecutive weekend games at Newcastle, Sunderland travelled to Edinburgh, where they drew 2–2 in a friendly with St Bernard's. Sunderland ultimately finished third, a point behind the champions.

Sunderland did take a trophy in 1903, though – and a huge one at that. As 1902 league champions they won the forerunner of the Community Shield, the giant Sheriff of London Shield, by beating Corinthians 3–0 at White Hart Lane. While the English Cup brought a heavy loss at old rivals Villa, the gate receipts of £1,793 from a crowd of 47,150 was the first time a Sunderland game had produced receipts of over £1,500. League games did not produce such high receipts for individual matches due to season-ticket holders not paying at the turnstile.

Despite topping the table early on the following season, and scoring more goals than in any year since the league and world championship campaign of 1894–95, Sunderland slipped to sixth in 1903–04, a year that would be Ted Doig's last at Sunderland. Doig was reunited with Watson at Liverpool and helped them to the league title in 1905–06.

Doig was not the only major figure to depart in 1903–04. A member of the 1902 title-winning side, Andy McCombie had played alongside Sunderland teammates Doig and Jimmy Watson as Scotland's full-backs and goalkeeper when they beat England at Bramall Lane in 1903. McCombie had been given or loaned £100 by the club in the summer of 1903 to help him start a business. This was not unprecedented: John Auld had received £150 in 1889 for the same purpose. After a league game with Middlesbrough in January 1904 was declared a benefit game for McCombie, he was subsequently asked to return the £100. This went down like a lead balloon with the Scot, who insisted that the sum had been a payment, not a loan. McCombie was subsequently sold to Newcastle United for a world record £700, but he was also taken to court by Sunderland as they sought the reimbursement of the £100.

Although the court found in SAFC's favour, the FA subsequently decided to investigate Sunderland's books and in October 1904 found the club guilty of making illegal payments to players. At the time, players in the Football League were subject to a maximum wage. Although this amount was occasionally modestly increased, it remained in place for almost another six decades, and in due course would result in further major problems for Sunderland. All but one of the players involved in 1904 admitted receiving illegal payments, with the club duly fined £250. Six directors, including chairman Sinclair Todd, were suspended for two and a half years. Todd had become chairman at the beginning of the season but would only serve a single year. For his part, Alex Mackie received a three-month suspension.

Mackie returned to take over after 1880s player Fred Dale oversaw fifteen mid-season games, but would only stay until the end of the 1904–05 season, when Sunderland finished fifth. During this time Mackie sold Alf Common to Middlesbrough for the world's first £1,000 transfer fee. Under a year earlier Mackie had re-signed the player from Sheffield United, having sold him to the Blades in 1901.

The chairman of Sheffield United was Charles Clegg, a former chairman of Wednesday. He was a man who had played in England's first ever international and refereed two English Cup finals. One of football's great early administrators, he was also chairman of the FA. Clegg remained vehemently against professionalism and transfer fees. He had tried to abolish transfer fees altogether in 1894 and 1899, and would attempt to do so again in 1908. To say he was miffed when Sunderland sold Common for almost twice what they had paid Sheffield United was an understatement. He was even less enamoured when, shortly after leaving Sunderland for Middlesbrough, Common pitched up at Bramall Lane and scored the winner.

Two of the more controversial but successful characters at Sunderland, McCombie and Mackie had completely different futures in the game after leaving Wearside. McCombie went on to serve Newcastle United for longer than any other individual, enjoying great success and staying with them in various capacities from 1904 to 1950, two years before his death. In contrast, after following Common in swapping Wearside for Teesside, Mackie lasted just one more year in the game. Having already served a three-month ban with Sunderland, he was permanently suspended by the FA after Boro were found guilty of making illegal payments. Disillusioned with the game, Mackie ended his involvement in football in June 1906 to become a publican, having resigned before his punishment was announced.

The departure of Mackie from Sunderland brought about the appointment of Bob Kyle. He would become the club's longest-serving manager, his tenure stretching from 1905 to 1928. A former goalkeeper and secretary of Distillery in Ireland, Kyle was installed as manager ahead of Fred Dale by chairman Frederick William Taylor. Eventually to become known as Mr Sunderland, F.W. Taylor had first been on the board in 1897, when the club were still at Newcastle Road. He had left the board a year after the move to Roker Park, but returned in 1903 and replaced Sinclair Todd as chairman in 1904, when Taylor became the only director to escape censure following the McCombie affair. Curiously, in 1906 he ran the line in a cup tie with Gainsborough Trinity at Roker Park, taking over after senior linesman Mr Morton replaced the referee, who had been injured.

In April 1908, four years after becoming chairman, F.W. Taylor made a key purchase in buying the land on which Roker Park was built, shipbuilder Theodore Doxford apparently being a main player in terms of the funding. One of the most influential leaders Sunderland ever had, F.W. Taylor remained as chairman until 1913 and a board member until 1946, a year before his death.

Kyle's first season saw Sunderland propping up the table after six games, having failed to take another point after beating champions Newcastle on the opening day. The Magpies had achieved their first league title in 1905 but to date have never held as many league titles as Sunderland. Although Kyle's team improved, they never got into the top half of the table and finished fourteenth out of twenty. Sunderland were mid-table again in 1906–07, this time finishing tenth. Gone were the days of the tight defence under Mackie. Kyle's team were trying to play more expansively. There were 131 goals in the 38 league games, 25 of Sunderland's 65 coming from left-winger Arthur Bridgett. The England international, who would not play on religious days, notched seventeen more than the second top scorer and single-handedly kept the club from a relegation battle. One of those goals came in what remains the club's joint-highest scoring draw, a 5–5 classic with league champions Liverpool in which Sunderland came back from being 4–1 down.

Although progress on the pitch was modest, the board seemed happy with the situation off it. The AGM of the club at the

Queen's Hotel in Fawcett Street on 19 June 1907 noted: 'The directors are pleased to report a good year in which the standard of play has been kept at a respectable average with the financial position of the club easily eclipsing all previous years.' A dividend of 5 per cent (the maximum allowed by the FA) was paid to shareholders.

Sunderland's first ever matchday programme (as opposed to a card listing the teams, surrounded by advertisements) was issued for the opening day of the 1907–08 season, when five players also made their debut. In total thirteen players would make their first appearances during the season, including legendary goalkeeper Leigh Richmond Roose. He added greatly to the entertainment on offer at Roker Park – if not any success. At this time goalkeepers were still allowed to handle the ball anywhere in their own half. Most restricted themselves to their own penalty area, but not Wales international Roose, who was something of a showman and a playboy. He was once said to have been found in bed with the winner of a beauty competition he had just judged, for example. Roose's penchant for bouncing the ball basketball-style to the halfway line and then launching it one-handed into the penalty area was a potent weapon, one he later put to use in the First World War as a grenade thrower. The laws of the game were changed in 1912 so that keepers could only handle in their own box, largely as a way of restricting Roose, although by then he had long since moved on from Roker. Roose was to become one of nine players to have been on Sunderland's books who would lose their lives in the Great War.

Kyle's third season was a disappointment. Before his arrival Sunderland had only once finished lower than seventh in fifteen seasons of league membership. Having finished fourteenth and tenth under the manager, in 1907–08 the side slumped to sixteenth and from time to time propped up the table. In the final analysis Sunderland finished just two points better off than Bolton Wanderers, who were relegated. Despite this, they were only outscored by Manchester United, who won their first ever league title; on the other hand, Sunderland conceded eleven goals more than anyone else.

A big improvement in 1908–09 saw the team rise to a much more acceptable third place, with the highlight of the season an incredible 9–1 away win on 5 December 1908 over a Newcastle United side who would finish as champions. Although equalled by Wolves at Cardiff in 1955, this remained the record away victory in the top flight of English football until Leicester beat a hapless Southampton 9–0 in 2019. Bridgett got two of the goals at Newcastle, with Billy Hogg (whose brother had been one of 183 children between the ages of three and fourteen killed at the Victoria Hall disaster in Sunderland in 1883) and George Holley both getting hat-tricks. Jackie Mordue also got on the scoresheet, meaning that all nine goals came from England internationals.

Sunderland were infuriated by the award of a contentious penalty for Newcastle on the stroke of half-time, which when converted made the interval score 1–1. Eight goals were then slammed home in the first twenty-eight minutes of the second half – probably the finest half hour in the entire history of the club. Spectators at Roker Park for the reserve game against Seaham White Star did not believe the score as it kept increasing on the scoreboard. The Tynesiders enjoyed some revenge later in the season when winning an FA Cup quarter-final replay at Roker Park, but the 9–1 victory remains the most astonishing result ever between the old rivals.

The summer of 1909 saw Sunderland depart on their first overseas trip. An eight-game tour of Hungary, Austria, Czechoslovakia and Germany brought seven wins, a single defeat, thirty-one goals scored and twelve conceded. George Holley missed the German leg of the tour, as he returned to Hungary and Austria to play for England, scoring braces against both countries. Back at Roker Park, work on renovating the stands and returfing the pitch began that summer while the team were away. On the newly turfed pitch, 1909–10 brought another improvement in defence, as for the second season running a dozen fewer goals were conceded than the year before, 51 being let in compared to 75 two seasons previously. At least some of this was down to the indefatigable Roose, who continued to be thanked in end of year board reports, as he always played as an amateur. However, with twelve goals fewer also being scored, the team finished in eight place, five places lower than the year before.

Sunderland understandably looked to boost their firepower in 1910–11. The signing of England forward 'Tim' Coleman brought to the club perhaps the only player with a personality to rival that of Roose. An example of Coleman's humour was when he wore a false moustache at the start of the second half at Preston, causing a delay, as the referee thought Sunderland had illegally substituted a player. Coleman stayed just one season, scoring 20 goals in 33 games, starting with an opening-day winner against Newcastle. Coleman also scored in the return 1–1 draw with the Magpies, but this was a sad day, as it proved to be Roose's last for Sunderland. A broken arm sustained in what was his ninety-ninth appearance for the club meant that Roose and Coleman only played together for Sunderland a dozen times. The dressing room must have been a lively place with both of them in it. Roose was presented with an 'illuminated address' by supporters in thanks for his contribution to the club, a popular way to commemorate outstanding service at the time. It consisted of a lengthy statement about the subject written in ornate calligraphy and presented as a scroll or already framed.

Tom Allan had replaced Roose in goal by the time the team went to Middlesbrough in early December. Unbeaten Sunderland were leading the table, with Boro in sixth position after a 5–0 thrashing at second-placed Villa. Teessiders chairman Gibson Poole was attempting to get into Parliament, with the election due to take place two days after the Tees–Wear derby. Desperate to be elected, he had Boro's players out canvassing for him in the run-up to the game. Equally desperate for a positive result ahead of the election, it appears that Poole's Teessiders attempted underhand methods, with Sunderland skipper Charlie Thomson being approached to throw the game. Thomson claimed Boro

The Greatest Season

manager Andy Walker had offered him £10, plus £2 for every other Sunderland player, to allow Boro to win in order to enhance Poole's election chances. Thomson flatly rejected the bribe and reported it to trainer Billy Williams before the match. Boro still won the game, but Poole lost the election.

In March of 1911 Sunderland signed a player who was to become one of the all-time greats: Charlie Buchan. He would go on to become Sunderland's record goal-scorer, and even after Bobby Gurney took that record, Buchan still retains the title as the club's record league goal-scorer, with 210 of his 223 goals for the club coming in the league. Buchan would be Sunderland's top scorer seven times, including the club's greatest season of 1912–13, the last season before the Football League stopped due to the First World War, 1914–15, and the first five seasons after it. Goodness knows how many goals Buchan would have plundered but for the four-season hiatus.

Coming in towards the end of the 1910–11 season, Buchan scored once in six games, the goal coming in a 1–1 draw with Notts County. This was one of 15 league draws that season, after only 11 of the previous 125 league games had ended all square. Those draws, only 8 defeats and an ever-tightening defence led to Kyle's Sunderland finishing third for the second time in three seasons. Third was decent, but pre-First World War Sunderland were expected to win trophies, not be among the also-rans. Indeed, third place was only marginally achieved on goal average from two other clubs who were level on points. Sunderland had topped the table for much of the season, but lost top spot to eventual champions Manchester United in a home Christmas Eve defeat and afterwards failed to last the pace, a 5–1 defeat at United on the final day clinching the title for the home club as they leapfrogged Aston Villa, who lost on the same afternoon at Liverpool.

After promising to become title contenders in 1910–11, Sunderland were off the pace in 1911–12. In the October of that season club founder James Allan passed away at the age of 54, sadly a few days after the death of his granddaughter

Daisy Louise. His funeral was attended by John Grayston, who 32 years earlier had helped Allan to start the club, but there was no representative from SAFC, who merely sent a wreath. Evidently the wounds between the club's founder and the club itself had not fully healed.

In the season of Allan's death Sunderland eventually finished eighth, but in terms of points were four closer to relegation than the title. Having become used to success, the supporters were disillusioned, the average gate of 13,105 being the sixth-lowest in the division, although three home cup ties had produced an average of just under 36,000. The *Titanic* sank in the last week of the season and it seemed Sunderland's hopes of regaining success were sinking too. After winning the league four times in their first twelve seasons, the best Sunderland had managed in the last ten was to finish third. Arthur Bridgett had also played his last game before becoming player-manager of South Shields. His departure was softened by the recruitment of Harry Martin, who would emulate Bridgett in going on to win England honours, as well as providing a potent supply line to Buchan.

The summer of 1912 saw the club undertake considerable investment in the stadium. The South Stand (later to become known as the Roker End) was significantly expanded at a cost of £20,000, the equivalent of £1,900,000 by 2024.

Excluding the years lost to the Great War, Bob Kyle took charge of nineteen seasons and only won a trophy in one of them. Nonetheless, his season of success was Sunderland's greatest ever, as they reached the English Cup final for the first time in addition to winning the league. As of the end of the 2023–24 season, Kyle remains the last manager from Northern Ireland to lead a team to the league title.

The 1912–13 season started horribly. After a good opening-day draw at Newcastle, only one more point was collected from the next six matches. Following defeat at Chelsea in early October, Sunderland were one off the bottom and already nine points behind three teams at the top of the table, including Villa, who that day beat Wednesday (who had started the day level with them) 10–0.

The Greatest Season

Sunderland's defeat at Chelsea saw the debut of new goalkeeper Joe Butler. A week later dominant defender Charlie Gladwin made his bow. This pair proceeded to have a major influence on the team turning the season around. Starting with a 4–0 home win over Middlesbrough on Gladwin's debut, only four of the last thirty-one league games were lost as Sunderland stormed to the title. In the final analysis Kyle's men were four points clear of their nearest rivals, and in bagging 86 goals scored more than any title-winning team other than Sunderland's wins of 1893 and 1892.

Winning a fifth league title to this point was something only Villa could match. The two giants of the game would stand in each other's way as both attempted to become the first team of the century to do the double of league and cup. Villa and Sunderland were due to meet in a key league contest on the day of the final, but instead found themselves in opposition in the cup final.

Having won the league regularly, the cup was the holy grail to Sunderland and their supporters. Twelve goals were scored in seeing off Clapton Orient, Manchester City and Swindon Town. In fact, an extra two were scored in a 2–0 win at City that was abandoned because of crowd trouble, with a replay ordered.

Three games were needed to dispose of Newcastle United in the quarter-final, Sunderland winning a second replay at St James' with the help of Harry Low, who turned down his only Scotland call-up in order to play in the second replay, which came four days before his benefit match, something he was entitled to for long-service. A replay was needed in the semi-final too, Burnley being beaten at St Andrew's in Birmingham following a goalless draw played in torrential rain at Bramall Lane. The replay ebbed and flowed before George Holley volleyed a spectacular winner and Sunderland won 3–2. A son of Seaham, Holley holds the record for the most goals scored for England by a player while on Sunderland's books, 8 in 10 appearances. With 157 goals for Sunderland he remains the club's fourth-highest ever scorer. In the season before the near double his 25 goals made him the country's top scorer, while that same year he also scored for England in all three British Championship games.

Just when they needed him most, Holley was injured for the cup final – but still played. A team photograph taken on the morning of the final shows the players in suits and ties, with a telltale sign in that Holley was wearing football boots. His fitness having been tested, he was ruled out of the game, only for his replacement, Walter Tinsley, to be overtaken with pre-match nerves, forcing Holley to be pressed into action.

Tinsley's anxiety was caused by the size of the crowd at Crystal Palace, an enormous 120,081 to see the first cup final between the two teams who would end the season at the top of the league. Only two previous finals had ever attracted crowds of over 100,000, while in 1912 the combined gate for the final and replay between Barnsley and West Bromwich Albion came to under six figures. Only the first ever Wembley final in 1923 (the 'White Horse' final between West Ham United and Bolton Wanderers) has ever drawn a higher attendance for a football match in England.

The final was packed with incident but only one goal. Southwick-born Charlie Wallace shot wide with a penalty for Villa, who had a goal disallowed and played part of the match down to ten men, with their keeper Sam Hardy off injured. Sunderland centre-half Charlie Thomson and Villa centre-forward Harry Hampton knocked lumps off each other, as they frequently did in the clubs' heavyweight clashes – so much so that they and the referee were all suspended for the opening month of the following season.

The only goal of the game was scored by West Stanley-born Tommy Barber, as had famously been dreamt the night before by Clem Stephenson. Villa's Blyth-born skipper revealed what proved to be his foresight as his team ate breakfast on the morning of the final. The nearest Sunderland came to a goal was when Harry Martin hit the inside of the post. Martin would be the only ever-present in 1912–13, although his meagre five league goals made him the only member of the five-man forward line not to reach double figures.

The Greatest Season

Losing the cup final brought enormous disappointment to the club and its supporters, who would have to wait for almost a quarter of a century for Sunderland to reach the final again. Thankfully, they only had to wait a week for the league title to come their way once more. Four days after the final, Sunderland and Villa met in the league at Villa Park. Sunderland were top of the table, level on points with Wednesday, but the Sheffield side had only one game to play compared to Sunderland's three. Third-placed Villa trailed Sunderland by four points but also had three to play. Effectively, this was a title decider: if Sunderland could avoid defeat Villa could potentially catch them on points but would need a near miracle to overtake the Wearsiders' goal average.

Having pulled out of the cup final, Tinsley redeemed himself by scoring as Sunderland drew 1–1, and when Sunderland won 3–1 at Bolton the following Saturday the title was secured with a match to spare. The Lads finished with 54 points, a record never beaten until the league was extended to 42 games. After beating Bradford City in their final fixture, the team then set off for another tour of Hungary, Austria and Germany, winning all seven games, including a victory over fellow tourists and 1912 league champions Blackburn Rovers in Budapest.

Unquestionably at this stage in history Sunderland were a leading light in the world of football. European competitions would not come along for over four more decades, but had they existed in this era the Lads would have been odds on to add European titles to their world title of 1895. Unfortunately, in the year after SAFC's near double, the world would have war to contend with rather than the joys of a game of football.

4

ALMOST ROARING TWENTIES

(1913–28)
The 1920s was the only decade between Sunderland's entry into the Football League in 1890 and the outbreak of the Second World War in 1939 in which the club failed to win a major trophy. Things had been going swimmingly with the acquisition of the league title and reaching of the cup final in the calendar year before the Great War began.

Millions died between 1914 and 1918 in the awful war that was meant to end all wars. Among them were Jack Huggins, James Chalmers, Thomas Rowlandson, L.R. Roose, Albert Milton, Sandy McAllister, Alexander Barrie, and reserve players John Shaw and Sammy Hartnell, who had all been on Sunderland's books. Albert Milton had been part of the team who won the league four years before he was killed in action during the first day of the Battle of Passchendaele. In no way do the ups and downs of a football club begin to compare with the horrors of war, but in football terms the war came at a bad time for Sunderland.

Having done so well in 1913, the club had committed to significant investment in Roker Park with the building of a new stand, shortly before funds dried up with the cessation of football during the war. Sunderland's attempts to retain their league title in 1913–14 saw a decent challenge after another slow start.

A highlight of the first home win over Aston Villa was some special entertainment as aviator Henri Salmet flew over the ground, having taken off from the cliffs at Roker in one of the earliest flights on Wearside. Salmet had been sponsored by the *Daily Mail* to visit over 120 towns to promote public interest in aviation.

By Christmas 1913, Sunderland's title challenge had taken off: they were in second place, only a point behind Blackburn Rovers. This position was maintained until mid-February, while once again the title charge was matched by a good cup run, which began with a 9–0 trouncing of non-league Chatham. The cup campaign ended in a quarter-final replay loss away to eventual winners Burnley. Cup defeat deflated the league campaign, as after the Turf Moor result six of the last nine games were lost, dropping the defending champions to an ultimately disappointing seventh.

By the time the 1914–15 season commenced the First World War had been underway for a month. Like so many other enduring wars, in the early stages of the conflict many felt it would be over within a few months, so football did not immediately stop. Indeed, the 1914–15 season was played to its conclusion. After three games Sunderland were third, but the season soon tailed away to become one of mid-table anonymity. Despite over 150 goals being scored in Sunderland's 38 games – they were the league's second-highest scorers and only four clubs had more porous defences – crowds dropped by 50 per cent as war became foremost in people's minds. Pressure had built on the football authorities to call the sport to a halt. Young men were losing their lives fighting on the continent while others kicked a ball around to the disgust of increasing amounts of people.

War's encroachment on life back in Britain was growing. Throughout the season Sunderland's squad undertook military training using broomsticks instead of rifles, while at the end of the campaign, in which Sunderland finished eighth, Charlie Buchan was among those to enlist, having completed a hat-trick on the final day of the season with what would be Sunderland's last league goal until 1919. He enlisted with the Sherwood Foresters and later served in the Grenadier Guards and gained the Military Medal.

Two days after the final match of the 1914–15 season, Jack Huggins became the first former Sunderland player to die in battle. A private in the 1st & 8th Battalion Durham Light Infantry, Huggins died at Ypres just five days after arriving in France. Nine years earlier he had scored one and made two on his debut in a 4–1 win over Manchester United. In December 2014, Sunderland's under-twelve team visited his grave near Roulers, Belgium, as part of the Premier League's 'Football Remembers' project. In the same month Huggins was named on a plaque placed next to the Fans' Statue outside the main entrance to the Stadium of Light.

In many parts of the country regional leagues were created throughout the war. In Scotland, although the Scottish Cup was not played, the league continued. In Sunderland's case football stopped almost totally for the duration of the war. The only games in 1915–16 and 1916–17 were two charity matches away to Newcastle in aid of the National War Fund and the Comrades of the Great War Fund. Additionally, some players appeared as 'guests' for other clubs, but many signed up, including Bobby Best who, after scoring a hat-trick against Newcastle on Christmas Day in 1914, joined the 3rd Durham Light Infantry.

Over 50 people who played for Sunderland either before or after the war served in the forces during the First World War. The son of 1880s financial secretary W.T. Wallace was killed in addition to the nine players, while reserve-team player Norman Gaudie became one of the country's best known conscientious objectors.

SAFC found themselves in dire financial straits. On 11 May 1915 (five days after the death of Tom Watson in Liverpool) an extraordinary general meeting of the club took place at the Palatine Hotel (later known as the Mowbray Park Hotel). Given the huge drop in attendances in this season, an average league gate of 11,158 compared to 21,879 the year before, combined with the costs of the new stand, the club were in such trouble that there was a possibility of it being wound up. It was thanks to people such as future chairman Sir Walter Raine and former Team of All

The Talents captain John Auld (by now a director of Newcastle United and a successful businessman), who acted as guarantors, that Sunderland stayed afloat. Player sales, such as that of Billy Cringan to Celtic for £600 in September 1917, also helped.

With the Great War coming to an end in November 1918, Sunderland took part in a hastily organised Victory League, which took place in the early months of 1919, finishing second to Middlesbrough in the eight-team league made up of North Eastern clubs. They also ended the decade with a trophy, having entered and won the Durham Senior Cup, beating Crook Town at Feethams (Darlington) in the final.

The 1919–20 season brought the resumption of the Football League and FA Cup, with the league expanded to 22 clubs. Following an internal warm-up match featuring two teams made up of existing players and a handful of triallists, plus friendlies against South Shields and Middlesbrough, the post-war era commenced with the glamourous visit of old foes Aston Villa. Newly appointed captain Charlie Buchan continued where he left off by scoring the club's first post-war league goal as Sunderland won 2–1. Over the course of the season sixteen new players were introduced to the team as manager Kyle looked for a new blend. Harry Low, George Philip and the legendary centre-half and captain Charlie Thomson had played their final games in the last league match before football stopped for the war. The new-look Sunderland did well in the first post-war campaign, finishing an encouraging fifth. They did so before a home crowd exceeding 25,000 on average for the first time, as people began to enjoy life and try and put the ravages of war and lost loved ones behind them.

If not for Buchan, Sunderland may well have struggled in 1920–21 and 1921–22 instead of finishing twelfth each year. Buchan netted 27 league goals in the first of those seasons and 21 in the second, each time the next highest scorer managing just 7. Despite those goals, Buchan was only a reserve when Roker Park staged an international, England beating Ireland 2–0 in October 1920. Sunderland suffered from inconsistency all season in

1920–21, for instance losing 1–0 at home to Aston Villa in the game after beating them 5–1 at Villa Park, which itself was on the back of another 5–1 win, over Arsenal.

With the financial troubles of the war years behind them, Sunderland ambitiously splashed the cash in what became the Roaring Twenties. While it would be in the fifties that Sunderland earned the nickname of 'the Bank of England Club', they were also big spenders in the early twenties.

Although a 5–1, fifth successive win on Bonfire Night in 1921 lifted the Lads to second place, any title challenge was short lived. In March, having fallen away into mid-table, Sunderland signed forward Jock Paterson for £3,790 from Leicester City, before smashing the world transfer record twice, on consecutive days. A record-busting £5,250 was invested in defender Michael Gilhooley from Hull, and 24 hours later £5,500 was paid to Second Division South Shields for full-back Warney Cresswell. Similar to September 2000, when big signings Don Hutchison, Julio Arca and Emerson Thome all made their home debuts in the same game, the expensive trio debuted together.

While the biggest crowd since Boxing Day came to see the new faces, it was old-stager Charlie Buchan who got the only goal of the game to beat Sheffield United. Buchan's goals that season were invaluable, but two thirds of them came in the first dozen games, after which the team tailed off, ultimately dropping into the bottom half of the table on the final day. Only three clubs won fewer away games, but only four won more at home.

With Bob Kyle still in charge, there was a big improvement in the middle of the twenties, as between 1922–23 and 1926–27 Sunderland finished in the top three in four years out of five. Only in the first of those seasons did they come close to actually winning the title. With a new goalkeeper in Ned Robson, signed from Portsmouth for £3,000, fewer goals were conceded in any season since 1913–14. Up front, with Paterson scoring 21 league goals, Buchan had some help and finished as the division's leading scorer with 30, inside-left Arthur 'Tricky' Hawes adding a dozen of his own.

Beating eventual champions Liverpool was the solitary win in the first five games before a change in style. The team were reported to have abandoned a close passing game to bring about a 5–1 win over Bolton, who would go on to win the first Wembley FA Cup final later in that 1922–23 season. The game's costliest goalkeeper, Dick 'Pincher' Pym made two stunning saves from Buchan, who still scored four and could easily have equalled his record as the only player to this date to score five league goals in a game for the Lads, something he had achieved in a 7–0 hammering of Liverpool in 1912–13.

After winning at third-placed Huddersfield in late January, thanks to a Buchan goal and a stern rearguard action, Sunderland were within two points of Liverpool. Although in the final analysis the Merseysiders took the title by a six-point margin, their only victory in their final seven fixtures came on the last day of the season. However, Sunderland slipped up, losing four of their last six matches. Perhaps the turning point came in mid-April when, despite a Buchan hat-trick, the unbeaten home record was lost in a 5–3 defeat to Sheffield United, Harry Johnson also scoring a hat-trick for the Blades, at a time when the Lads were four points behind Liverpool but with a game in hand.

Although Sunderland finished third in 1923–24, they were two points closer to the title than the year before. New goalkeeper Albert 'The Great' McInroy (to summer 2024 the only goalkeeper to be capped by England while on Sunderland's books) arrived in 1923, having been signed in the toilets of the Grand Hotel in Manchester at midnight. Kyle had got wind from the club's Manchester scout, Harry Bedford, that McInroy's contract with Leyland Motors was to expire then, and arranged a meeting there to avoid other suitors snapping him up. From early March until Easter in mid-April, Kyle's men topped the table, but Huddersfield always had games in hand and duly gained the necessary points as they commenced their three-year domination of the championship.

The title would probably have gone to Cardiff rather than Huddersfield but for a refereeing mistake in the Huddersfield–Sunderland game. With most of the season's fixtures played in pairs, Sunderland had beaten Huddersfield at Roker seven days before the 8 December encounter in Yorkshire. The only goal Huddersfield had conceded at home so far in the season was against defending champions Liverpool, but Sunderland had scored twice and were drawing 2–2 when they had a glorious chance to go ahead. Buchan had the ball at his feet and was unmarked in front of goal when referee H.V. Stott of Tamworth blew for offside. To be fair to the referee, he could have just let Huddersfield take the free-kick and get on with the game, but realising he had made a mistake and Buchan was onside, he restarted with a drop-ball, which of course came to nothing. The home side went on to win the match with a speculative shot from Charlie Wilson four minutes from time. Had the referee not erroneously blown for a phantom offside, Sunderland would have almost certainly led 3–2 and may well have won or drawn the match instead of losing it. That season Sunderland had the best away record in the top-flight and were top-scorers on the road. Huddersfield went on to win the league by pipping Cardiff City on goal average.

Defeat at Huddersfield motivated Sunderland, who did the double over Newcastle United in the next two games to begin a fourteen-game unbeaten run that sprung them to the top of the league. As supporters left Roker Park after a drawn final home game of the season against Arsenal on Easter Saturday, Sunderland were still top of the table, although the two teams beneath them were just a point behind with games in hand. Two days later Sunderland had to win at West Brom, who they had beaten on Good Friday, but in the days before substitutes in league games, an injury to Michael Gilhooley in the opening quarter of an hour left them a man short in a gruelling third game in four days, and they were duly beaten.

The 1924–25 campaign saw a fall back to seventh place. It was a season when, three days before the derby with Newcastle, Roker Park was used for a rugby match between Durham County and the touring All Blacks, who won 43–7. It was also the season that marked the end of the Sunderland career of the imperious Charlie

Buchan. Approaching his thirty-fourth birthday, he was wanted by Arsenal. The Gunners offered only half of Sunderland's £4,000 asking price, but agreed to pay £100 for every goal he scored in his first season on top of the £2,000 they were willing to pay. Arsenal could have saved themselves £100 by paying the asking price, as Charlie netted 21 times in his first season at Highbury. Buchan had scored a record 223 goals for Sunderland, and while that record would be overtaken, Buchan's 210 league goals has never been surpassed by a Sunderland player.

Buchan left Sunderland just as the offside law was changed to make it easier to score. From 1925–26 there only needed to be two opponents between the attacker and the goal instead of three. In 1926–27 Durham-born George Camsell would score 59 Second Division goals and 63 in all for Middlesbrough, while a year later Dixie Dean would score 60 top-flight goals for Everton.

Astonishingly, Buchan was booed when he returned to Roker for the first time towards the end of the 1925–26 season. His £4,000 replacement Dave Halliday had made a sensational start with ten goals, including two hat-tricks, in his first four games. Halliday ended up with 42 goals, playing all 46 league and cup matches of the season. However, when Buchan next returned to Roker, Halliday was sent off and the pair were upstaged by a youngster by the name of Bobby Gurney, making his fourth appearance. Buchan had deservedly been given an ovation when he led the Gunners out, but when he brought down Charlie Parker late on, the already irate crowd were further infuriated.

Halliday was dismissed after clashing with Gunners' goalkeeper Dan Lewis, who was also sent off. Ten minutes earlier Gurney had levelled Jimmy Brain's opener for the visitors, and he took full advantage of winger Joe Hulme going in goal for the last twelve minutes by scoring a late winner. Halliday's sending off infuriated the crowd, with chairman Fred Taylor demonstrating that he disagreed with referee Mr Mee's decision by shaking Halliday's hand as he left the pitch.

Gurney would go on to take Buchan's record as Sunderland's leading goal-scorer, with 228 goals, while Halliday ended up with

165 goals in 175 games for the club. This makes him the player with the highest goals per game ratio in Sunderland's history, 0.943 goals per game. On this day when 'Boy' Gurney's brace beat Arsenal 2–1, the top three goal-scorers in Sunderland's history were on the pitch at the same time: Gurney, Buchan and Halliday, who scored a combined 616 goals for the club in 976 games.

Arsenal finished the season above Sunderland, who were third. The Wearsiders were nine points adrift of Huddersfield, who completed their third successive title. With 96 goals Sunderland were the division's second-top scorers, behind Sheffield United, but the Blades were the only team in the top half to concede more than Sunderland's 80. For all this attacking play, the goals of Halliday and the potential of Gurney, Sunderland also paid another world-record fee of £6,550 to bring in centre-forward Bob Kelly. He had scored at Roker Park for England in 1920 and would win one of his fourteen caps while with Sunderland three months after joining, but after just 15 goals in 53 games he moved on to Huddersfield Town for slightly more than half of what had been paid to Burnley for his signature.

Sunderland were even more prolific in front of goal in 1926–27, with 98 goals making them the league's leading scorers. They finished third again, but Newcastle took what, at the time of writing, remains their most recent league title. Despite a slow start to the season, the side spent chunks of the first half of the campaign at the top of the table. Halliday missed 9 games through suspension or injury, but still bagged 37 goals in 34 games, Bobby Marshall chipped in with 20, Gurney added 7, and Stan Ramsay came into the team late on and notched 8 in 9 appearances.

The 1927–28 season would prove to be Bob Kyle's last, having been in charge since 1905. He announced his resignation in March, a day after a 5–1 win over Arsenal in which Gurney grabbed a hat-trick. After a bright start Sunderland had briefly topped the table after five games, but they then crashed to earth, suffering six successive defeats. A mid-season run of one reverse in eleven lifted them back to mid-table. By mid-March they were still eleventh, but in a table so tight that, come the end of the campaign, only fifteen points separated champions Everton and relegated Spurs.

As the final fixture of the season came around, Sunderland went into it on the back of four successive defeats. The spectre of relegation haunted what was officially Bob Kyle's last match in charge. This would be at Middlesbrough, who were also in deep relegation trouble. But while a draw would keep Boro up, Sunderland needed nothing less than a win at Ayresome Park.

Missing Gurney through injury, Sunderland were also in danger of going into the decider minus goalkeeper Albert McInroy. He got himself strapped up and went out to play in place of Paddy Bell, who had been deputising for him and been subject to criticism after a home defeat to Wednesday. Sunderland won the Boro game 3–0, with McInroy producing a tremendous performance highlighted by a double save from Jackie Carr and Bobby Bruce, which seems to have been as good and as important as Jim Montgomery's famous double save at Wembley 45 years to the day later in the 1973 FA Cup final. Despite the convincing scoreline, Boro battered Sunderland for much of the match, with SAFC centre-half Adam Allan and full-backs Ernie England and Bill Murray all having storming games to help keep them at bay.

This would be one of an unmatched 838 games Murray was involved with for Sunderland, either as player or manager. He had arrived from Cowdenbeath the year before, and other than a two-year stint back in Scotland, remained with Sunderland until 1957. Years after this famous 1928 game on Teesside, Murray told the great North East football historian Arthur Appleton that after the match was won: 'There was the drama of strong men weeping. The atmosphere was unreal.' It wasn't just the players who were crying. 'It was the only time I saw old Billy crying,' McInroy told Appleton, speaking of trainer Billy Williams, who organised the team that day, having been with the club since 1897. Williams would stay with Sunderland for another season, but as Kyle left and the end of the decade approached, a new era was about to begin on Wearside.

5

RAICH AND THE THIRTIES

Sunderland's return to the top (1928–46)
With the appointment as manager of Scotsman Johnny Cochrane, Sunderland came under new leadership for the first time in almost a quarter of a century. Cochrane had managed St Mirren to Scottish Cup triumph in 1926, having beaten Rangers in the semi-final and then triumphing in a Hampden Park final against a Celtic side that included the mercurial Tommy McInally, whom Cochrane would subsequently bring to Wearside.

Cochrane's first season revolved around Dave Halliday. Now in his fourth term at Sunderland, the forward broke his own record of goals for the season, hitting 43 from his 42 league appearances. This made him the country's leading scorer, in what was his last full campaign at the club. No one has ever scored as many goals in a season for SAFC as Halliday did even in his least-productive full campaign at Sunderland. He scored at least 35 top-flight goals in four consecutive seasons at Sunderland. To 2024, no other player at any club has managed as many as 30 top-division goals in four successive seasons, while Halliday is one of only two players (with David McLean of Wednesday and Rangers) to be top scorer in England as well as Scotland. Halliday's son Ian accepted his father's induction into the Sunderland Hall of Fame in 2020.

Raich and the Thirties

After the big threat of relegation the previous season, home fans were encouraged by wins in the new manager's first three home games of the 1928–29 season. However, despite Halliday's eight goals from the first nine matches, Cochrane's club were eighteenth after four defeats in a row, thirteen goals being conceded in the final three of those. Powered by Halliday, the season would ebb and flow with runs of wins, draws and defeats. Either side of the turn of the year, a twelve-game unbeaten league sequence lifted them to second, albeit they were still four points adrift of Wednesday at the summit; the league leaders were beaten 4–3 at Roker Park in January in the match of the season, which extended the unbeaten run to eleven league games. A final placing of fourth, five points off the top, could have been so much better for Sunderland but for a tame ending, which brought six losses in the last ten fixtures.

This would be a year of change both at the club and in the town. Although Halliday scored a hat-trick in the opening home match of the 1929–30 season, just two months later he followed the path trodden by Charlie Buchan in going to Arsenal. The summer of 1929 had already seen the departure of inspirational skipper Charlie Parker, while the early part of the season also brought the final appearance of goalkeeper Albert McInroy. The club were also rocked by the untimely death of twenty-year-old Jack Bartley. He passed away of laryngeal diphtheria just five days after playing against Leeds United in the First Division.

Cochrane, meanwhile, was bringing in a stream of new faces to go with the impressive new grandstand designed by the renowned football stadia architect Archibald Leitch. The opening of this allowed former chairman Samuel Wilson to donate to the club the huge Thomas M.M. Hemy oil painting of the match with Aston Villa from an 1895 meeting at Newcastle Road. In recent years this had been housed in Bells Restaurant in Bridge Street in the town centre.

To get to Roker Park in 1929 the painting had to cross the brand new Wear Bridge. This had taken two years to construct and replaced the previous iron bridge built in 1796, when it had been the biggest single-span bridge in the world. The new bridge accompanied the adjacent railway bridge, which had opened as the club began life in 1879. It wasn't just a new bridge and a new main stand Sunderland had in 1929, a new general hospital opened too.

On the pitch it was a season of struggle, but in contrast to many campaigns of the twenties, which featured poor ends to the season, the start of the thirties brought a strong closing stage. For almost all of the season up to March, Sunderland struggled in the bottom four, being bottom at Christmas and for much of the winter. Had there been a manager-of-the-month award in March, Cochrane would have been a shoe-in, as his team suddenly won all five games. Soon, another run of four wins in a row began with a 6–0 win over Liverpool at Anfield, where Gurney got four, helping the team to an unlikely finishing place of ninth.

The following season, 1930–31, saw Sunderland join in with a goal-fest in Division One. There were 174 goals in the club's 42 league games, but having scored just 4 more than were conceded, Cochrane's side finished eleventh. The top three netted 357 between them, while bottom of the table Manchester United leaked 115 – 10 fewer than Blackpool, who stayed up. Blackpool had won 4–2 at Roker Park in Sunderland's eighth game of the season. It was a fifth consecutive loss after three draws, which left winless Sunderland one off the bottom.

In this season of high-scoring games, an 8–2 win over Blackburn Rovers featured hat-tricks for Jimmy 'Hookey' Leonard and Billy Eden, in a match where it was 7–0 by half-time. There was also a Bobby Gurney hat-trick in a 6–5 win over Liverpool. When Gurney got two in a 4–2 win in the Anfield return, it became part of a four-game winning run that lifted the Lads from the lower reaches into mid-table as the season ended.

While it was a disappointing though entertaining league campaign, Sunderland did better in the cup. In years to come, when Sunderland won the FA Cup in 1973, much was made of the numbers of the years being transposed from the previous cup triumph of 1937. In 1931, in reaching the semi-finals, Sunderland enjoyed their best run since being finalists in 1913.

A record Roker Park crowd of over 63,000 saw Sheffield United beaten in the fifth round, before Exeter City's record gate of 20,984 saw the Wearsiders win a quarter-final replay 4–2. In a match that was the first Sunderland game to be broadcast on radio, the semi-final was lost 2–0 to Birmingham at Leeds, despite Sunderland dominating proceedings. Cochrane's team had provided plenty of excitement, but there would be better to come in what was to be one of the club's great decades.

Winger Jimmy Connor and half-back Alex Hastings would become two of the side's stalwarts, after Cochrane returned to Scotland to bring them in from St Mirren and Stenhousemuir, both debuting in the opening three fixtures of this 1930–31 campaign. The great Raich Carter was also signed during this season but would have to wait until October 1932 for his debut, by which time he was eighteen. Another local youngster to arrive was goalkeeper Jimmy Thorpe, who debuted in October 1930. He was to become a tragic figure.

As Cochrane continued to build, right-winger Bert Davis from Bradford Park Avenue and Charlie Thomson from Glasgow Pollok were among the new faces in 1931–32, although Davis would not break into the first team until the opening day of the following season. Thomson was also the namesake of the 1913 captain. Both were half-backs who played for Scotland, with the Thomson of the thirties managing one fewer game than the 264 of the earlier incarnation. The thirties version was more of a schemer than the earlier stopper, although both possessed plenty of bite in the tackle.

There was yet to be an improvement in results, the team finishing one point and two places lower than the previous year, while in the cup three attempts at beating Second Division Stoke ended in a second-replay defeat in the fourth round. Undoubtedly Sunderland's position would have been much worse had it not been for the twelve goals scored by diminutive striker Benny Yorston, including seven in his first five games. He had signed from Aberdeen in late January after reputedly being involved in a betting scandal.

Sunderland were locked on 40 points again the next year (1932–33), although once again there was a promising cup run. Having reached the quarter-final without conceding a goal, Sunderland drew 4–4 at Derby County. The Wednesday afternoon replay brought a record attendance of 75,118, with the gates locked an hour before kick-off and thousands unable to gain admittance. However, the gigantic crowd were left disappointed and infuriated in equal measure. A 1–0 defeat was suffered after extra-time in a game mired in controversy. London referee Mr Gould initially gave a goal for Gurney, only to disallow it for offside. He then irked the huge crowd further by failing to give a penalty for a foul on Patsy Gallacher, even though the challenge saw the inside forward have to retire from the match, leaving Sunderland down to ten men.

Four days after the end of the season, Sunderland experienced two firsts in a game in France against Racing Club de Paris. Wearing numbered shirts for the first time, the team who would eventually host games at the Stadium of Light played their inaugural match under floodlights, winning 3–0. Despite the cup runs of 1933 and 1931, there was little sign of Sunderland stepping back up to the highest levels of the game, or even the consistent top three places of the mid-twenties. On the surface, a rise to sixth spot in 1934 failed to disguise the fact that just four points more than the year before had been gained, or that Sunderland were a massive fifteen points behind Arsenal, who retained the title. In the FA Cup a record 7–2 defeat in the competition was suffered in the fourth round at Aston Villa.

If there is one Sunderland player who would be likeliest to get into an all-time England XI it would be Raich Carter, even more so than Len Shackleton, whose maverick approach after the war failed to endear him to the game's authorities. April 1934 saw Carter's international debut in a 3–0 Wembley win over a Scotland side featuring Carter's clubmate Jimmy Connor.

The previous month, playing for 'The Rest', Raich had scored four goals, with Bobby Gurney bagging two, as England were beaten 7–1 at Roker Park.

The only player to win the FA Cup on both sides of the Second World War, Carter captained Sunderland in 1937, scoring in the final, and won the trophy again with Derby County in 1946. A majestic, two-footed inside-forward, Carter's career lost its best years to the war, but he nonetheless became a legendary figure in the game, scoring 31 goals as Sunderland became champions in 1936. Raich later enjoyed success as player-manager of Hull City, won the FAI Cup with Cork Athletic, managed Leeds United to promotion and also played first-class cricket for Derbyshire.

As the mid-thirties approached, Carter and the Sunderland team of the era were reaching their peak. Although there have been other notably successful years, such as 1973 and 1902, Sunderland have had three periods where they dominated English football: The Team of All The Talents of the 1890s; the 1912–13 side who won the league and reached the cup final; and Carter's side of the mid-thirties.

There was gradual improvement as Johnny Cochrane built his team. Having been a creditable fourth in his first campaign of 1928–29, on the back of Dave Halliday's record 43 goals, four mid-table finishes had led to the 1934 rise to sixth. But it was in 1934–35 that Sunderland signalled they were ready to challenge for honours again.

The summer of 1934 saw the first European staging of the FIFA World Cup. The inaugural tournament had been held in Uruguay in 1930. In 1934, Spain knocked out Brazil and only lost to hosts and eventual winners Italy in a replayed quarter-final. Just a week before Spain beat Brazil, Sunderland beat a Spanish XI 3–1 in Valencia in what was Spain's final warm-up match for the tournament. Earlier in the week Sunderland twice drew with Spain XIs at the homes of Real Madrid and Athletic Bilbao, in games refereed by Spanish officials and with the home side utilising substitutions to bring on fresh legs while Sunderland did not. The players Sunderland faced were basically the Spain World Cup squad: only four of those who played in the trio of games against the Wearsiders failed to make it into their country's squad for Italy. Notably, Sunderland achieved all of these results without their best player, Raich Carter. He was away on international duty with England. A year later Sunderland were invited back to Spain for a pair of friendlies, in which a Catalonia Select XI were thrashed 7–1 in Barcelona before a Madrid Select XI were beaten 2–1 in the capital.

By the time of the 1935 games in Spain, Sunderland had finished runners-up to the great Arsenal team of the era. Always a club of class, the Gunners invited Sunderland to their championship dinner held in the capital. Two Carter goals had beaten Arsenal at Roker, while late in the season Sunderland had held the champions to a draw on their own patch in front of Highbury's record crowd of 73,295. Despite scoring 90 goals, Sunderland scored 25 fewer than Arsenal, who were four points clear of Cochrane's men.

When Roker Park closed after 99 years in 1997, a poll in the *Sunderland Echo* saw supporters vote the 1973 FA Cup replay with Manchester City as the Match of the Century. That game with City was indeed a fabulously special occasion, but had more people been around who remembered it, the clash with Arsenal between Christmas and New Year in 1935 might have rivalled the City replay for that accolade. The Gunners arrived on Wearside in third place and with the tightest defence in the country. They had only conceded nine goals in their eleven away league trips. Table-toppers Sunderland, though, were rampant and boasted a 100 per cent home record from their ten games. With Carter conducting matters, Sunderland tore into the champions they were looking to usurp and raced into a 4–1 half-time lead. Looking to retain their league title for a fourth-successive season, Arsenal showed their mettle and fought back after the break only for Sunderland to emerge as 5–4 winners.

Johnny Cochrane's side strode to the title. They finished eight points clear of the chasing pack and remarkably did so despite conceding more goals than anyone in the top half of the table.

The 74 goals conceded were more than any team had ever let in while winning the title. However, with Gurney and Carter scoring 31 times each, Sunderland scored 109. Four of Gurney's goals came in a 7–2 win away to Birmingham that sealed the league championship with three games to spare. Bobby Gurney, who passed away in 1994, told me in 1992 that he remembered the leaky defence of the championship season: 'We used to play hell with them! We used to say: "What's the use of us scoring goals if you lot are letting them in?" But they'd just say, "You'll have to make up for it."'

At this point in history only Aston Villa could equal Sunderland's tally of six league titles. As Sunderland were crowned champions Villa and Blackburn Rovers were relegated. They were the last two of the league's twelve founder members to go down. This left Sunderland as the one club to have only ever played league football at the top level. It was a boast the club would hang on to for more than two further decades.

Sadly, the title triumph was tinged with sadness. Young goalkeeper Jimmy Thorpe's championship medal was awarded to his widow. A diabetic, Thorpe was only 22 when he was subjected to substantial rough treatment in a home game with Chelsea. Although Thorpe walked out of Roker Park unaided that afternoon, he soon took ill and died in hospital a few days later. Thorpe's death, together with that of another 22-year-old keeper earlier in the decade – John Thomson of Celtic – led to the laws of the game being changed so that a player was not allowed to raise their foot to the goalkeeper.

Following the death of Thorpe, Matt Middleton took over in goal, but after a bad run that culminated in a 6–0 defeat at Middlesbrough, teenager Johnny Mapson was signed from Reading. Mapson died in 1999, but earlier that year I interviewed him for a book on Sunderland goalkeepers. He told me of the surprise he faced when arriving in the North East to find children running about barefoot: 'I'd never been so far north before, and coming from the country we didn't see much of that. It rather shocked me to see kids running about with no shoes on.

There was a lot of unemployment about. It seemed to be proper morbid when I first got up there, and it took a bit of getting used to.' During the thirties unemployment was up to 31 per cent in Sunderland, while it reached an incredible 80 per cent in nearby Jarrow in 1936 during the period that Sunderland were dominating on the football pitch.

Despite the lack of money around, Sunderland marked the winning of the title with investment in a new stand, just as they had following the previous league title triumph in 1913. The Clock Stand opened officially for the start of the 1936–37 season. It provided covered terracing for 10,000 supporters, with seats added later. Once again it was a creation of the architect Archibald Leitch.

Mapson would go on to become one of Sunderland's great goalkeepers. In October 1936 he kept goal as cup holders Arsenal were beaten 2–1 in the Charity Shield at Roker Park, and the young goalkeeper would be central to Sunderland going on to win the FA Cup for the first time a year later. Having helped Sunderland to two draws with Wolves in the quarter-final, he was approached with the offer of a bribe to throw the tie in the second replay. 'Before the game I got a letter asking me if I'd be interested in earning some money by giving Wolverhampton the chance of winning,' Mapson told me. 'Of course I wasn't interested at all, I wouldn't have cared if they'd offered me thousands of pounds. Although it was a lot of money, I wasn't interested, so I just took it to the manager and that was the last I heard of it. That was the only time I was offered a bribe. I was young and full of enthusiasm and football was the only thing for me, I wouldn't bother with anything like that. I never looked at it from the financial side until I got a lot older. I was more interested in playing.'

Mapson kept a clean sheet as Wolves were walloped 4–0 in the decisive game of the tie, and he went on to set a record as the youngest winning Wembley goalkeeper, playing in the final on the last day of his teens. This record stood until 1975, when Mervyn Day of West Ham became an even younger cup-winning keeper. After beating Millwall in the semi-final, Sunderland met Preston North End in the final. Despite trailing at half-time to a goal from Frank O'Donnell, Sunderland came back to win with goals from Gurney, captain Carter and Eddie Burbanks. Carter and Burbanks had scored in the Charity Shield game earlier in the campaign.

With Gurney as his best man, Carter had been married a few days before the final. In his autobiography, *Footballer's Progress*, Raich remembered that as the Queen handed him the coveted cup she did so with the words: 'That's a nice wedding present for you!'

Folklore has it that in February 1892, Jimmy Hannah – a member of The Team of All The Talents – had been told of a curse that Sunderland would never win the cup until a 'Scotch lass' became queen of England. He was told this on the day Sunderland lost the cup semi-final despite a goal from Jock Scott. Queen Elizabeth, who handed over the trophy, had become queen a month before Sunderland started their cup run and was crowned in the month of the final – the first ever final to be held in May. Although born in Hertfordshire, she was the daughter of the Earl of Strathmore, a landowner whose main residence of Glamis Castle in Angus had been his family's home since the fourteenth century. Just for good measure, both managers and over half the players in the 1937 final were Scottish.

Sunderland's pride in its football team has always been strong. During the dark days of the Depression during the thirties it was stronger than ever. Unemployment was rife. October 1936 had seen the Jarrow March. Bairns often had no shoes on their feet and many had empty stomachs, housing conditions were horrendous, but the football team was the best in the land. In just over twelve months Cochrane, Carter and co. had delivered the only three pieces of silverware available: the league championship, the Charity Shield and now, at last, the FA Cup. As Carter remembered, when the team returned to Sunderland with the trophy: 'The tugs and ships in the river were hooting and blowing their sirens, railway engines shrilled their whistles, bells rang and rattles clacked, there was shouting and cheering. It was like a thick, concrete wall of deafening din. Then the cheering resolved itself into a Sunderland roar: "Ha'way, the Lads!" And the cry was taken up and surged around, echoing and re-echoing through the crowd, who spread further than the eye could see. "Ha'way, ha'way, ha'way!" cried half a million throats.'

In their defence of the cup, Sunderland got as far as the semi-finals in 1937–38, winning every match up to then 1–0 and setting new attendance records at Everton and Tottenham Hotspur along the way. Knocked out by Huddersfield, and having been beaten by Manchester City in the Charity Shield, the season would be a barren one, but Sunderland did have a significant role to play in the destiny of the league title. Although they could only manage eighth place, victory over Wolves on the final day denied Wanderers the title, Arsenal leapfrogging the men in old gold to pip them at the post.

With Adolf Hitler beginning to wreak havoc in Europe, the 1938–39 season would be the last to be completed before the Second World War. Although Sunderland had enjoyed a halcyon period in the mid-thirties, this golden era for the club had come to a close before war brought a cessation of the Football League. Sunderland finished a dismal sixteenth in the league, albeit level on points with the two clubs above them. Home form was particularly disappointing, with no team winning fewer home games and only one scoring fewer goals in front of their own supporters.

As with The Team of All The Talents four decades earlier, a great era ended with a substantial chunk of the team coming to the end of their time with the club. Patsy Gallacher left for Stoke, Jimmy Connor and Bobby Gurney made what were their final official appearances during peace-time in a cup tie with Blackburn, and notwithstanding appearances in what would become the cancelled 1939–40 campaign, Alec Hall and Raich Carter made what were their last officially counted Sunderland appearances in the final official pre-war match, a goalless draw at Wolves. Thirteen other players also officially bowed out in the final seven fixtures. Some of these players appeared in later war-time games, but – as with all clubs – these do not count in terms of official appearances in club records, so for many greats their final outings in major competitions ended with the outbreak of war.

The 1938–39 season also saw the end of manager Johnny Cochrane's time in charge. He had taken charge of exactly 500 games, winning 212 of them and bringing every available piece of silverware to the club. He signed off at the end of February, ironically with a 3–0 defeat at Middlesbrough, the same ground that had witnessed a vital win by the same scoreline as he sat in the stand, about to take over, eleven years earlier.

After George Crow stood in for a couple of matches as caretaker-manager, the board appointed Bill Murray, bringing back the club's long-serving defender after he completed his playing days with St Mirren. Murray would win just one of his first nine games after taking charge. He would then be faced with a seven-year wait for a tenth Football League fixture to actually count in the records.

He did have three games in what was supposed to be the 1939–40 season, but with Britain entering the Second World War 24 hours after Murray's men had lost 5–2 at Arsenal, the season was brought to an immediate halt. Acutely aware of the heavy criticism football faced when choosing to play the season to conclusion in the first year of the First World War, the footballing authorities wasted no time in suspending the Football League.

Clubs retained player registrations, but all player contracts were suspended. However, within a couple of weeks of the league being brought to a halt – with Sunderland fifteenth after three games – friendlies were allowed to be played, providing local police gave their blessing.

Only seven weeks had elapsed between the Football League being suspended and eight regional leagues being set up. Along with a handful of clubs including Aston Villa and Derby County, Sunderland decided not to join one of the regional leagues, so the club did not play a game until 22 March 1940, when they won 8–2 at South Shields, four players scoring twice each. The match at South Shields was a warm-up game as Sunderland had elected to play in a League War Cup competition. Roker Park was not used for any of the nine games the Lads played in this competition, as Sunderland was in a designated evacuation zone due to its shipyards. Home games against Darlington and Leeds United were staged at St James' Park, a ground Sunderland had used for a home game against Middlesbrough in 1903.

Sunderland again declined to participate in regional leagues in 1940–41. Supporters would have only been allowed to attend matches if they lived within five miles of Roker Park, but the club did enter a Durham Wartime Cup in which they reached the final, only to lose 2–1 to Chopwell Colliery at Gateshead. Some players were getting games elsewhere: Johnny Mapson, for instance, playing for Reading and for England against Wales at Nottingham in April.

Bill Murray occupied himself with providing fitness programmes for troops based in County Durham. In his role as honorary sports welfare officer for the county, at the end of May 1941 he launched a 'Fitness for Service' programme for men waiting to be called up or working in civil defence or essential industries.

Football returned to Roker Park in 1941–42. A wartime league saw Raich Carter kick the season off with an opening-day hat-trick in a 7–1 win over Sheffield United watched by 10,500 people. With a team featuring a lot of local youngsters, many of whom only played in wartime games, tenth place was achieved in this league before the commencement of a League War Cup. Sunderland reached the two-legged final against Wolverhampton Wanderers. Almost 35,000 saw the first leg, which was drawn 2–2, with Carter being joined on the scoresheet by Albert Stubbins, a 'guest' player and the only footballer to feature on the cover of the Beatles' seminal album *Sgt. Pepper's Lonely Hearts Club Band*. Carter would also score in the second leg of the final at Molineux, where Wolves won 4–1, to the delight of over 43,000.

Stubbins, incidentally, would not be SAFC's only connection with the Beatles. Fifties player Colin Grainger was nicknamed 'the singing winger'. As well as playing for England he sang professionally, recorded on the HMV label and on 13 June 1963 appeared on the same bill as the Fab Four in Manchester, in a week when the Beatles were number one in the charts. Moreover, Sunderland's record league goal-scorer Charlie Buchan later went into publishing. Most famous for what was once the world's top-selling football magazine, *Charles Buchan's Football Monthly*, Buchan also published music magazines *Melody Maker* and *Disc*. At one point Buchan briefly employed a young Cliff Richard as his office boy, while it was claimed that John Lennon once attended one of Buchan's publishing parties!

Of course, the frivolity of the swinging sixties and Beatlemania was a world away as the Second World War raged. In contrast with the nine footballers who had been on Sunderland's books and lost their lives in the First World War, only one perished in the Second World War. This was Percy Saunders, a man born during the First World War who had been given the middle name Kitchener after the Great War Field Marshal Earl Kitchener, who had been killed a month before Saunders's birth. A forward who played 26 times for Sunderland between 1937 and 1939, at the age of just 35 Saunders died when his Dutch ship, the SS *Rooseboom*, was torpedoed in the Indian Ocean on 1 March 1942. There is a memorial to Saunders in a cemetery in Singapore.

Some 27 per cent of merchant shipping built in Britain during the Second World War was built on the Wear, which made Sunderland a target for German bombing raids, and 267 people are known to have been killed by bombing in Sunderland, with 1,000 houses destroyed and three times that number damaged. Roker Park was also bombed, with Special Constable Lancelot Slawther killed outside the club house and a crater left in the pitch after another bomb came through the roof of the Main Stand in May 1943.

A fortnight before that bomb landed, Roker Park had staged another cup final, this time the first leg of the West Riding Combined Counties Cup. Cliff Whitelum scored all six goals – five of them before half-time at the Fulwell End – as Huddersfield

Town were beaten 6–2. Sunderland still needed a goal from Johnny Spuhler in the second leg to take the trophy, as a 4–1 reverse was suffered in Yorkshire. Once again, goals were scored as if they were going out of fashion, 204 being netted in Sunderland's 40 games, 111 of them in the 'right' net.

Sunderland continued to play in a wartime competition called Football League North. Rather like some modern-day South American championships, this was a complicated arrangement that featured pre- and post-Christmas tables. Up to sixty teams took part in these competitions, and in each half-season Sunderland would play eighteen or nineteen games. Across 1942–43 and 1943–44, finishes of twenty-first, twenty-second, ninth and forty-fifth were registered, but ultimately people were just pleased to have football to play and watch.

The last year of the war saw Sunderland finish third in the pre-Christmas league, but thirty-first after Christmas. Cliff Whitelum continued to score freely. His seasonal tally of 42 from 36 appearances included four hat-tricks. There was another cup final, but ultimately a 6–3 defeat to Gateshead at St James' Park in the Tyne–Wear–Tees Cup.

Just two games of the 1945–46 Football League North season had been played when Japan formally surrendered to bring about the end of the Second World War on 2 September 1945. This surrender had been agreed a couple of weeks earlier, before the football season kicked off, but with troops still in service and often still overseas, and many players still to return to their clubs, the recommencement of the Football League was delayed by a year. The Football League North carried on, while the FA Cup restarted immediately.

Sunderland struggled in the league, finishing 18th out of 22. For the only time in its history the FA Cup was played as two-legged ties. But for this, Sunderland would have reached the quarter-finals and maybe beyond. Having eliminated Grimsby Town and Bury (which they would have done after the first match anyway), Birmingham City were beaten 1–0 at Roker Park, 1937 cup-final winger Len Duns getting the goal in front of 44,820, the first post-war crowd to surpass 40,000. But a second-leg scoreline of 3–1 to Birmingham eliminated Sunderland.

Raich Carter went on to win the cup with Derby County, scoring for the Rams against Birmingham City in the semi-final. Carter had left Sunderland just before Christmas, his very last game in red and white having come on 15 December against Manchester United at Manchester City's Maine Road. As with all players, Carter's appearances in the Football League North and other wartime competitions do not count on official records, so his last official game for the club remained his last pre-war outing.

Carter would be the big draw in the opening Football League game after the war when Derby County were the visitors to Roker Park for the resumption of the league at the end of August in 1946. The war was thankfully behind everyone, and Sunderland could set out on maintaining their position as one of the country's leading and most successful clubs. However, in the years after the Second World War, Sunderland have – with the glorious exception of FA Cup triumph in 1973 – failed to maintain that position. They have slid down the soccer hierarchy, despite commanding outstanding support brought up on the football folklore of what had happened up to this point.

6

THE BANK OF ENGLAND CLUB

Post-war problems on and off the pitch (1946–58)
The post-war boom in attendances saw over 900,000 people pass through the turnstiles for Sunderland league games alone in each of three successive seasons from 1947 to 1950. Over a million came to see the team in 1949–50, when an average of 47,785 watched a season that could and should have brought a first post-war league title. Had Sunderland achieved that, then perhaps such success could have led to further silverware in an era when Sunderland spent so much money they became known as 'the Bank of England Club'. In all of Sunderland's history that Bank of England Club moniker is the only one to have become as common as The Team of All The Talents nickname of the 1890s. However, whereas the Talents produced phenomenal success, the stars of the fifties ultimately failed to produce anything other than a first ever relegation, due largely to their being a set of talented individuals who simply did not gel well enough as a team on a consistent basis.

Just under 50,000 saw the first post-war league game, when Raich Carter's Derby County were beaten 3–2, Carter's fellow 1937 FA Cup final scorer Eddie Burbanks notching the first post-war goal with a penalty. And the crowd could have been larger. At least 5,000 spectators failed to gain admission, as there was a lack of staff to operate all the turnstiles (the Roker End was claimed to have fewer than 15,000 spectators present). Burbanks's fellow winger Len Duns and goalkeeper Johnny Mapson were the other survivors of the cup-winning side. One of three debutants in the opening-day line-up was a man who would get more England caps than Carter – although all but four of half-back Willie Watson's twenty-seven international appearances would be as a cricketer! The eleventh of twelve dual football and cricket internationals, Watson once scored a century against Australia at Lord's, although his cricketing duties often led to him missing the start or end of the football season.

Despite a disappointing cup exit to Second Division promotion-chasers Chesterfield at the first hurdle, Sunderland did okay in the opening league campaign after the war. Wartime goal-machine Cliff Whitelum and new signing Jackie Robinson got 33 goals between them, but overall goalscoring was a problem, and the team finished a modest ninth. The most notable result of the season saw a Whitelum hat-trick as Manchester United suffered their solitary home defeat of the campaign, in a match played at Maine Road because of bomb damage to Old Trafford. United were to miss out on the title by a point to rivals Liverpool.

The 1947–48 season was hugely disappointing. Once again there was an immediate cup exit away to a Second Division outfit, this time Southampton. More worryingly, the team finished third from bottom, although four points clear of the relegation places. At home they won as many games as runners-up Manchester United, but only newly promoted Manchester City won as few as Sunderland's two away victories.

Sunderland were already splashing the cash in search of success. Unlike football today, clubs did not obtain most of their finance from TV and sponsorship money. Most of their resources came from the paying supporter, and Sunderland had plenty of those. On the other hand, at this time gate money was shared with the visitors, unlike nowadays, when clubs retain the money from their home fixtures. Brandishing their chequebook, Sunderland twice broke their transfer record during 1947 and

1948. In January 1947 this was for Third Division Crystal Palace defender Arthur Hudgell, who went on to play 275 games for Sunderland, until retiring to become one of the club's coaches in 1957. This was followed in November when almost the same amount was paid to Dundee for Ronnie Turnbull. This initially looked like a bargain when he bagged four goals on his debut, although Turnbull would score just four more in the rest of the season.

That record was more than doubled just over a year after Hudgell's arrival. Known as 'the Clown Prince of Soccer', Len Shackleton was one of the game's great mavericks and one of the most talented individuals to grace the sport. Having joined Newcastle United for a club record £13,000 fee after the war, 'Shack' scored six goals on his United debut in their record 13–0 Division Two win over Newport County. Nonetheless, Shack spent only eighteen months with the Magpies before United wanted to move him on, apparently due to his fractious relationship with the club's management. Sealed bids were invited, with a friendly Newcastle director tipping off his Sunderland counterpart that the highest bid was £20,000. Sunderland duly bid £20,050 and secured the signature of a player who was to become one of the all-time greats on Wearside.

Tales of Shack playing one-twos off the corner flag, putting back-spin on the old heavy leather ball so that defenders would be tempted to lunge for it while – like an obedient dog – it came back towards him, or impudently sitting on the ball while it was in play are commonplace among supporters of the era. In the history of the club only L.R. Roose and, to some extent, Tommy McInally could begin to rival Shackleton for showmanship. Len's sheer talent warranted far more than the five England caps he got, but again his face did not fit with officialdom, and despite scoring a wonderful individual goal against reigning world champions West Germany at Wembley in 1954, he was never selected again. Infamously, but typically, in his autobiography Len left a blank page under the chapter-heading: 'The Average Director's Knowledge of Football.'

Shackleton was upstaged on his debut at Derby, where Raich Carter scored four as Sunderland were thrashed 5–1, but goals in his first two home games swiftly endeared him to his new audience. His first full season of 1948–49 brought one of the most ignominious results in the club's existence, when non-league Yeovil Town bundled moneybags Sunderland out of the FA Cup on their infamous sloping pitch. The match was drawn over 90 minutes, but instead of a replay went straight to extra-time on a day that was one of the most humiliating in the club's history. It was not the first time Sunderland had been dumped out of the cup by a team who were not members of the Football League. In 1908, for example, defeat had been tasted at Southern League New Brompton, a club who later became Gillingham.

Manager Bill Murray would have hoped for a reaction to that Yeovil defeat, but he did not immediately get one. A 5–0 reverse at Arsenal next time out was the first of four consecutive league losses, before a Dicky Davis hat-trick against Preston sparked an eleven-match unbeaten run (which included a club record six successive draws) to the end of the season that saw Sunderland climb to eighth.

A schoolboy international teammate of Shackleton's, Davis had come to Sunderland as a teenager a few months before the war. In 1949–50 he would be Division One's top scorer as his 25 goals powered Sunderland to third in the league table. Crucially, injury ruled the hot-shot out of five late-season games before he returned with a brace on the final day. During his absence, three games in a row were lost, including one where relegated Manchester City won their only away game of the season, which featured Jack Stelling missing a twice-taken penalty for Sunderland. Frustratingly, that afternoon Sunderland were without the influential Willie Watson, who was even more frustratingly not used by England as they beat Scotland at Hampden Park. In the final analysis Sunderland were a point behind champions Portsmouth, although Pompey also had a superior goal average. Sunderland had started the season poorly and been in the bottom half of the table in mid-November.

While they only briefly topped the table at Easter, in reality it was a golden chance to add a post-war title and set the tone for the decade to come. England entered the FIFA World Cup for the first time that summer, and Watson was a member of the squad in Brazil, although again he did not play.

Despite Davis being the division's top scorer, Sunderland replaced him early the following 1950–51 season with Wales international Trevor Ford. He arrived from Aston Villa for a national record fee of £29,500 and made a stunning entrance on his home debut against Sheffield Wednesday. Not content with scoring a hat-trick, Ford made himself the talk of the town by also dislodging a goal post and breaking an opponent's jaw. Before his next home game Trevor scored twice more at Roker Park, this time for Wales, who lost 4–2 to an England side that included Watson.

With the addition of Ford it was hoped that the team would be further improved. The near miss of 1949–50 was only the seventh season of league football played since the title had last resided at Roker Park, in 1936. With Irish winger Billy Bingham also having been purchased to supply Ford, and with Shackleton and the sublime Ivor Broadis as inside-forwards, Sunderland were assembling a star-studded side that kept the turnstiles clicking, but 1950–51 saw the team marooned in mid-table. At least there was a cup run for the first time since league football resumed, the challenge ending in a quarter-final replay against Wolves at Molineux.

Having impressed in 1949–50, the following three seasons were disappointing, despite continued investment in the team. With no notable cup success, league finishes of twelfth, twelfth and ninth preceded a poor year in 1953–54, when eighteenth place was only secured on goal average and maximum points from the final two games after the team had been bottom of the 22-team table for much of the autumn.

The calendar year of 1953 actually saw Sunderland top of the league in the opening week, just a few weeks after Roker Park had staged its first ever floodlit match with the visit of Dundee.

Nine days earlier Sunderland had played under lights in a friendly at Southampton. But an injury to Ford saw Sunderland's title challenge fade quicker than those early floodlights. By the end of the calendar year only back-markers Liverpool were keeping the Lads off the bottom of the table.

Failure on the pitch could not be laid at the feet of the board, who kept bankrolling the Bank of England Club. In 1953–54, Billy Elliott, Ray Daniel, Ken Chisholm, Ted Purdon, Joe McDonald and two goalkeepers in James Cowan and Willie Fraser arrived for combined fees totalling £112,000, an astronomical amount for the time. Occasionally, the team clicked into gear. Never more so than when a Ford hat-trick combined with a superlative display by Shackleton inflicted a 7–1 hammering on champions Arsenal. Approaching the end of the 2023–24 season, no reigning champions have since suffered such a heavy defeat. For good measure the Gunners were also blasted 4–1 at Highbury, where Ted Purdon's hat-trick began with Sunderland's quickest-ever goal, registered after just ten seconds.

While the overall failure of Sunderland at this time can by no means be purely put down to a clash of personalities, it was no secret that star forwards Shackleton and Ford didn't see eye to eye. Both admitted as much in their autobiographies, with Ford feeling that Shackleton would often deliberately under- or over-hit a pass to him, whereas passes to other players would be made to measure. By the time of Purdon's hat-trick at Highbury, Ford had moved on, joining Cardiff City for a record £30,000. Ford was a brilliant battering ram of a centre-forward, one who would put 100 per cent into every game, but without him the following season Sunderland did the best they had since the season before he arrived.

With full-backs Jack Hedley and Joe McDonald contributing to the top flight's tightest defence, until February 1955 there was a serious chance of doing the double. The line was now being led by new centre-forward Charlie 'Cannonball' Fleming, and his brace in a win at Newcastle left Sunderland just a point behind leaders Wolves. Two weeks later it was Purdon's turn to score a brace as Wolves were beaten in the cup quarter-final. Perhaps the excitement of the cup run clouded the league challenge, as after the win at St James' a meagre five points were accrued from the next nine games. Despite winning the last three fixtures, Murray's men finished fourth, four points behind champions Chelsea, who won what was their only league title until half a century later.

The cup run came to an end in the semi-final at Villa Park, when a 1–0 defeat was suffered to a Manchester City side managed by Les McDowall, who had played a handful of games for Sunderland in the mid-thirties. Had Sunderland won that match it would have set up a derby Wembley final with Newcastle United, who progressed after winning their own semi-final in a replay at Roker Park against York City.

Rekindling memories of the club's past, when they cashed in on being a star attraction by playing many lucrative friendlies, the Bank of England Club embarked on an extensive nine-game tour of the USA and Canada, four of these games being exhibition matches against fellow top-flight tourists Huddersfield Town.

Huddersfield would be one of the teams well beaten early in the 1955–56 season, as Sunderland made a positive start, even topping the table after an October win at Tottenham. The team could turn on the style from time to time. The previous month – for the only time in history to 2023 – Sunderland came back to win after being 3–0 down, and did so against reigning champions Chelsea. The fact that they did this a week after conceding seven goals in a 42-minute spell at Blackpool illustrates the lack of consistency that saw them finish ninth, albeit just three points adrift of Manchester City in fourth place. Some awful defeats were suffered, including an 8–2 loss at Luton a week after regaining top spot in the league. What was worse was a record 6–1 home defeat to Newcastle on Boxing Day, a result that ruined many a red and white Christmas, especially as the following day, in the reverse fixture, there was another loss, this time 3–1 after the Lads led at half-time.

New £12,000 signing from Burnley Bill Holden marked his debut in that game at St James' with a goal. Just over

The Bank of England Club

two months later he returned to St James' to score both in a 2–0 FA Cup quarter-final win that knocked out holders Newcastle. Going into 2025, United were still searching for their first domestic trophy since then, albeit they were increasingly confident of ending that drought due to their newfound riches. For Sunderland, the Holden-inspired cup triumph on Tyneside set up a semi-final defeat to Birmingham City at Hillsborough. To 2025, Birmingham had reached two FA Cup finals, on both occasions defeating Sunderland in the semi-final, the previous time being in 1931.

The Blues lost the first of those finals to local rivals West Bromwich Albion, and it was Albion who snuffed out Sunderland's hopes of a third successive cup run in the fourth round of the next season of 1956–57. After three seasons in the mid-fifties when the Bank of England Club had threatened to cash in with a trophy, 1956–57 became the beginning of a dreadful period in Sunderland's history.

The club was torn to shreds after the football authorities received a letter signed by a 'Mr. Smith'. This alleged that Sunderland had been making illegal payments to players still bound by the maximum wage. Certainly, Sunderland were an attractive club, not least because of the fantastic support they commanded, but when so many of the game's top stars had been lured to a corner of the country relatively geographically isolated, it caused some to wonder how Sunderland were managing to persuade so many famous players to up sticks and move to the North East. Sunderland were still brandishing their chequebook in the search for success: £24,000 had been lavished on centre-forward Don Revie, who had played against Sunderland in the 1955 cup semi-final and would cross Sunderland's path later as a manager. Another newcomer was Colin Grainger, an England international known as 'the singing winger'.

Way back in 1904, SAFC had been fined the then sizeable sum of £250 for paying bonuses to players contrary to regulations. All but one of the players questioned confessed to receiving bonuses. Sunderland's club secretary and directors were duly punished with suspensions ranging from one to three seasons, but far worse was to come following the 'Mr. Smith' letter.

The issue of a maximum wage was a bone of contention for footballers across the land until the early 1960s, when it was abolished. Derby County had first proposed a maximum wage of £4 per week for players in 1893, at a time when Sunderland were league champions and top players could command up to two and a half times Derby's proposed maximum. Five years after the 1904 revelations, the FA instructed all players to leave the Association Football Players' Union (today known as the Professional Footballers' Association), and seventeen Sunderland players are believed to have refused. Charlie Buchan had been among those to call for strike action in 1920 when the maximum wage was actually reduced from £10 a week to £9. All that happened is that, astonishingly, it was reduced again the following season to £8, with £6 a week in the close season. So much for the 'roaring twenties'.

Those figures remained the same until after the Second World War, when the close-season wage was raised by a pound a week. In 1948 the wages of professional footballers were increased to £12 a week, with £10 a week allowable in the close season. Increases to £14 in 1951, £15 in 1953 and £17 in 1957 did little to impress the high calibre of players being attracted to Sunderland during this period.

Clubs found ways around the maximum wage. Sunderland were one of many to fix their players up with jobs outside of football, often for the firms of directors or friends of the club. Players employed to be car salesmen, for example, might do relatively little work but be handsomely rewarded. Players also often lived in houses owned by clubs while paying a token rent. However, the issue at Sunderland was not down to such legitimate ways in which players might be helped financially. The problem was that many of Sunderland's players had been illegally receiving more than they were allowed to for playing football.

The club had generated the extra cash needed for these payments by claiming that they had paid more than they

The Bank of England Club

really had for straw and tarmac. Straw was an old-fashioned but effective way of protecting pitches in icy conditions. The Thomas M.M. Hemy painting that dominates the entrance hall of the Stadium of Light, from a match in January 1895, shows the pitch surrounded by straw, which had been used to help get the game on. When SAFC's books were inspected in 1957 they showed a £3,000 expenditure on straw. The day before the Sunderland story broke in the press, Alan Hardaker had begun his new post as Football League secretary. He was suspicious of Sunderland's straw bill and telephoned his brother Ernest, who was the chairman of Hull FC, a rugby league club. Asking if £3,000 was a reasonable amount to pay for a winter's worth of straw, Alan Hardaker was informed that £3,000 would cover a quarter of a century's worth. The (black) cat was out of the bag, and Sunderland's subterfuge began to unravel.

SAFC had produced the money to make illegal payments by placing goods orders that were much in excess of what was needed. Evidently wanting to assist the club in the search for success, the suppliers had been delivering what was really required then issuing credit notes, which had been cashed in order to circumvent the club's accounts. Over five years, just under £5,250 had been raised in this way.

In his 1977 autobiography, *Hardaker of the League*, Hardaker explained that he felt he knew who the author of the anonymous 'Mr. Smith' letters were. 'I am very sure I knew who sent them,' he wrote. 'I compared type faces and style with one or two other letters I had received and there was no doubt in my mind that they tallied. His name, if I revealed it, would cause enormous surprise even now.'

Hardaker chose not to reveal the mystery of Mr Smith, with Simon Inglis adding in his 1985 book *Soccer in the Dock*: 'Without proof we cannot put in print the suspicions of several people who were close to the affair. Suffice it to say that they are still personally convinced of "Mr. Smith's" true identity and allege that he was in fact a member of the Sunderland board as it existed in early 1957.'

This squares with the name I was given as the identity of 'Mr. Smith' one day when I was out for lunch with Len Ashurst, who joined the club late in 1957; Malcolm Bramley, who was a young office boy at Roker Park in the early sixties and was later secretary to former Sunderland players Brian Clough at Derby as well as Ashurst at Gillingham; and Ian Mills, whose firm had been the club's solicitors. Ian Mills named who he believed 'Mr. Smith' was and was adamant about it, but, like Simon Inglis, I will not print the name without proof. Unsurprisingly, given how long ago this all took place, the person identified as 'Mr. Smith' is long-since dead.

The motives of 'Mr. Smith' can be guessed at. In his excellent *Soccer in the Dock*, Inglis argued: 'It was strongly suspected that he was either one of the directors himself or was at least being fed information by one of the board', while adding the inevitable question, 'But why would a director wish to inform on his colleagues?' In *Soccer in the Dock* Inglis explains that in particular the *Daily Express* and the *People* chased the story. The sports editor of the *Express* claimed to have seen what were two anonymous letters. The sensational story first appeared in the public domain on 7 January 1957, at a time when the team were struggling near the bottom of the division. The *Express* claimed that 'Smith' 'gives enough facts to show he is well acquainted with the Sunderland club and that his object is the punishment of individuals'.

As a consequence of the 'Mr. Smith' letters, FA chairman Arthur Drewry CBE and Football League president Arthur H. Oakley led a six-man joint FA and Football League commission into Sunderland's affairs. This meeting, at the Royal Victoria Station Hotel in Sheffield on 7 March 1957, saw Sunderland represented by chairman Bill Ditchburn, director Bill Martin and club secretary George Crow, seven weeks after the club's financial records had been requested and examined.

As a follow-up, all of the club's board, along with the manager, secretary and club accountant, were called before a commission at York just over three weeks later. The commission

The Bank of England Club

then met again on 6 April, four days before their conclusions were made public. Sunderland had endured many bad results in their history to this point, not least another recent heavy defeat to Newcastle United, who had swept Sunderland aside to the tune of 6–2 on Tyneside just before Christmas. But the result of the commission was even worse. Found guilty of making illegal payments to players, chairman Ditchburn and director Martin were permanently suspended from football. Vice-chairman Stan Ritson and director Laurie Evans were suspended indefinitely, and the club, as well as being ordered to pay the costs of the inquiry, were fined £5,000, a figure more than six times higher than any punishment previously handed out by the FA. The inquiry also handed down punishments to a total of fourteen players in the form of the loss of qualifications and benefits and indefinite suspensions.

Not all of the players punished were still with Sunderland at the time, and the suspension effectively lasted for just one match. This was an end-of-season game at Portsmouth, whose winner came from former Sunderland striker Derek Weddle as Pompey leapfrogged the Lads, leaving them third from bottom, but fortunately still in an age when only two clubs went down. The club were in total disarray on and off the pitch. Bill Murray was fined the relatively modest sum of £200, the inquiry having accepted that he was working under instructions from the board. George Crow was exonerated totally and remained with the club, but Murray tendered his resignation as manager five weeks after his fine and passed away four and a half years later.

Player suspensions were quickly lifted when they owned up to having received illegal payments. In November 1958 five players sued the commission, claiming they did not have the authority to hand out the punishments they did. The lifetime bans on Ditchburn and Evans were rescinded in 1962, the year in which Bill Murray's fine was returned to his widow. Bill Ditchburn's son Jack was a solicitor. He felt that the FA had overreached themselves by suspending company directors, because the FA did not possess the power to override company law. Determined not to let the matter drop, Bill Ditchburn sought to unearth illegal payments at the clubs of members of the League Management Committee and FA Council. Later, one of the accused Sunderland players, Ken Chisholm, revealed details of additional payments he had received from Partick Thistle, Leicester City and Leeds United. Leicester and Leeds were represented on the League Management Committee although no action was taken against those clubs.

Bill Ditchburn tried and failed to regain a place on the club's board of directors, although his son Jack later became vice-chairman, with Laurie Evans's son also becoming a director. Syd Collings was also on the board at the time of the 'Mr. Smith' letters. He went on to become chairman of SAFC and the FA representative who introduced captain Bobby Moore and the England team to Queen Elizabeth II ahead of the 1966 FIFA World Cup final at Wembley. His son Keith Collings later became chairman of Sunderland, being in charge when the FA Cup was won in 1973.

By the time the protests of Sunderland's directors and players were upheld in April 1962, the maximum wage had been abolished (in January 1961). However, by then the damage had been done to the club. Quite apart from the loss of face nationally to one of the greatest and most successful clubs in the history of the game, in the season after the 'Mr. Smith' revelations, Sunderland were finally relegated for the first time. In going down SAFC duly lost the proud tag of being the only club to have only ever played top-flight football since being admitted into the Football League in 1890.

The match programme of the time appears to have seen that relegation coming. From 1955–56 until the end of the 1956–57 season, the cover of the club's official programme showed an aerial photograph of Roker Park and a list of the club's major honours, under which was placed the boast: 'Only Club which has never played in any other than the First Division.' However, on the opening day of 1957–58, while the photograph and list of honours remained within exactly the same page design, the boast had disappeared.

Also disappearing was the legendary Len Shackleton, who retired after one match under new manager Alan Brown, in which Arsenal left Roker Park with both points after inflicting a 1–0 defeat in front of over 56,000 on the first day of the season. A native of Northumberland, Brown was steeped in football, having had a lifetime in the game as a player and manager. A strict disciplinarian, Brown placed his faith very much in youth while looking to move on more experienced players. Among the ten players to make debuts during the season was Brown's best signing, one of the greatest acquisitions in the club's history. This was the colossal centre-half Charlie Hurley, who would be voted the club's player of the century in the centenary year of 1979. A tower of strength in the air, but beautifully balanced and in control when bringing the ball out of defence with his feet, Hurley became the hero of the terraces soon after their darling Shackleton had retired.

However, he had a less than glorious start. Beaten 7–0 on his debut at Blackpool and 6–0 second time out, a week later at Burnley, Charlie revealed his supreme inner confidence with the cheeky remark that he had already made a difference, as the second defeat hadn't been as heavy as the first. That is not to suggest the Irish-born, London-raised man signed from Millwall didn't take his football seriously. He would quickly become the king-pin around which the team revolved. Nonetheless, he was unable to halt the slide that saw proud Sunderland slip into Division Two for the first time.

Nineteenth following a Good Friday draw at Manchester United, shortly after the Old Trafford club had experienced the devasting horror of the Munich disaster, Sunderland were a point clear of local rivals Newcastle United and Leicester City, who were managed by Sunderland's goal-scoring hero of the twenties Dave Halliday. The Magpies, though, had three games in hand, with the Foxes also having a game in hand. Propping up the table with two points fewer than Sunderland were Sheffield Wednesday.

Twenty-four hours after bringing back that point from Old Trafford, Sunderland were hammered 6–1 at home by mid-table

Birmingham City, with worse to follow when Manchester United won the Easter Monday return at Roker Park. Another loss followed at Manchester City the following weekend, and though Nottingham Forest were beaten in the penultimate match, it left Sunderland dangling over the precipice. As had happened a year earlier, the final game of the campaign saw Sunderland on the south coast – at Portsmouth where they had ended the previous season.

Going into the final day Sunderland were in the bottom two, a point ahead of Wednesday, but one behind Leicester and two adrift of Pompey and Newcastle, with everyone having a far superior goal average to Sunderland. Sunderland needed to win and hope other results went their way. Leicester were away to Birmingham, who had recently scored six at Sunderland, but the Foxes won 1–0 to render Sunderland's 2–0 win at Portsmouth redundant. Although Newcastle lost at home to Leeds, they still had another game to play (which they lost), but like Leicester they had a superior goal average to the red and whites. Finally, the club who had spawned The Team of All The Talents, the near-double team of Charlie Buchan and co. and the all-conquering side of the thirties were now to play in Division Two. The *Sunderland Football Echo* marked the relegation by changing from being printed on pink paper to blue, only changing it back when Sunderland were promoted six years later. Sunderland had often been a tough place to live, with many people struggling financially. However, throughout the hardest of times for many, through the late Victorian age, the depression of the thirties and the world wars, the people had always been proud of their football team. Now, in the aftermath of the 'Mr. Smith' revelations, that team would no longer be at the top level of English football. It was to be a long road back.

7

BROWNED OFF

The beginning of the 'yo-yo' years (1958–72)
Colin Grainger got Sunderland's first Second Division goal, but any hopes of an immediate return to the top flight were quickly replaced by the anguish and fear that, while Sunderland's stay in Division Two might be short, it could end with an exit through the trapdoor into Division Three. Grainger's opening-day goal did not even warrant the term consolation, as Sunderland lost 3–1 at Lincoln City in August. By the end of the following month Sunderland were, astonishingly, bottom of the table, having suffered four defeats in a row, including 5–0 and 6–0 hammerings, the heaviest of these at Sheffield Wednesday, who had been relegated with the red and whites.

The third of this run of four defeats saw the start of new manager Alan Brown's revolution of youth. Debuts were given to three teenagers who between them would go on to amass over 1,100 appearances for the club. Cec Irwin's debut made him Sunderland's youngest-ever player up to that point at 16 years and 165 days. Fellow full-back Len Ashurst went on to become the club's record outfield appearance-maker, while in front of him, left-half Jim McNab ensured the left side of the Roker rearguard was locked down.

While Irwin waited almost a year for a second appearance, before going on to establish himself, McNab enjoyed a ten-game run in the side and Ashurst immediately made the number-three shirt his own, missing just one match for the rest of the season. Alongside the blossoming Charlie Hurley and the superb Stan Anderson, who had bucked the trend of the Bank of England side by being a home-grown thoroughbred, Sunderland actually had the makings of a promising team. Although the end-of-season report showed that the club was tightening its belt after the financial largesse that had led to so much trouble, Brown was still backed in the transfer market. The sum of £15,000 was invested in goalkeeper Peter Wakeham, with £9,000 spent on veteran Sunderland-born winger Ernie Taylor. He became one of five players who would represent England during their careers to play for Sunderland that season, along with Anderson, Grainger, Don Revie and Billy Elliott.

In between Wakeham and Taylor's debuts came Revie's final appearance. He had come to blows with Brown in the dressing room after scoring in a 4–0 win at Rotherham, when South African Don Kichenbrand netted a hat-trick. Revie requested to make his own way home, but Brown would have none of it as he asserted the iron discipline he was renowned for. Taylor's debut six weeks after Wakeham's corresponded with the final match of the redoubtable Billy Elliott, who had been such a whole-hearted player for the club. Revie and Elliott would cross paths again in the 1973 FA Cup final, when Don was manager of Leeds and Billy was Sunderland's trainer.

Sunderland backed up that win at Rotherham with a 4–1 victory over promotion-chasing Sheffield United, Johnny Goodchild getting a hat-trick this time, with ex-Blade Grainger also on the scoresheet. Soon after Christmas a sequence of five wins in six league games improved the league standing, although the team never climbed above eleventh and finished a disappointing fifteenth: twelve points clear of relegation but with a chasm of twenty points separating Sunderland from the last of the promotion spots. It was to be a long road back to the top level, with a 4–0 defeat at top-flight Everton in the FA Cup's first hurdle emphasising that Sunderland were well behind the required standard.

Having gone down with Sunderland, Sheffield Wednesday won the league, scoring over a hundred goals, and would start the 1959–60 season in the First Division. If it was hoped that the Rokermen had reached rock bottom and could now begin to muster a first ever promotion campaign to herald the start of the 1960s, those ambitions were dashed when Brown's men finished a place lower than the year before.

After starting badly, taking just three points from the first four games, the dropping of just a single point from the next four briefly raised spirits, only for a 6–1 slaughtering at Ipswich to start another sequence of three points from four fixtures. By the beginning of April the team were third from bottom, after defeat at second-bottom Bristol City, where Amby Fogarty was guilty of missing numerous good chances. Thankfully, a week later Fogarty got a winner against Scunthorpe United, which signalled the start of a five-game unbeaten run that took the team to safety. Nonetheless, Brown was quietly transforming the side, with older experienced players such as Kichenbrand and Grainger moving on, while youngsters such as Martin Harvey and Nick Sharkey were blooded.

Had play-offs existed in 1960–61 there would have been reason to get excited about the prospect of promotion, as sixth place was achieved. Sunderland actually topped the table after just two games, but shortly afterwards dropped to nineteenth after a run of seven games brought just a single point. As the crowd of 19,240 made their way over Wearmouth Bridge after a home draw with Rotherham United a week later, now into a third season out of Division One following the 'Mr. Smith' disgrace, supporters were at a low point in following a club whose trademark had been success rather than sorrow.

Little were people to know that – despite a 4–3 defeat at Brentford in Sunderland's first ever League Cup tie a few days after the trip to Rotherham – the draw with the Millers was to be the first of a sixteen-game unbeaten league run that would climax with six successive wins, including a 7–1 thrashing of Luton and, more importantly, two classic cup wins. During this run Brown was able to name an unchanged team for ten successive games, and a settled side reaped the rewards. They developed a never-say-die spirit that even brought an equaliser deep into injury time at Swansea, where they had come back from being 3–0 down within quarter of an hour.

In one of Stan Anderson's most famous matches the wing-half scored both goals as top-flight Arsenal were beaten 2–1 in front of over 58,000 on Wearside, before promotion-chasers Liverpool were beaten in the fourth round at Anfield. Tragically, four young supporters would lose their lives in a road accident on the way home from that tie. After Hurley headed a late winner at Norwich City, cup fever gripped supporters who until this season had seen Sunderland win just one cup tie since the semi-finals of the mid-fifties. Given a home draw with Division One leaders Tottenham Hotspur, the stage was set for Sunderland to make it a North London double, after knocking out Arsenal, and to re-assert themselves on the national stage. Over 61,000 squeezed into Roker Park for a match where, even according to the official history of Spurs, Sunderland came closest to derailing them as Tottenham went on to become the first team of the twentieth century to capture the double of league and cup.

Tottenham and Northern Ireland skipper Danny Blanchflower was found after the match wandering the stands. Asked what he was looking for, the genial Blanchflower explained that he was looking for the loudspeakers that had amplified the crowd. There was no such crowd amplification: Blanchflower had simply heard the 'Roker Roar', the famous atmosphere that made Sunderland renowned throughout the game for sheer passion and unsurpassable noise. Remember that at this time both ends of the ground were uncovered, so the noise generated could not echo back from the overhanging roof. The Fulwell End would be covered later in the decade in preparation for the 1966 FIFA World Cup.

Having taken an early lead in the cup quarter-final through Cliff Jones, Spurs were pegged back soon after half-time when teenager Willie McPheat scored on the rebound after keeper Bill Brown could only parry a Hurley header. With fever pitch now reached in the crowd, many, mainly children, invaded the pitch in excitement. The hold-up in play gave the Londoners an opportunity to regroup and try to hang on against a rampant Sunderland, who went closest to a winner through young winger John Dillon before the game ended 1–1. Spurs comfortably saw off Sunderland in the replay.

No one has ever scored more goals as a teenager for Sunderland than the 23 Willie McPheat managed. Willie had his top-class career ended by a terrible tackle from Leeds' Bobby Collins seventeen months later. In later years McPheat suffered badly from dementia, seeing out his days in a Glasgow care home. Every Friday his old teammate John Dillon would take two buses across Glasgow to visit him and talk about the pair of them playing for Sunderland as young lads, even when John thought that Willie could probably no longer understand what he was talking about. McPheat and Dillon passed away within four months of each other in 2019.

A combination of reaching the cup quarter-final and the long unbeaten league run in 1960–61 offered renewed hope that Sunderland could look to mount a promotion challenge the following year. Such hope was boosted when, on the last day of the 1960–61 campaign, a debut was given to a new record signing. This was Scotland international forward George Herd, bought for £42,500 from Clyde. Herd was to become one of Sunderland's stars of the sixties. He was a fitness fanatic in the days before substitutes were introduced to the Football League, and teams would sometimes attempt to man-mark him. He would simply spend 75 minutes running all over the pitch to tire his marker out and then look to strike in the closing stages once he had freed himself from their shackles.

Herd would hit thirteen goals in his first full season of 1961–62, but none of those games would see him paraded as Sunderland's record buy. Brian Clough had arrived from Middlesbrough in the summer for £48,000 and would proceed to shatter scoring records, Herd being one of Cloughie's chief supply lines. Setting a post-war scoring record of 34 goals in his first season, Clough was on course to smash that record when he had hit 28 goals going into his 28th game of 1962–63 on Boxing Day at home to Bury.

With Clough's firepower Sunderland had gone close to promotion in 1962, finishing third, a point behind Leyton Orient, who also had a slightly better goal average. For good measure there had also been a decent run in what was only the second season of the Football League Cup, where the quarter-final had been reached. During that run a Clough hat-trick against Walsall had corresponded with the first-team debut of goalkeeper Jim Montgomery. 'Monty' waited until the following February for a league debut, whereupon he immediately established himself as first choice.

Montgomery was ever-present in Clough's second season, which crashed to a halt in that Boxing Day fixture. Chasing down a long ball from Ashurst, Clough collided with Shakers' keeper Chris Harker. Tearing his medial and cruciate ligaments, Clough's career was effectively over in an instant. 'Malc, that's me, I'm done,' he said as he waited for the ambulance called by Malcolm Bramley, who you might recall earlier from the 'Mr. Smith' episode. Clough's wasn't the only disastrous injury to affect a forward during the season, either. Just three games in had come Willie McPheat's injury against Leeds.

After striving tirelessly to try to regain fitness, Clough did attempt a comeback 21 months later, managing one goal in three appearances before being forced to retire. He began his coaching career at Sunderland, helping the youth team to their first ever FA Youth Cup semi-final in 1965. The controversial, confrontational and charismatic Clough was to find phenomenal success as a manager elsewhere, two Sunderland chairmen (Keith Collings and Tom Cowie) turning down the opportunity to appoint him following interviews.

Without Clough in the second half of 1962–63, Sunderland missed out on promotion by a whisker, finishing a point behind champions Stoke City and behind Chelsea on goal average. Chelsea were final-day visitors to Roker Park. Sunderland needed a draw to guarantee promotion, but despite battering the Londoners' goal fell to a 1–0 home defeat thanks to a scrappy effort by Tommy Harmer. At the final whistle Sunderland were still two points clear of Chelsea, but the Stamford Bridge side still had a game to play. Hopes that Chelsea might slip up against Portsmouth the following Tuesday were dashed when Chelsea took just two minutes to open the scoring in what proved to be a 7–0 annihilation. Sunderland were condemned to a sixth season of Second Division soccer.

Clough had been replaced by teenage striker Nick Sharkey. The Scot soon became only the fourth Sunderland player ever – and the first since the Second World War – to score five times in a game, something he achieved in a 7–1 victory over Norwich City. That match was Sunderland's twenty-ninth league game of the season. A bonus system for the players meant extra payments were due (the maximum wage had ended in 1961), depending upon league positions at certain points. The Norwich result took SAFC to joint top of the table, resulting in a substantial payment to all of the players bar Sharkey. The youngster did not have this bonus scheme in his contract and had to settle for the souvenir of the match ball!

Sharkey also found the back of the net in a League Cup semi-final first leg match, which was lost 3–1 at home to Aston Villa in January. The winter of 1962–63 brought a big freeze that meant Sunderland did not play a league game between 29 December and 23 February 1963. If only the freeze had come a few days earlier that injury to Clough might never have occurred. Three FA Cup games and the League Cup meeting with Villa were staged in that fallow league period, but there were no fewer than 100 days between the two legs of the League Cup semi-final, a goalless draw at Villa Park safely seeing the home team through to the final.

Although there was huge disappointment at missing out on promotion again after finishing in third place for a second successive season, the club had done their best to strengthen despite the blow of losing Clough. Fees of between £22,500 and £26,700 were spent on Andy Kerr, Johnny Crossan and George Mulhall. Crossan and Mulhall would become major figures as promotion was finally secured in a stupendous 1963–64 season that also brought another fabulous run in the FA Cup.

Four wins out of five, three of them on the road, was a positive start. From mid-September to the end of the season Sunderland were in the top two for every week except one, in mid-October. Battles with the talented but tough Leeds team of the era had begun before this season but came to the fore in the promotion year as the clubs contested top spot. Leeds eventually topped the table two points clear of the Lads, who were comfortably five points ahead of third-placed Preston North End. Meeting Leeds twice between Christmas and the new year, Sunderland took a draw from Elland Road before goals from Herd and Sharkey secured a 2–0 victory in the return 24 hours later in front of over 55,000.

The sides narrowly missed out on an FA Cup meeting too. Leeds and reigning league champions Everton played out a fourth-round draw, with the winner of the replay pitted against Sunderland in the fifth round. The Toffees were too good for Leeds, however, though not for Sunderland, who beat them 3–1 in front of just under 63,000 at Roker Park.

Throughout the season, success was based on having a settled side. Of the regular eleven players, four played in every league game, and another five barely missed a match, while both Martin Harvey and Nick Sharkey played the final thirty-plus games without missing a game after coming into the side. The regular promotion side of Jim Montgomery, Cec Irwin, Len Ashurst, Martin Harvey, captain Charlie Hurley, Jim McNab, Brian Usher, George Herd, Nicky Sharkey, Johnny Crossan and George Mulhall became an eleven that virtually picked itself. Sharkey took over from Andy Kerr after nine league games, with Harvey taking over from Stan Anderson a game later. The legendary Anderson was sensationally sold to Newcastle United, whom he captained to promotion the following year.

It ultimately didn't matter that Leeds finished ahead of Sunderland, given that both sides were promoted, but the cup run definitely contributed to Sunderland having to settle for runners-up spot. Having knocked out Everton, Sunderland's reward was a tie away to cup holders Manchester United. Outplaying a United side that included Bobby Charlton, George Best and Denis Law in their own backyard, Sunderland led 3–1 with four minutes left, Johnny Crossan having scored twice. A late injury to Jim Montgomery led to goals from Charlton and Best that forced a replay, which brought another really late goal when Charlton levelled for the holders in the last minute of extra-time. Long before the introduction of penalty shoot-outs, this meant a second replay, which was scheduled for Huddersfield Town's Leeds Road ground, where United were finally convincing winners.

Sunderland's record attendance is officially the 75,118 who witnessed an FA Cup quarter-final replay with Derby County 31 years to the week earlier than the replay with Manchester United. Unofficially, this record attendance was well beaten with the replay against the men from Old Trafford. While the official number attending was under 47,000, tens of thousands poured into the ground without paying after the gates were broken down, with estimates of the number watching the match varying from 75,000 to over 90,000. It was reported that there was a continuous line of traffic stretching from Newcastle to Roker Park prior to the game. Sadly, not all who attended made it home, as two people were reported to have died from heart attacks that night.

Once the cup run was over there were still nine league games to play. The first home fixture in that run brought third-placed Preston North End to Wearside. They were just a point behind Sunderland, who turned on the style to romp into a 4–0 half-time lead. That was also the final score, and from then on Sunderland remained unbeaten. Promotion was mathematically secured with a game to spare, former Sunderland goalkeeper Peter Wakeham having a blinder for Charlton Athletic at Roker Park, before a late winner from the season's leading scorer

Crossan sparked scenes of wild joy. Charlie Hurley led his team on a glorious lap of honour, and Sunderland, the club whose proud boast had previously been that they had never played at a lower division than the top level, were now back where they felt they belonged after six long years in the wilderness of Division Two.

After seven seasons transforming a team made up of big-name players from the Bank of England era into a vibrant, young attacking side who earned a return to the big time, Alan Brown would surely have been chomping at the bit to lead that team back in the top flight. Instead, he submitted a shock resignation following a dispute over the board's refusal to allow him to purchase the house he lived in (which was the property of the club) at a preferential rate, something that had been on offer to some of the players.

Having seen the way Brown had resurrected Sunderland in the aftermath of the 'Mr. Smith' scandal, Sheffield Wednesday appointed him to clean up their club after an even bigger sensation that involved some of their top players – including England international Peter Swan – being found guilty in a match-fixing scandal. Brown led the Owls to eighth place in his first season and to the FA Cup final in his second.

With Brown gone, Sunderland started their first season back in the big league in 1964–65 without a manager – and with a fifteen-year-old in goal. Montgomery had not missed a match for over two seasons, but was injured as the campaign commenced. In his place came Derek Forster, at 15 years and 185 days still to the summer of 2024 remains Sunderland's youngest ever player. Forster's record as the youngest person to appear in the top flight of English football stood until September 2022, when Ethan Nwaneri came on as a last-minute substitute for Arsenal in a Premier League match against Brentford as the Gunners led 3–0. Nwaneri was four days younger than Forster when the England schoolboy keeper took to the pitch for a home game with Leicester City, who had England's Gordon Banks between the sticks at the other end.

With the directors picking the team, Forster conceded ten goals in his first three matches before £12,000 was paid to Kilmarnock for the experienced Sandy McLaughlan. Former Sunderland stalwart Arthur Wright and Jack Jones were in charge of coaching the side as they tried to adapt to life in Division One without the guiding hand of a manager. According to many players of the period, the team looked to captain Charlie Hurley for leadership in the dressing room, but there was plenty of significant interest in the vacant manager's position as Sunderland stumbled through sixteen league games and three League Cup ties minus a manager.

Given the blank page entitled 'The Average Director's Knowledge of Football' in his autobiography, Len Shackleton might have allowed himself a wry smile at the fact that for the entire spell with the directors in charge, the team occupied between eighteenth and twentieth place in the table. Sunderland were without a win from the opening eight league games when the club received an application for the manager's job from none other than former Sunderland forward Don Revie, who had led Leeds United to promotion alongside Sunderland the previous season. Revie was a year into a three-year contract at Elland Road, and his written application for the Sunderland job prompted Leeds chairman Harry Reynolds, despite being in hospital following a car crash, to declare: 'Under no circumstances will Leeds United release Don Revie from his contract.' Revie stayed at Leeds once he had been offered the better contract he wanted. His application for the Sunderland job might have been his way of nudging his employers into that agreement.

Sunderland were still without a manager when the club signed Northern Ireland international defender John Parke from Hibernian. Hoping to be offered the Sunderland manager's job, Hibs boss Jock Stein travelled with Parke to complete the deal, but the man who in 1967 would lead Celtic to become the first British team to win the European Cup was evidently not considered. Five days after Parke's arrival at Roker, former

England international George Hardwick was surprised to be invited to speak to the Sunderland chairman. As he explained in his autobiography, *Gentleman George*:

> In November 1964 I was in the Roker Park press room, simply collecting information for my column, when my career was to take yet another twist. Sunderland's club secretary, George Crow, called in to inform me that the chairman, Syd Collings, wished to speak to me. As I sat down in the plush surroundings of the chairman's office, I automatically presumed he was about to reveal the name of the club's new managerial appointment … It was a bit of a scoop to be selected as the journalist who was exclusively invited into the chairman's office to be given the name of the new boss. I eagerly awaited to see who it was going to be. So, you could have knocked me down with a feather when, right out of the blue, Syd Collings offered the position to me. I was the main character in the exclusive story I'd hoped to scoop.
>
> I'd been given no previous indication that my name was even under consideration for the vacant position. There was no formal interview process. Sunderland didn't want me to give them my CV or to try to explain why I was the right man for the job. The chairman simply said that the club would be pleased if I accepted the position. To say that I was taken aback by Mr Collings' offer was a complete understatement.

Hardwick lifted Sunderland from twentieth to fifteenth, seven points clear of the drop, only to be dismissed at the end of the season. While unsubstantiated rumours circulated that Hardwick's dismissal was due to womanising close to home, in his opinion his removal as manager was at least in part down to his plans to promote Brian Clough to work alongside him with the first team. Clough's attempt at a comeback had failed, so Hardwick had put him in charge of the Sunderland youth team alongside long-serving coach Bill Scott.

Clough and Scott led Sunderland to a first ever FA Youth Cup semi-final in 1965, Newcastle and Leeds being among their victims. This was to herald a golden age of a youth policy set up by the departed Alan Brown. After Clough left, Sunderland reached the final in 1966, losing over two legs to Arsenal, and the trophy would be won in 1967 and 1969. The first of those finals would see Birmingham City beaten in both legs. In 1969, following a 3–0 first-leg loss at West Bromwich Albion, the team then turned on the style to win the second leg 6–0, with Paddy Lowrey scoring a hat-trick as the Baggies had two men sent off. The FA Cup winning team of 1973 would include five men who played in these youth cup runs, as well as the previously home-grown Jim Montgomery. With the youth sides of this period also producing stars of the calibre of Colin Todd, Colin Suggett and John O'Hare, it was a golden era for home-produced talent almost always originating from the North East and Scotland.

By the time of the second of those FA Youth Cup triumphs, Alan Brown had been reinstated as manager, but before then, from May 1965 until February 1968, the club was managed by Ian McColl.

McColl had played for and managed Scotland. Sunderland were to be the only club side he took charge of. As a player he had been steeped in the Ibrox traditions of Rangers, whom he had served from 1945 to 1960. Under McColl, SAFC became a divided club, as he brought in Rangers legend Jim Baxter together with players such as former Rangers man Ralph Brand and Baxter's second cousin George Kinnell. Within the dressing room two cliques developed.

Whereas in the Bank of England era the rivalry between Len Shackleton and Trevor Ford is not known to have led to the creation of two distinctly separate camps within the playing staff, during McColl's time the longer-serving players remained loyal to Charlie Hurley as their captain and leader, while a number of newcomers followed the lead of Baxter. Hurley and co. were by no means saints, but they were good professionals who had developed a bond from the promotion campaign. Baxter, on the other hand, came to Sunderland with the nickname 'Slim Jim', but by the time he left was better known as 'Bacardi Jim'. A world-class talent whose ability places him at the top table of the most gifted players to have donned the red and white stripes, unfortunately Baxter's ability was not matched by a world-class attitude.

This was most notably witnessed in 1967 when, amazingly, Sunderland spent the entire summer playing under the name of the Vancouver Royal Canadians in a twelve-game league across the USA and Canada. In an attempt to get the game of soccer up and running in North America, a league had been set up whereby teams from Europe and South America represented various American and Canadian cities. For example, Stoke City became the Cleveland Stokers and Wolverhampton Wanderers became the Los Angeles Wolves. Teams from Scotland, Ireland, Italy, the Netherlands, Uruguay and Brazil also took part.

Split into Eastern and Western divisions, Sunderland/Vancouver finished second-bottom of the six-club Western Division. Tales of drunkenness involved Baxter's cohort being visited by the police in British Columbia after allegations of using counterfeit money to buy alcohol. Reportedly, an apparently fun thing to do was to throw empty bottles from Bacardi Jim's window at the Georgian Towers hotel, aiming to knock out the bulbs on the hotel's neon sign. On a trip to Washington for a game with the Washington Whips (Aberdeen), Baxter and Parke even managed to get themselves arrested. It was unbecoming of a club of Sunderland's stature, but it was not the biggest problem. Under ex-Rangers man McColl, a dividing line of Protestant and Catholic players occurred. Nick Sharkey had an excellent goal-scoring record of 62 goals in 117 games in his time at Sunderland, better than a goal every other game. Nonetheless, Sharkey recalled to me that McColl got rid of him because of his religion. Speaking to me for the book *Sunderland: Match of My Life*, Sharkey explained:

The thing is, when he was appointed manager, I knew I was gone right away. I knew my time was up. I kept playing in the team and I kept scoring, but he made it evident he didn't want me. The directors couldn't believe it. People don't believe me when I tell the full story, there's a lot more to it. He'd spent fifteen years playing for Rangers and I was a Catholic. That is the truth. Check how many Catholic players transferred from Sunderland when he joined. Mike Hellawell, Harry Hood, John O'Hare – just check. Three quarters of the players who left were Catholics. People don't believe me – but it's the God's honest truth.

Baxter himself moved on not long after the Vancouver trip, becoming Sunderland's first £100,000 transfer when he went to Nottingham Forest shortly before Christmas 1967. Baxter was on the way down from his peak and was given a free transfer by Forest less than eighteen months after arriving from SAFC.

McColl lasted little longer: in February 1968, following a run of thirteen games without a victory, he was sacked after a win away to Alan Brown's Sheffield Wednesday, which lifted the team to eighteenth place. Five days later, Brown was sensationally reinstated for a second spell at Roker Park.

The stadium looked somewhat different from the one the manager had left in 1964. The Fulwell End had been roofed, a 'boys' enclosure' had been created in the Roker End, while seats had been installed in the Clock Stand. All this had been done for the 1966 FIFA World Cup, when there had also been temporary seats fitted in the Fulwell End. Roker Park hosted four games in the tournament. Back then only sixteen countries contested the finals, with a quarter of them appearing on Wearside. The Union of Soviet Socialist Republics, Chile and Italy played at Roker in group games, before Hungary lost to the USSR in the quarter-final. Less than a decade on from the 'Mr. Smith' letters, Sunderland were evidently now so well thought of at the FA that SAFC chairman Syd Collings was the official introducing the England team to Queen Elizabeth II on the Wembley pitch at the 1966 World Cup final. Collings had chaired the International Select Committee he served on between 1963 and 1966.

Brown's second spell began with four defeats, which left the team a point and a place off the foot of the table, before a bright end to the campaign lifted the Lads to fifteenth position after a fabulous final-day victory at Manchester United. This was shortly before the Red Devils became the first English team to win the European Cup. 'We were very good that day. It was a superb game' said Colin Suggett, who scored one and made the other for George Mulhall in a 2–1 win.

As in his first period in charge, Brown turned to youth. In his first full season all five debutants came through the ranks – including Ritchie Pitt and Dennis Tueart, who went on to be FA Cup winners in 1973. Brown's first full campaign of his second stint saw the side finish in seventeenth place, avoiding relegation. Sadly, this wasn't the case in the following 1969–70 campaign when – having been in charge on the only other occasion Sunderland were relegated – Brown's side went down again.

Bottom for much of the season having failed to win any of their first ten games, Brown's men went down on the final day, losing to a late goal at home to Liverpool. Had Sunderland been able to win that match they would have stayed up by leapfrogging Crystal Palace, who had already completed their fixtures.

For many supporters Alan Brown was something of a jinx. Renowned as the only club never to have been relegated from the top flight prior to his appointment, Sunderland had now suffered the first two relegations in their history during his two spells in charge. But despite being a strict disciplinarian, many players from both of his periods as manager remain fiercely loyal to him. Dennis Tueart, for example, invariably extols Brown's virtues as a coach ahead of his time, and Brown was a huge influence on Brian Clough. Roy Keane played for Clough at Nottingham Forest. Whenever I visited the Republic of Ireland legend in his office when he was manager of Sunderland, he frequently had a book or DVD on Clough on his desk, but never one about Sir Alex Ferguson. Several times Roy asked me to give him background information on Brown as a boss, because he was aware that Brown had been such a big influence on Clough. Regardless of his later failure at

Browned Off

Sunderland, Lawrie McMenemy was also a successful manager and again someone who admits that Brown was his mentor – Brown having given McMenemy his first coaching position in the professional game at Sheffield Wednesday.

Brown had, of course, resurrected a failing club at Sunderland during his first spell and led the side to promotion. Although the team were struggling badly when he was sacked late in 1972, come the end of that season, when Sunderland sensationally won the FA Cup under Bob Stokoe, all but two of the cup final XI had been assembled and nurtured by Brown. 'For me the cup-winning side was Alan Brown's team,' Jim Montgomery told me in 2023. 'Bob Stokoe came in and brought in Vic Halom, Ron Guthrie and [substitute] David Young, but it was Brownie's side. All of the ethics brought in by Alan Brown were there.'

Nonetheless, in his first season after that 1970 relegation Brown's team struggled to finish in thirteenth position. Backing in the transfer market came in the shape of the payment of the club's first six-figure transfer fee, the £100,000 signing of Dave Watson from Rotherham United, with £30,000 also invested in right-back Dick Malone from Ayr United.

In his first full season of 1971–72 Watson was joint-top scorer with Tueart. It was an improved showing, as Sunderland finished fifth, six points behind the second and last promotion place at a time when play-offs were still a decade and a half away. Hopes that Sunderland would succeed in mounting a promotion campaign in 1972–73 proved to be unfounded. After a fair start, the beginning of the end for Brown came at Oxford United, where a hat-trick in the last eleven minutes by Scotland international Hugh Curran contributed to a crushing 5–1 defeat. Eight players who would be in the starting line-up at Wembley later in the season were in the side that afternoon. A ninth member of that cup-winning side would be on display at Roker Park in the next game, but at the time Vic Halom would score for Luton as they beat Brown's men. When a third consecutive loss suffered at QPR was followed by a tame goalless draw at home to Fulham in front of a crowd of just 11,618, Brown had reached the end of the road and was sacked.

Earlier in that month of October 1972, questions had been asked in Parliament about unemployment in Sunderland. Male unemployment in Sunderland was at 11 per cent , and only 11,000 stalwarts were still turning up to watch matches; 1972 had seen unemployment in Britain reach a million for the first time since the 1930s. The figure had almost doubled in the two years since Edward Heath's Conservative Party had been in government. It was a shocking year that had witnessed what became known as Bloody Sunday in Northern Ireland, when British troops opened fire and killed fourteen Catholic citizens in Derry. A seven-week miners' strike was added to by a dockers' strike, which led to the government declaring a state of emergency, while 1972 also brought a pay freeze. Britain was not a happy place and Wearside was suffering more than most.

But barely six months later Sunderland was the happiest place in the world!

8

STOKOE'S STARS

The 1973 FA Cup win (1972–87)
Sunderland needed change. The story of how Bob Stokoe arrived and magically turned a struggling Second Division side into the most glorious FA Cup winners almost overnight is one of football's most romantic tales. Stokoe warrants an enormous amount of credit for his achievement, and indeed his statue is the only one of an individual at the Stadium of Light. However, in between the sacking of Alan Brown and Stokoe's arrival, someone else played a key role.

To many outside the region, the name Billy Elliot brings to mind the famous film of the young boy who takes up ballet in the North East during the miners' strike of 1984–85. However, the real Billy Elliott was a Sunderland stalwart. Brought in as a £26,000 signing from Burnley in 1953 during the Bank of England era, Elliott was a former England international who by 1972 was working as first-team trainer at the club. During his own playing days Elliott had seen his position switch from left-winger to left-half and finally left-back. Given a four-game spell as caretaker-manager between Brown and Stokoe, Elliott took a decision that would have a major impact.

Having kept Dave Watson in his regular position of centre-forward for a home draw with Aston Villa, the following week, at Carlisle, Elliott switched Watson to centre-half. It was a position

Watson had played earlier in his career. In the early stages at Brunton Park Sunderland's defence were all at sea, 2–0 down within quarter of an hour. Although two more were conceded in what proved to be a 4–3 defeat, the longer the game went on, the more it became apparent that Watson's future lay in the number five shirt rather than the number nine. Watson was a very good centre-forward, but he was to prove to be an exceptional centre-half. By September 1973 he had been called up for an England squad for a Wembley win over Austria. Later that season came Dave's international debut. It was the first of 65 full caps Watson won with England, the initial 14 of these won with Sunderland, making him the club's most-capped England international.

Two home draws and two away defeats came in what was Elliott's first spell as caretaker manager (he would return later in the decade). Defeat to a late goal at Bristol City in his fourth game in charge left the Lads languishing level on points with second-bottom Cardiff City. The line-up at Ashton Gate included eight players (with a ninth on the bench) who would become Wembley heroes less than six months later. No one left Bristol's ground that night thinking they had just seen that season's FA Cup winners.

Four days after the defeat at Bristol City there was a new man in the manager's office at Roker Park. An FA Cup winner as a centre-half with Newcastle United in 1955, Bob Stokoe hailed from Mickley, just south of the Tyne. He was 43 when he took over at Sunderland. Like Dave Watson, he had played as a centre-forward before becoming a centre-half. Having moved into management when he was only 31, Stokoe had been in charge of Bury, Charlton Athletic, Rochdale, Carlisle United and Blackpool, winning the Anglo-Italian Cup with the Tangerines in 1971. Almost exactly a decade before becoming Sunderland boss, Stokoe had been on the pitch at Roker Park as Bury's player-manager on the fateful Boxing Day when Brian Clough sustained the injury that was to end his playing days.

Stokoe's appointment initially underwhelmed a disillusioned fanbase, but his first decision met with widespread approval.

As the teams took to the pitch for the new manager's first match, against league leaders Burnley (who were managed by Jimmy Adamson, Stokoe's eventual successor at SAFC), Sunderland were wearing black shorts instead of the white ones they had worn since the early sixties. Although white shorts, or knickerbockers, had been originally paired with red and white stripes when Sunderland first adopted that strip in September 1887, black shorts had long been established as the club's traditional kit. White had been reintroduced in August 1961 under Alan Brown.

Losing 1–0 at home to high-flying Burnley was no disgrace, but it was a relief to learn that none of the clubs below Sunderland had picked up a point, so the team were still above the relegation places, albeit only on goal average. Next up was a trip to Portsmouth, who were immediately behind Sunderland, on the same points. It was a game Sunderland could not afford to lose, but despite taking the lead thanks to centre-half Watson, with four minutes to go Stokoe's side trailed 2–1. Had the team lost both of the new manager's first two games, any hope of a new-manager bounce would have been flattened. Had the score stayed 2–1 at Fratton Park, Sunderland would have dropped into the bottom two, as on the same afternoon lowly Cardiff thrashed Sheffield Wednesday 4–1.

Those final four minutes on the south coast were among the most influential in the club's history. Goals from Scots pair Billy Hughes and Bobby Kerr transformed defeat into a win and gave Stokoe his first victory in the town that hosts the ship of that name. Good fortune awaited, as after a home goalless draw with Preston, the team was decimated by a flu bug. That might not seem like good luck, but it gave Stokoe time to take stock and work with the players who were well before the side next took to the field three weeks later. The fixture gods presented Sunderland with an ideal opportunity at home to bottom-of-the-table Brighton, who duly suffered a tenth consecutive defeat as Sunderland hammered them 4–0.

It was Sunderland's biggest win of the season so far, a second successive clean sheet and a third match unbeaten. All well-timed signs for the start of a cup campaign that was due to begin seven days later. It was to be the most famous cup run not just in the history of Sunderland, but in the history of football. The FA Cup is the world's oldest football competition, but only the finals of 1923 (the White Horse final and Wembley's first) and 1953 (known as the Matthews final, despite South Shields-born Stan Mortensen scoring a hat-trick) can rival Sunderland's accomplishment of 1973 in terms of fame and sheer romance.

Jim Montgomery's world-famous double save in the final is renowned as being one of the greatest saves ever seen. Spectacular reflex saves were the stock in trade of the marvellous Montgomery. His Wembley heroics gained global glory because of the stature of the game. Had it not been for another fabulous save from Monty, the cup run would never have got going, the stardust Stokoe sprinkled on Sunderland in 1973 would never have been seen and Sunderland's history in the latter quarter of the twentieth century would have been notably different.

Away to Notts County, Sunderland, who were already in a relegation battle, trailed 1–0 and looked like going out of the cup at the first hurdle to a team from the division below. Notts' goal had come from their all-time top scorer Les Bradd. He looked like scoring again when thundering another header goalwards. That evening's *Nottingham Football Post* recorded, 'Montgomery certainly saved Sunderland when he made a fantastic save from a close-range header from Bradd,' while the *Sunderland Football Echo* noted that the header 'whipped past Montgomery and looked a certain goal until the goalkeeper, diving back to the far post, managed to palm the ball out'.

Shortly afterwards, having been moved up front for the latter stages as an equaliser was sought, Watson brought Sunderland level. Disposing of Notts comfortably in the replay set up a fourth-round tie with Reading of Division Four. At first glance that might have looked like a run-of-the-mill match, but Reading were managed by Charlie Hurley. It was four years since the Irishman had left Sunderland and six before he would be voted player of the century when the club celebrated its centenary. Inevitably, 'the King' received the most tumultuous of welcomes.

Hurley's side earned a replay thanks to the heroics of their diminutive but athletic goalkeeper Steve Death, but short work was made of Reading in the replay, where Sunderland raced into an early three-goal lead and won without any on-pitch drama.

There was plenty of drama off it. Centre-forward Vic Halom was signed that night, while two members of the squad did not return home with the team. Young defenders Ritchie Pitt and Keith Coleman were allowed to join Arsenal on loan immediately after the replay at Reading. To his surprise Pitt had played at Reading, having not previously appeared since the game before Watson's switch to centre-half. He still did not play alongside Watson on this occasion. Having seen the problems Watson had caused Hurley's rearguard at Roker when he moved forward late on, Stokoe selected him to lead the attack in the replay. It was a decision that reaped immediate dividends when Watson scored after only 80 seconds and soon afterwards created a goal for Tueart.

Playing alongside Pitt at the heart of the defence was David Young. Along with left-back Ron Guthrie, Young was one of a pair of surplus Newcastle United defenders that Stokoe had swiftly recruited to add experience to the youthful side he had inherited from Brown. Pitt and Coleman duly went off to Arsenal, where they played in the reserves, before Pitt was recalled due to an injury to Young. Stokoe had told Pitt he wanted to cup-tie him before his loan. It was perhaps impressive foresight from Stokoe. The Gunners were a top side. Two seasons earlier they had become only the second team of the century to do the 'double' of winning the league and cup. Not only did they go on to face Sunderland in the semi-final, they did so with an injury problem at centre-half, which meant Jeff Blockley was drafted into the side having not played for a month and a half. Blockley would be at fault for the first goal, but had Pitt not been cup-tied, Young not got injured and Pitt signed for Arsenal, the Gunners centre-half that day could have been Pitt.

The draw for the fifth round had already been made before the replay at Reading, so it was known that the winners would face a trip to big-hitters Manchester City or Liverpool. As Sunderland overcame Reading, City came out on top in the replay in Manchester in front of a crowd 5,000 short of the 54,500 Sunderland would pull in.

While cup fever was beginning to build, there was still plenty of work to be done in the league. Three points had been taken out of four available since the cup run began, but on the weekend after the Reading victory defeat at Sheffield Wednesday still left the Lads just a point clear of the relegation trapdoor. There was an upside to that situation, thankfully. Sunderland were the highest ranked of four teams on 23 points, with Stokoe's side having three or even four games in hand. By the time Sunderland returned to Hillsborough for the semi-final two months later, they were still in the bottom half of the table but comfortably clear of the fear of relegation, and still with between two and five games in hand on the rest of the division.

Any lingering relegation worries were ended in the only other league game before the fifth round. Middlesbrough arrived on Wearside after back-to-back wins, but were trounced 4-0 as an increasingly confident Sunderland turned on the style. It was the first time the eleven who would line up in the cup final started a match together. The outcome was a sign of things to come. The same side would start every remaining cup tie.

Regardless of the manner in which Middlesbrough had been beaten, Sunderland travelled to Manchester as rank underdogs. City's ground had seen the end of Sunderland's cup hopes the previous season in a second replay with Cardiff, and given the Manchester side's stellar array of top talent, all heads said Sunderland would once again travel home from Maine Road with only the cliché of being able to 'concentrate on the league' for solace.

Sure enough, City took an early lead through Tony Towers and all seemed to be going according to conventional wisdom. Nine minutes before half-time came the turning point. Micky Horswill, the youngest member of the team, was in the side to stop others playing. It was a job he did with energy and effectiveness. On this occasion he brought inventiveness to his game. Reading a short pass from a free-kick from City goalkeeper Joe Corrigan, the ginger-haired Horswill swooped upon left-back Willie Donachie, lifted the ball over the defender and gleefully rifled it beyond the despairing Corrigan. One–one, and the huge Sunderland support in the crowd – boosted by Manchester United fans who had arrived as their league game with Crystal Palace had been postponed – had reason to roar even louder than the din they had already been making. Standing in two big blocks of red and white they provided the Roker Roar in stereo. It was an atmosphere befitting of the occasion, but nothing compared to what was to come in the replay.

That replay was earned with a stirring second-half display that warranted a win. However, had City's controversial equaliser in a 2–2 draw not been allowed to stand, the history of SAFC would have been denied the match which, when Roker Park closed in 1997, supporters voted to be the Match of the Century. While all such votes result in things from living memory being selected, and there is an extremely strong case for the 5–4 meeting with Arsenal in 1935 being the Match of the Century, there is no question that the replay with Manchester City was one of the most magical games in the Sunderland story.

Sunderland took the lead in the second half at Maine Road with a stunning goal. Speed merchants Tueart and Hughes combined to rip City apart, Hughes applying the finish. While that goal was a thing of beauty, City's equaliser was a beast. As in the quarter-final across Manchester nine years earlier, the home side netted their second goal from a corner. Back in 1964, Bobby Charlton's header came moments after Jim Montgomery had received treatment for a head injury. On this occasion Rodney Marsh looked to have fouled Monty as he came for Mike Summerbee's corner. The ball ended up in the back of the net, but there was still time for future Sunderland skipper Towers to be sent off for City in the climax of a pulsating drama.

Cup fever can be an intoxicating and thrilling feeling. Wearside was becoming overwhelmed by it even before the replay. When City rocked up at Roker ready to show Sunderland that the big boys were in town and they might have had an off day on their own patch, they swaggered in with their eyes already on the semi-final. All they had to do was dismiss Second Division Sunderland and then see off another second-tier team in Luton Town, who had been drawn away to the winners of the Roker replay. Since 1968, City had won all four domestic trophies, as well as a European one. They could see the glint of more silverware coming their way, but like so many before them they were blown away by the Roker Roar.

While City had been showered with success in recent seasons, Sunderland supporters had had nothing to cheer since before the war, other than the 1964 promotion brought about after the trauma of the club's first ever relegation in the aftermath of the 'Mr. Smith' affair. Stokoe had prodded the sleeping giant of SAFC back to life. The last home fixture before 'the Messiah' – as Stokoe was being called – arrived had been witnessed by a meagre 11,141. Now over four and a half times that many squeezed into Roker Park: 51,782 came to be part of the red and white revolution.

The match produced record receipts of £26,048, but the value was in passion, not pounds. Over half a century after those receipts were spent, the memories of those who were there live on. Those memories were burned into the psyche of what it means to be a supporter of Sunderland, this grandest of clubs but one that had come to resemble the Miss Havisham of soccer, one that had seen better days. Now, though, there was every reason to have great expectations, as, regardless of the talented opposition before them, Sunderland were ready to sweep them aside.

Billy Hughes was a swashbuckling forward. In Stokoe's setup he played on the right, with Dennis Tueart on the left and the battering ram of Vic Halom in the centre. Woe betide you if you suggested to Billy he was a winger. 'I'm a centre-forward!' he would almost snarl. This was his finest night. He would score the second and third goals in a 3–1 win, sandwiching England striker Francis Lee's retort. The goal of the game, though, was the opener, blasted in by Halom in only his fourth appearance for the club. It was a goal that made Vic an overnight legend. Arguably the finest team of all time were the Brazil side that won their third FIFA World Cup in four tournaments three years earlier. Destroying Italy 4–1 in the 1970 final, they brought that phenomenal display to a climax with a sensational team goal finished off by Carlos Alberto (the man who would later contribute the foreword to Tueart's autobiography, having been a teammate at New York Cosmos, where Tueart was signed to replace Pelé!). Halom's goal was reminiscent of the final phase of the Carlos Alberto classic, but with Vic's shot being even more of a rocket.

Sunderland had not just beaten Manchester City, they had played football comparable with the world champions. They had shown steely resolve when City showed their class and tried to get back into the game, and the Lads had demonstrated that at long last the supporters had a team to be proud of and a side capable of beating anyone. People who not long ago felt that the team couldn't beat an egg were now adamant that they now had a new team with the ability and attitude to live up to the club's finest traditions.

Such was the clamour to see the quarter-final with Luton Town, it was announced that vouchers enabling people to buy a cup quarter-final ticket would be issued at the turnstiles for a league game with Oxford. Subsequently, just under 40,000 showed up. This was a third higher than the previous league high of the season, which had come in the most recent home game against near-neighbours Middlesbrough. After beating Oxford there was a dress rehearsal for the cup-tie when Sunderland travelled to Luton for a league game. While Sunderland lost that fixture, both managers kept their cards close to their chests, as Stokoe changed over half of his side and the Hatters' Harry Haslam left out a quartet of key men.

A crowd even bigger than that for the replay with Manchester City packed Roker Park for the big day, which was preceded by chairman Keith Collings making a presentation to Jim Montgomery, as the keeper had now overtaken Len Ashurst in making the most starts for the club. In typical fashion, 'the Mighty Jim' responded with a clean sheet as Sunderland progressed to the semi-final with second-half goals from defenders Dave Watson and Ron Guthrie, both from Roker End corners.

While relegation fears were no longer an issue, any thoughts that cup concerns would mean a fall-off in league form were banished by the fact that only one point was dropped from the next six games. The team were still only eleventh. Had play-offs existed then, Sunderland surely could have made it a cup and promotion double, considering the form they were in. At this point they were just three points behind sixth-placed Fulham, with four games in hand.

More importantly, by this time they were also through to the cup final, after beating Arsenal. The Gunners had been bidding to become the first team since Blackburn Rovers in 1886 to reach three consecutive finals. At the time they were second in the top flight, a point behind leaders Liverpool. They were a tougher nut to crack than even Manchester City, but Sunderland outplayed and outpowered them. Dubbed 'the H-bombers', Halom and Hughes got the goals, as they had in the replay with City. Monty was forced into one of his trademark miracle saves, thwarting a deflected effort from George Armstrong, and when he was finally beaten, Charlie George's goal came with just six minutes left, too little for the Gunners to level.

In modern-day football, players and managers applaud crowds at the end of virtually every game. This was not the case in 1973, but with legions of Wearsiders refusing to leave the ground in Sheffield, the police had to ask Bob Stokoe to come out and acknowledge the fans and their endless chants of, 'Stokoe, Stokoe, Stokoe, Stokoe.' The moment when the Messiah came out to accept the adulation stands as one of the highlights of a cup run that was becoming a fairytale.

Sunderland was bouncing. Productivity in local industries was soaring, sick days were at a minimum and the place which a few months earlier had been an economically struggling grey town on the North East's coast was now a place where everyone was walking on air. The following Friday night many of the team were at the Mecca in Sunderland (where the giant Tesco near the Stadium of Light now stands) to join Rod Stewart and the Faces on stage in a gig later described by legendary Radio 1 DJ John Peel as the best he'd ever been to. Being out just before a match didn't bother the team, who promptly beat Portsmouth that weekend.

Whereas this group of young footballers had been under the control of strict disciplinarian Alan Brown at a time when the cultural revolution of the swinging sixties and the early glam-rock days of the early seventies were going on around them, Stokoe had come in and taken the shackles off. Players were allowed to express themselves off the pitch, and this was very much reflected on it. This was never better demonstrated than on the day of the cup final against Leeds United. In the TV interviews from the team hotels on the morning of the match, the experienced cup holders Leeds looked stiff and nervous in their club suits, whereas at Sunderland's Selsdon Hall base players relaxed in their own clothes – many of them picked up that week on Carnaby Street or the King's Road. Famously, Sunderland's interviews degenerated into riotous laughter, as Billy Hughes had obtained a laughing box, which he kept in his pocket and set off every time anyone was asked a question.

'Without question, Billy's laughing box illustrated that we weren't at all phased by the occasion,' explained Dennis Tueart, 'We were very relaxed during our television interview, whereas Leeds were all very regimental in their club suits. We didn't have to wear club suits. We were told we could wear what we liked for the final. We had the free expression to be ourselves, and that free expression was reflected in the way Billy brought out the laughing box and in the way we played.'

Tueart, Hughes and Ian Porterfield, the Scottish midfielder who would score the winning goal in the cup final, attended that week's recording of the flagship BBC music programme *Top of the Pops*, while the whole team went to the Football Writers' Association Player of the Year dinner just two nights before the final. It was an unconventional build-up to the big game, but Stokoe believed in relaxing his players and his approach worked wonderfully.

It wasn't a total case of 'do what you like', however. Stokoe kept a close eye on his new signing Vic Halom. Stokoe had given Halom his debut as a young lad at Charlton, and to some extent he confined Vic to barracks: 'I got banned from going out when we went to London in the week of the final. Stokoe wouldn't even let me go out to the bank ... Bob had a point – I used to go from wherever I'd been the night before to training!' Never one to miss out on having a good time, Halom made sure his parents savoured the big day. He hired the hotel's Rolls-Royce to take them for a champagne lunch on the morning of the final before delivering them to the stadium.

While Sunderland prepared for Wembley in a way that some might have felt looked as if they were simply happy to have reached the final, they swiftly made it clear that they had not come just for a day out. In the opening moments of the match Ritchie Pitt wiped out England striker Allan Clarke with a high tackle that signalled Sunderland meant business. In today's football it would be a definite yellow card, possibly red. This was not today's football, though. It was 1973 and Ritchie received no more than a stern word from the referee.

Having Leeds United as cup-final opponents could not have been better scripted. Since the clubs had vied with each other for the promotion they both won in 1963–64, a fierce rivalry had built up. Leeds had developed into a leading side. Since promotion they had been league champions, and runners-up no fewer than five times. The 1973 FA Cup final was the fourth they had reached since promotion, and they were the holders. In this recent period Leeds had also won the League Cup, the Charity Shield and had been in three European finals, winning two of them. Moreover, eleven days after their Wembley clash with Sunderland, Leeds had a date with AC Milan in the final of the European Cup Winners' Cup.

Unquestionably, Leeds were admired for the success of their supremely talented team. But they were also reviled in equal measure by many football supporters for the way in which they played. They were known for their gamesmanship, the pushing of the boundaries of the game's laws, and had earned the moniker 'Dirty Leeds'. Willie McPheat was not the only Sunderland player to have his leg broken against them in the past decade. The last time Sunderland met Leeds in the FA Cup the same thing had happened to Bobby Kerr. This was at a time when Kerr had just broken into the team and had scored seven times in his first ten games going into the tie.

This cup meeting had ended in controversy in a second replay at Hull, following a first replay at Leeds that pulled in United's record crowd of 57,892. That match was held up for seventeen minutes when a crush barrier collapsed and thirty-two people were rushed to hospital. Three minutes from the end of a hard-fought second replay, Leeds were given a penalty so contentious that Sunderland fans invaded the pitch in fury, and in the dying minutes Sunderland had George Herd and George Mulhall sent off, with after-match suggestions flying about that referee Ken Stokes might have been 'got at'. In his autobiography, Leeds forward Peter Lorimer wrote that manager Don Revie had instructed: 'If anybody gets anywhere near the box, get down.' Even the website mightyleeds.co.uk states that Jimmy Greenhoff, who won the penalty, 'was fully five yards outside the penalty area when he was brought down'.

To add further spice to the 1973 cup final, there was no love lost between the managers. Revie had been accused by Bob Stokoe of offering him a bribe in the early sixties, when Revie was at Leeds and Stokoe manager of Bury. And they had been direct opponents in the 1955 FA Cup final, when Stokoe's Newcastle defeated a Manchester City team who had beaten Sunderland in the semi-final.

As the teams entered the pitch for the FA Cup final, the stage was set with Stokoe and Revie's personal dislike for one another, the recent history between the clubs and with broken-leg victim Bobby Kerr now Sunderland's captain. The media tried to build the match up as a David and Goliath clash between successful

Leeds and Second Division Sunderland, but as far as Wearside was concerned there was no doubt that the giants were Sunderland.

The game revolved around three key moments, in the second, thirty-second and seventieth minutes: Pitt's challenge on Clarke, the only goal of the game from Ian Porterfield and the double save from Jim Montgomery still rated as one of the greatest saves in the history of football. Having parried a header from Trevor Cherry, the ball fell to Peter Lorimer. He was the man with the hardest shot in football. With the goal open Lorimer lashed the ball from within the six-yard box. Miraculously, Monty materialised seemingly from nowhere to knock the ball onto the crossbar and to safety via Dick Malone's clearance. From Ted Doig through L.R. Roose, Albert McInroy and Johnny Mapson, Sunderland had a tradition of great goalkeepers that continued after Montgomery, but this was the greatest and most important save in Sunderland's history, not forgetting McInroy's double save in a key relegation battle at Middlesbrough 45 years to the day earlier.

Montgomery's save secured Sunderland's FA Cup triumph. To this day, it remains the only major trophy won since the Second World War by the club who entered that conflict having won as many league titles as anyone. At the final whistle Stokoe sprinted to Montgomery in recognition of the role the keeper had played in winning the trophy. The victory was celebrated throughout the country, outside Leeds. Even in Newcastle there was some joy. The *Newcastle Evening Chronicle*'s banner headlines screamed 'WE'VE WON', although Magpies fans' reactions were more mixed when the cup was paraded with a lap of honour at St James' Park nine days later, ahead of a testimonial for United defender Ollie Burton.

By then Sunderland had fulfilled two outstanding league fixtures since winning the cup. They had also played at Orient in London on the Monday of cup-final week as the fixture pile-up was whittled down. In between matches on the Monday and Wednesday after Wembley, the side returned to Wearside with the trophy. Estimates of anything between three-quarters of a million and a million supporters greeted 'Stokoe's Stars' as they made the thirteen-mile trip from Carrville in Durham to Sunderland, finishing up at a packed Roker Park.

Given the fact that this cup journey had started when the Lads were languishing in the lower reaches of Division Two having just sacked their manager, supporters had just witnessed the most incredible few months in the entire history of the club. Sunderland were the darlings of the world. Even Soviet Union gymnast Olga Korbut, the heroine of the previous year's Olympics, proclaimed herself to be a Sunderland fan. In this era before wall-to-wall television coverage of football, only the annual England–Scotland game and the FA and European finals were regularly screened on live TV. Sunderland became a household name throughout the world. Goal-scorer Ian Porterfield subsequently managed in Zambia, Zimbabwe, Oman, Trinidad and Tobago, Ghana, South Korea and Armenia, as well as England and his native Scotland, no doubt helped by his worldwide fame as the man who scored Sunderland's winner in the most romantic of cup finals.

As cup winners, Sunderland were expected to stroll to promotion. Pre-season brought a thrilling 2–1 win away to a Celtic side about to go on and win their ninth successive league title, but once the league got under way, being held to a home draw by Orient was a sign of things to come. Sunderland were the scalp every team in the division craved. Although the first away fixture was won in style at Notts County, where the pace of Hughes and Tueart ripped the home side apart, it was to prove a frustrating campaign.

Although the team were third and unbeaten after the first five games, they soon dropped into mid-table and never again got higher than the sixth they managed in the cup-winning campaign. The FA Cup was meekly defended, tamely going out in a third-round replay at home to Carlisle United. That defeat was the tenth cup match of the season. The side's cup form had continued in the League Cup. A three-game marathon with a top Derby side (league champions in 1972 and '75) brought a scintillating 2–2 draw at the Baseball Ground followed by one of the best exhibitions of football at Roker Park, in a replay that was again drawn – Dennis Tueart having a penalty saved. Having won the toss to host a second replay, 48 hours later a Vic Halom hat-trick secured a 3–0 win, Halom outpowering England centre-half Roy McFarland, a player who would soon lose his international place to Sunderland's Dave Watson.

Amidst industrial action by mineworkers and railwaymen shortly before the introduction of the 'three-day week' by Ted Heath's Conservative government, which restricted companies to using electricity only three days per week, the next round of Sunderland's League Cup campaign against Liverpool took place on a Wednesday afternoon, as floodlights were banned. With the help of a fluke goal that looked to be intended as a cross and another scored while Watson was off the pitch receiving treatment, the visitors ended Sunderland's hopes by winning 2–0.

Since Stokoe's arrival a week short of a year earlier, Sunderland had lost just twice in seventeen cup games. The other defeat had brought an end to what remains the club's solitary venture into a major continental competition. As FA Cup winners, Sunderland took part in the European Cup Winners' Cup. In the midweek after Dennis Tueart's acrobatic scissor kick at Oxford took the team to third in the league very early in the season, Tueart followed Billy Hughes' first goal in Europe with a stunning solo goal as he dribbled from his own half to seal a 2–0 win in Budapest against Vasas.

Tueart netted the only goal of the second leg from the penalty spot in front of a crowd of under 23,000. Crowd numbers had been restricted by the doubling of admission prices in order to help fund new floodlights to assist with colour-television broadcasts, at a time when many supporters were struggling financially. Having been drawn against former holders of the Cup Winners' Cup Sporting Lisbon, Sunderland won the first leg 2–1 but lacked the nous of experienced European campaigners in the return. The Portuguese side took a 3–2 aggregate lead, at which point the ball boys mysteriously disappeared or went on a go-slow, as Sporting eventually succeeded in eliminating Sunderland, who hit the post through Porterfield. Club director Maurice Bewick and vice-president Stan Ritson had their pockets picked on the way to the stadium, and the team felt similarly hard done by. Perhaps they might have been given some advice about the potential local petty thieving from Fulham chairman Ernie Clay, who owned the house the Sunderland party stayed in.

The first of the four European games was the last time the complete cup-final side played together. The following weekend – with Ron Guthrie missing – Ritchie Pitt suffered a career-ending injury against Luton Town at Roker Park. It was to be the beginning of the break-up of the cup team. Within five years, when captain Kerr made his final appearance against Stoke City in August 1978, 'the Little General' became the last of the cup-final side to play a first-team game for the club.

Dennis Tueart and Micky Horswill departed for Manchester City in March 1974, with Tony Towers coming in the opposite direction. Dave Watson also went to Manchester City, at the end of the following 1974–75 season, after a promotion near-miss when Sunderland finished a place outside what were now three automatic promotion slots. With Ron Guthrie retiring from the professional game at the same time, Sunderland had lost half of the outfield players from the final within two seasons. A sixth had been temporarily lost when Ian Porterfield suffered a near-fatal car crash in December 1974. Just before the collision the Scottish schemer was in supreme form when he imperiously controlled a 4–1 home win over Portsmouth that left Sunderland second in the table. From early November 1974 onwards, Sunderland sat in the automatic promotion berths until the final day, when defeat at promoted Aston Villa saw them overtaken by Norwich City.

Porterfield would return the following season, but he was never the same player. He made his final appearance in December 1975, although, following a loan to Reading, it would not be until the summer of 1977 that he left the club, signing for Len Ashurst at Division Three Sheffield Wednesday. Porterfield at least got to play in a promotion season, as Sunderland won Division Two in 1976 on the back of an undefeated home record. The two Bristol sides escaped Roker Park with a point, while every other visitor was defeated in the league. As in the previous promotion season of 1963–64, there was also a run to the quarter-final of the FA Cup. There were dreams of a repeat of Stokoe's success of three years earlier, but Sunderland were beaten by a strong wind as much as a Crystal Palace side featuring future SAFC assistant manager (to Mick McCarthy) Ian 'Taff' Evans. Managed by Malcolm Allison, who along with Joe Mercer had been in charge of Manchester City in 1973, Division Three Palace upset the Roker form book with a win on Wearside. Later that month Vic Halom – who would later stand for Parliament in Sunderland North – made his farewell appearance, so that when Sunderland did step out for their first game back in the top flight, only Jim Montgomery, Dick Malone, Bobby Kerr and Billy Hughes survived from the cup-winning team.

Astonishingly, by January all but Kerr had played for the club for the final time, with Stokoe himself having resigned. The season back in Division One had begun solidly enough, with three draws and a comfortable League Cup win over Division Two Luton Town. The first sign of trouble came in a heavy 4–1 defeat at fellow promoted side Bristol City, a club who would feature in the campaign's controversial denouement. By mid-October, Sunderland were still without a league win, they were propping up the table and were without a manager, as the messiah Stokoe submitted his resignation, having increasingly been troubled by migraine attacks as well as his team's results. The manager had recently delved into the transfer market, making Leicester City striker Bob Lee the club's first £200,000 purchase, and surprisingly replacing Montgomery with the purchase of Bolton keeper Barry Siddall.

The 627th and ultimately final game of Montgomery's time at Sunderland came in a 1–0 defeat at Manchester United in a

League Cup third-round second replay. Monty was a few days short of his 33rd birthday, still a young age for a goalkeeper. After a loan to Birmingham City, Jim signed for Southampton and went on to win a European Cup winner's medal as an unused substitute for Brian Clough's Nottingham Forest. He subsequently returned to Sunderland, although he was never able to add to his first-team appearances tally. Monty went on to coach the youth team on more than one occasion, and in the 1990s did so alongside his sixties teammate George Herd. Montgomery later spent many years as club ambassador, a role he still held in 2024.

After a seven-game spell under caretaker-manager Ian MacFarlane, which featured a couple of wins – the first at Coventry – Jimmy Adamson stepped into the managerial hotseat with the team one off the bottom. Having lost the last two matches of MacFarlane's spell, the first seven league games under Adamson were also lost, leaving Sunderland marooned at the bottom of the league. The run of consecutive defeats had been punctuated by a 2–2 draw with Division Three Wrexham in the FA Cup. Those goals were the first scored since the first of the run of losses, when Billy Hughes had converted a penalty. The draw with Wrexham was Hughes' final game. With Malone having been discarded after Adamson's third match, it left Kerr as the only survivor of the 1973 cup heroes.

As one era came to an end, a new one began. In the replay at Wrexham, Adamson gave debuts to youngsters Shaun Elliott and Kevin Arnott, while centre-half Jim Holton made his final appearance in a 1–0 defeat. A couple of months later, Holton joined Coventry and would play in the match that eventually sent Sunderland down. After the Wrexham reverse there was a ninth consecutive league defeat before a goalless draw at home to lowly Stoke City stopped the rot. Like a cricket team who manage a series of dot balls before claiming a wicket, Sunderland totted up another goalless draw before Mel Holden finally scored the team's first league goal after ten blanks. Holden's goal provided a 1–0 win over Bristol City in a rare Friday night fixture. Sunderland had gone into that match not only six points adrift of safety, but also having played between two and five games more than every other club in the bottom eight. To compound matters, in the season where goal difference replaced goal average, Sunderland's was by far the worst.

'Sunderland are back!' quickly became the terrace chant as, after the narrow win over Bristol City, Sunderland's forwards found that following the spell where every shot seemed to be saved, just miss or strike the woodwork, suddenly everything went in. The team who couldn't score promptly netted sixteen goals in the next three games, with scorelines of 4–0, 6–1 and 6–0. A quarter of those goals were bagged by Gary Rowell, a third home-grown youngster, who along with Elliott and Arnott became collectively known as 'Charlie's Angels'. The name came from a popular new TV show, but was also in recognition of the renowned Sunderland scout Charlie Ferguson. A consummate penalty taker, Rowell was an attacking midfielder rather than an out and out forward. He would go on to top a century of goals and take over from Len Shackleton as the club's record post-war scorer, until Kevin Phillips took that particular record.

Revitalised, the red and whites won nine of the last seventeen league games, having taken just two victories from the first twenty-five league fixtures. Going into the final match, just two games had been lost out of sixteen, as Adamson's team had put themselves into a position where they had a great chance of survival after previously being no-hopers. At Everton on the final night Sunderland's support lifted the gate at Goodison to over 36,000. The Toffees had attracted just 20,102 for their previous home game. A point would keep Sunderland up, and the only way they could go down was if they lost and on the same night a match between Coventry City and Bristol City ended in a draw. Coventry needed to win to secure their own safety.

On a hugely controversial evening, Coventry delayed their kick-off, claiming they could not get the crowd of 36,903 in on time – even though they had kicked off on time in front of over 38,000 against Liverpool ten days earlier. Unaccountably, Adamson omitted skipper Towers at Everton, where Sunderland slipped to a 2–0 defeat, the second goal coming in the last minute as the visitors pushed for an equaliser. Meanwhile at Coventry, the home side had led 2–0 but been pegged back to 2–2 and were in serious danger of losing and going down.

Once Sunderland's defeat was known, however, Coventry's chairman Jimmy Hill had the result announced on the scoreboard and PA system while the score was also relayed to the players. At this point the players of both sides effectively killed the game, playing out the remaining minutes by simply passing the ball around between them and making no attempt to score. They did so in the knowledge that if there were no further goals, both were safe and it would be Sunderland who crashed through the relegation trapdoor. As tears were shed at Goodison, Bristol City's manager Alan Dicks – who had previously been assistant manager to Hill at Coventry – shared champagne with his Sky Blues counterparts at Highfield Road.

Spending much of 1977–78 in mid-table in the Second Division, five wins in the last six games propelled the team to a final placing of sixth. During the season, Roly Gregoire, a young lad signed from Halifax Town after impressing against Sunderland for their reserves, became the first player of colour to play for the club. Sadly, the amount of discrimination at the time meant that a black player would have had to be brilliant to win over some racially prejudiced people. Gregoire was a willing runner, but with the odds stacked against him he failed to make the grade. It would not be until the mid-eighties and the arrival of Gary Bennett and Howard Gayle that the club started to make progress in terms of welcoming black players. It had been at Sunderland that a black footballer first played in the top-flight of English football. That distinction went to Sheffield United goalkeeper Arthur Wharton as far back as February 1895 at Newcastle Road. The first black players of Tottenham Hotspur, Leyton Orient and Notts County all subsequently made their first appearances at Sunderland.

Cup captain Bobby Kerr's final appearance at the end of the first month of the 1978–79 campaign was the last of any of the cup winners, as the decade neared its end with Sunderland searching for a new set of heroes. It wasn't to come under Adamson, as midway through October the Ashington-born manager jumped ship to take over at top-flight Leeds United. After eight games as caretaker-manager, Adamson's assistant Dave Merrington left to link up with him at Elland Road. At the time Sunderland were fourth. They were still fourth at the end of the season after Billy Elliott was handed the reigns, just as they had been before Bob Stokoe arrived.

With Rowell scoring a famous hat-trick in a 4–1 win at Newcastle, Elliott's charges went close to promotion. Needing to win by four goals to go top for the first time in the season, a late penalty save by Barry Siddall secured a 6–2 win over Sheffield United in the third from last match, only for the good work to be undone three days later with a home defeat at the hands of mid-table Cardiff City. Six years to the day from the 1973 FA Cup final, Sunderland's final fixture of the season brought a win at Wrexham, but it was not enough, as news filtered through that promotion rivals Crystal Palace, Stoke City and Brighton & Hove Albion had all won away, the latter at Newcastle. As fans travelled home Sunderland remained third, a point behind both Stoke and Brighton, who were duly promoted. Sunderland were level on points with Palace and ahead of them by just a single goal on goal difference, but crucially the Londoners still had a game to play. They say it's the hope that kills you, and Sunderland's agony was prolonged until the following Friday night, when Palace secured their promotion and indeed the title by beating Burnley, with future Sunderland striker David Swindlehurst getting on the scoresheet. Sunderland missed out, finishing just two points behind the champions. Three seasons later, in 1981–82, the system of three points for a win was introduced. Had it already been in place Sunderland would have been promoted in second place, with Palace missing out on promotion on goals scored.

Having done well, Elliott was expected by many to be appointed manager, but the directors had a surprise in store when first-team coach Ken Knighton was placed in the hot seat. This decision was reached after the board tried and failed to bring County Durham-born manager Bobby Robson in from Ipswich, although they did initially get as far as Robson shaking hands on the deal. Knighton's appointment ahead of Elliott was unpopular with the players, as the new boss established he was now the man in charge instead of largely being the link between players and management.

Nonetheless, Knighton delivered the goods. Backed in the transfer market, he twice broke the club record, with the £300,000 and £380,000 signings of Stan Cummins and Argentinian Claudio Marangoni, though Marangoni's fee was reportedly never paid in full, as he left the club before his contract had ended. Sizeable fees were also paid for goalkeeper Chris Turner and centre-forward John Hawley, while shortly before the transfer deadline of the time, a record for a Fourth Division defender was paid when £135,000 was invested in Wigan Athletic full-back Joe Hinnigan.

Early in the season Sunderland's first penalty shoot-out victory came in a League Cup second-leg match at Newcastle United. The Magpies were also beaten 4–0 in a cup semi-final at Wembley in November. This was the then prestigious *Daily Express* five-a-side tournament at Wembley Arena, where with Kevin Arnott dictating matters Sunderland took the trophy – the final seeing them overcome Brighton & Hove Albion. While five-a-side trophies were not what the club was about, the win was a nice way to mark the club's centenary celebrations. These began with a Grand Dinner Dance at the Roker Hotel on 10 October 1979 and concluded with a Centenary Banquet at the Mecca Centre on Sunday, 25 November 1979, three days before that Wembley Arena tournament victory. Centenary celebrations included Charlie Hurley being voted the club's player of the century, a photographic exhibition at Roker Park, a star cabaret evening featuring pop singer Tony Christie, a supporters' association dance and, most importantly, the Grand Centenary Football Match against an England XI. This took place on 7 November 1979 at Roker Park. Managed by Ron Greenwood, the experimental England XI did not show the fixture the greatest respect. Over half of the side had never won a full cap, and of those that had, between them they mustered a meagre 33 caps by the end of their careers. The most senior member of the squad was Everton's Bob Latchford, who got both goals as the England XI won 2–0. He had won what proved to be the last of his dozen full caps the previous June.

Fittingly for the centenary season, the Lads went on to win promotion as runners-up, with Joe Hinnigan debuting in the first of the final fourteen games, in which the team were unbeaten. This time it was Sunderland's turn to have a game to play after everyone else. With Leicester assured of the title, Birmingham guaranteed promotion on 53 points and Chelsea on the same number, Sunderland were a point behind but with the best goal difference in the division and a game to play. There was a nine-day wait for the outstanding fixture, when FA Cup finalists West Ham United were due at Roker Park 48 hours after the final, in which they beat Arsenal.

Thousands were locked out of Roker Park after the gates were closed when the capacity – 47,000 at the time – had been reached. Some of those who missed the game were already halfway over the Atlantic. The club had organised an end-of-season trip to America. With this confirmed before the fixture with cup finalists West Ham was re-arranged, three busloads of supporters left Roker Park for Heathrow airport at 6am on the day of the match. Ken Knighton was there to wave them and his family off! When they finally caught their fans up, two days after playing West Ham, Sunderland won in Florida against Fort Lauderdale Strikers, with Kevin Arnott scoring, as he had against the Hammers, who were comfortably beaten 2–0 with Stan Cummins netting the second.

Having been relegated in the first season after the previous promotion, Sunderland were desperate to consolidate being back in the top flight. Sunderland did survive, although Knighton did not. Winning the first two games handsomely actually had SAFC top of the pile, and although that blistering pace could not be maintained, it was late November before the side slid into the bottom half of the table. Knighton got the bullet with four games to go after a loss at Stoke, a third successive defeat that left the team in seventeenth place, albeit with a four-point gap to the drop zone. Knighton had been allowed to spend big on the spine of the side. Sam Allardyce had come in as centre-half at the start of the campaign from Bolton, midfielder Ian Bowyer had arrived mid-season from Nottingham Forest, and in January Knighton had looked to add to the team's firepower with the purchase of Tom Ritchie from Bristol City. The striker had failed to score in his dozen games leading to Knighton's departure, but promptly scored a hat-trick as Birmingham were beaten 3–0 in the first match under caretaker boss Mick Docherty. A reporter who rang Knighton to tell him Ritchie had scored three and ask the ex-manager how he felt was promptly told to 'piss off!'

Ritchie scored again in the next match, which ended in defeat, as did the last home game against Brighton & Hove Albion. Rarely, if ever, did the noise at Roker Park plummet so suddenly as it did when Albion's Gary Williams scored a last-minute winner at the Fulwell End. The one remaining fixture was away to Liverpool, and while Sunderland were in the same seventeenth place they were when Knighton was dismissed, they were staring another immediate relegation straight in the eye. Brighton were one of two clubs behind Sunderland only on goal difference. Both had winnable home games to come, in Norwich's case against second-bottom Leicester City, who could conceivably survive if they won. With Crystal Palace already down, the other team in the mix were Wolves. They were a point behind the triumvirate on 33 points, but they had two games in hand.

With Wolves winning in midweek before Sunderland went to Anfield, the Lads arrived on Merseyside knowing that a draw might not be enough to stay up. Just as he had scored in the promotion-winning match against West Ham, Cummins came up trumps with the winner at Liverpool, although with Leicester winning at Norwich, both of those clubs went down and Sunderland would have stayed up even if they had lost. Nonetheless, it was a close shave and a big win. The champagne left in the Sunderland dressing room by Liverpool's Hetton-le-Hole-born boss Bob Paisley was consumed with relief.

It is questionable what the people who came up with the strip for the coming 1981–82 season were thinking when they made the decision. The traditional red and white stripes were abandoned in favour of a white shirt with thin red candy-stripes, while, less than a decade after Bob Stokoe's popular move to return to black shorts rather than white ones, the shorts were now red. It was a kit that lasted two years. Two years too many in traditionalists' eyes.

New manager Alan Durban – a protégé of Brian Clough's, having played for him at Derby – was handed the toughest of starts with games away to new UEFA Cup holders Ipswich Town and at home to league champions Aston Villa. With expensive new signing Ally McCoist providing an impudent back-heel to set up midfielder Mick Buckley for one of his two goals, a highly creditable 3–3 draw was taken from Portman Road, before champions Villa were beaten 2–0 at Roker Park: for the very first time Sunderland collected three points from one game, following another major rule change.

It was to be the solitary league win in the first third of the season as Sunderland slumped to the bottom of the table. In October admission prices were reduced by a third (seat prices, for instance, dropping to £3 from £4.50) in the light of financial difficulties due to inflation, redundancies and unemployment. According to Hansard, in the year leading up to October 1981, unemployment in County Durham rose by 39 per cent. Unemployment stood at over 16 per cent in both County Durham and Tyne and Wear (Sunderland had been part of the newly created Tyne and Wear since 1974). Times were hard and the football team were doing little to alleviate the suffering as Thatcherism bit into the North East in particular. Although there was the occasional away win, supporters had to wait until March to witness three points being won in a match on home soil again.

That second home league win brought goals for McCoist and Nick Pickering as league leaders Southampton were defeated 2–0. It was only McCoist's second strike of the campaign. Although he went on to become Rangers' all-time top scorer, the youngster found the switch from part-time soccer at St Johnstone to the pressures of top-flight football with Sunderland to be tough. Nonetheless, he remained endlessly popular with the fans who could see there was a genuine talent there, just waiting to be unleashed. Pickering was a home-grown youngster who had come into the team on the opening day and would go on to play for England, as would Barry Venison, another local lad introduced to the side that season.

Gradually, Durban improved the team, establishing a blend of youthful energy and veteran players of international calibre. Colin West, another home-grown product, came into the side to score six late-season goals – including one against Everton in the first Saturday home win in one day short of exactly a year – and stave off relegation as Sunderland finished fourth from bottom, after six months had been spent in the bottom two.

Having beaten league champions Villa in the first home game of 1981–82, Sunderland travelled to Villa for the curtain raiser of 1982–83 with the Midlands club now crowned as European champions. With Villa fan Ian Atkins debuting, having been signed from Shrewsbury Town, where he had played for Durban, Sunderland shocked maybe even themselves by winning 3–1. Astonishingly, after three games Sunderland were fourth, but decline set in and by the end of November they were back at the foot of the table.

As had become usual, times were hard at the club and in the region. From the start of the season the Roker End was closed, as two thirds of it was demolished in line with the requirements of the Safety of Sports Grounds Act. In his definitive book *The Football Grounds of England and Wales*, published the year after the Roker End was restructured and reduced, Simon Inglis wrote: 'Rising 50 feet above the street, the Roker End was like an unfinished tower block, its guts exposed to the passer-by, who could see deep into a dark cavernous web of beams. Truly there was never terracing like it, nor ever will be again.'

Limited to 17,150 before the remedial work, from its peak of 23,000, the Roker End reopened in early December for a fixture with Ipswich Town with its capacity cut to 7,500, after two thirds of it was demolished for safety reasons. It was emblematic of the decline of the club. Once a giant that contested the top honours in the sport, since the first relegation following the 'Mr. Smith' revelations of a quarter of a century earlier, Sunderland now struggled to stay in the top flight. Relegation had been suffered in 1958, 1970, 1977 and now seemed imminent every season.

Soon after the Roker End reopened Gary Rowell plundered a hat-trick in a 3–0 win over Arsenal to start a run of fourteen league games with just one defeat. This lifted Durban's team to fifteenth, and although there was a late-season slump before the double was done over the Gunners, the team survived, finishing three places better off than the year before. Slowly but surely Durban was developing a decent side. He made perhaps his best signing in the summer of 1983, when spending £225,000 to bring in midfielder Paul Bracewell from Stoke, a club where 'Durbs' had given 'Brace' his league debut.

Although 1983–84 was spent bumbling around in the lower reaches of mid-table, unlike the previous couple of campaigns, when substantial periods had been spent at the foot of the league, this time Sunderland never dropped into the bottom three at all. Nonetheless, chairman Tom Cowie OBE (later Sir Tom) pulled the plug on Durban after a narrow defeat at Manchester United in late February, as the board of directors grew frustrated with what they perceived as a lack of sufficient progress. With the benefit of hindsight many fans now look back on that period as a time when the club should have been more patient with Durban's gradual improvements. The plug had also been pulled on TV coverage of the home game with Manchester United the previous October due to an industrial dispute affecting *Match of the Day*. Aiming to capitalise on such coverage, Cowie's company name Cowies had been emblazoned on the front of the team's shirts. Shirt sponsorship at Sunderland had arrived.

Following the departure of Durban, the evergreen goal-scorer Bryan 'Pop' Robson had one game in charge before Cowie handed the reins to the club's record outfield-appearance holder, Len Ashurst. Len had enjoyed a lengthy managerial career mostly in the lower leagues. He had taken minnows Newport County to the quarter-finals of the European Cup Winners' Cup in 1981 after triumphing in the Welsh Cup, as well as winning promotion from Division Three with Cardiff City in 1983.

Notts County were relegated after a goalless draw in Sunderland's final home game, but the Lads were not sure of their own status as they headed to their remaining match at Leicester City. Victory lifted them to thirteenth, which was the highest since 1956, although because of results elsewhere they would have been safe even with defeat.

Ashurst made wholesale changes. There were eight debutants in the first four games of the following season. These included Gary Bennett, brought in from Ashurst's old club Cardiff. Bennett would go on to join Ashurst in Sunderland's all-time top-five appearance makers and later would spend over two decades summarising Sunderland games on local radio, a job he was still doing in 2024. Bennett eventually earned the Freedom of the City of Sunderland and a host of other honours for his sterling work in fighting racism. He became Sunderland's captain and led by example in more ways than one. Gary took just two minutes to score on his debut against Southampton – and England keeper Peter Shilton – as the 1984–85 season started with a 3–1 win.

It was the fourth time in five seasons since promotion that three goals had been scored on the first day, but as in previous years it was a false dawn. Although Ashurst's side were seventh in early November, there was a slow but steady slide to relegation amidst constant boardroom turmoil as rebel director Barry Batey fought, unsuccessfully, for control of the club. Sunderland eventually went down with Stoke City and Norwich City, the latter having beaten Sunderland at Wembley in SAFC's first ever League Cup final. The cup run had seen goalkeeper Chris Turner in outstanding form, particularly in a pair of games against Tottenham Hotspur. Chelsea were beaten home and away in a semi-final played at the height of eighties hooliganism. Such were the scenes at Stamford Bridge that one of Sunderland's goals was scored while a police horse was on the pitch!

Eleven days before the Sunderland–Norwich City final at Wembley, Millwall and Luton Town fans badly rioted in a game at Kenilworth Road, while in May of 1985, thirty-nine people died after crushing at the European Cup final between Liverpool and Juventus at the Heysel Stadium in Belgium. In contrast, Sunderland's final with Norwich was played in such good spirit it became known as 'the friendly final'. The game itself was a dull one in which Norwich won 1–0 with a goal that took a deflection off Sunderland defender Gordon Chisholm, after rookie defender David Corner – in for suspended skipper Shaun Elliott – was robbed trying to shepherd a ball out for a goal-kick. The normally reliable Clive Walker also missed a penalty on a day that definitely was not Sunderland's. Though Sunderland fans at least witnessed the trophy being raised in their direction. Gary Rowell, who was on crutches thanks to a long-term injury, had joined Norwich after being released by Ashurst, but evidently with very mixed feelings, as he lifted his team's trophy towards the red and white legions.

Whereas at most cup finals the losing team's supporters leave immediately, the red and white army sportingly stayed to salute their own side as well as the winners on their lap of honour. Afterwards, outside the stadium, scarves and best wishes were exchanged. As a consequence a Norwich car dealership provided a trophy called the 'Friendly Cup' which thereafter has been played for between the clubs when they meet. Norwich supporters showed the same sort of class in defeat seven years later when they lost to Sunderland in the FA Cup semi-final at Hillsborough.

Among those leaving Sunderland after relegation was Chris Turner. He captained the team in the final game of the season at home to Ipswich in front of a sub-10,000 crowd. It also proved to be Ashurst's last match, he was sacked with relegation having been confirmed.

Fans had long craved a big-name manager. Brian Clough was the man they wanted but could never get. Don Revie and Bobby Robson had been among the other big names in the frame for the post since the initial promotion in 1964, but in 1985 the Sunderland board finally got their man. Cowie lured Southampton boss Lawrie McMenemy back to his native North East by dangling an astronomical salary and the position of managing director. McMenemy's time proved to be disastrous, but Cowie could not be accused of lacking ambition in bringing him in. Having emulated Stokoe in winning the FA Cup with a Second Division side in Southampton in 1976, McMenemy had led the Saints to promotion two years later, and as recently as 1983–84 had led his side to runners-up spot in the top flight. He had a track record of success wherever he had been and possessed one of the biggest media profiles in the game.

McMenemy's recipe for success failed at Sunderland. In direct contrast to the turning to youth that was the approach of Alan Brown, and would be under the leadership of sporting director Kristjaan Speakman in the 2020s, 'Big Mac' went for experience: top-quality older heads. A succession of big-name – but past their best – players were brought in, but on the opening day of the season they were played off their own pitch by a Blackburn Rovers side managed by Bobby Saxton, who would later excel at Sunderland as Peter Reid's right-hand man. By the time the first five games were lost without even a goal being scored, Sunderland were rock bottom of the second tier.

Although they improved a little it was a season of struggle. Four goalkeepers were used, with on loan Andy 'Officer' Dibble proving to be the 'Top Cat' late in the season, when back-to-back clean sheets contributed to 2–0 home wins that staved off a second successive relegation. In the second of those, against mid-table Stoke, the crucial opening goal came from the penalty spot as early as the second minute, after Stoke player-manager Mick Mills – who had played for McMenemy at Southampton – uncharacteristically dived into a challenge on his old Ipswich teammate Eric Gates. Once the final whistle went McMenemy appeared in front of a relieved crowd waving a white handkerchief of surrender. He hoped for better second time around, but 1986–87 was to become the worst season in the club's history.

Stoke returned in the sixth league game of the new term, when another 2–0 win left Sunderland sixth and hoping at least for a place in the play-offs, which were being introduced in this season. Teams aiming for promotion had to be at least fifth to qualify. That position was reached briefly at the end of October, and while Sunderland did go on to qualify for the play-offs, they did so at the wrong end of the table after decline set in. The new system was that the team finishing third from bottom would participate in play-offs with the clubs third, fourth and fifth from the division below.

Totally disillusioned, a meagre 8,544 populated Roker Park for what proved to be McMenemy's last match in April. After Sheffield United came from behind to win with a late goal from ex-Newcastle striker Peter Withe, many of those fans congregated in protest outside the main entrance. Stones were hurled at office windows and directors' cars were damaged before order was restored. That evening McMenemy performed what became known as his 'midnight flit', heading back to the south of England and letting fans discover his resignation via a newspaper column, despite his son Chris remaining on the club's coaching staff.

These were truly desperate times at the club. At the start of the season Bob Murray had taken over as chairman from Tom Cowie and inherited McMenemy as manager, but he couldn't afford to sack him due to the lucrative contract he was on. The club was already over its overdraft limit. The bank got tough with Sunderland after

Cowie left; they had tolerated SAFC's financial difficulties as the banking from Cowie's car-leasing business was worth so much more than that from the club. Within a week of Murray becoming chairman, the Midland Bank withdrew the club's overdraft. In the same period Middlesbrough FC were served a winding-up order, with the gates at their Ayresome Park home locked five days before Murray became Sunderland chairman.

Murray went on to become SAFC's longest-serving chairman and managed to prevent the club going the same way as their Teesside neighbours. Once McMenemy went, Murray needed someone to take over and try to save the club on the pitch. He turned to Bob Stokoe, hoping the Messiah could provide one more miracle.

After a narrow defeat at Bradford City, which left the team one off the foot of the table, Stokoe's first home game of his second spell was against 1973 FA Cup finalists Leeds United. Sunderland were leading 1–0 at half-time, but the match ended 1–1 after keeper Iain Hesford, who was having an immensely difficult season, was beaten from long distance by John Pearson. Taking seven points from the next four games meant Stokoe's side went into the last league game, against Barnsley, as the highest placed of three teams on forty-eight points trying to avoid third-bottom spot, but knowing that because of fixtures elsewhere a win was required to guarantee survival. Leading 2–0, they managed to lose 3–2, one of the Tykes goals coming from recent Sunderland old boy Rodger Wylde.

Doomed to the first year of the play-offs – a modern-day revival of the Victorian-era Test Matches, albeit with a different format – Sunderland were paired with Gillingham, who had finished fifth in Division Three. Losing the first leg 3–2 in Kent, Sunderland won 3–2 at home thanks to a dramatic late Bennett header. Both keepers saved penalties, Sunderland's Mark Proctor having also failed to score with one in the Barnsley game. With the horrific possibility of a first ever relegation to Division Three looming, the game went to extra-time, during which both teams scored once more to tie the aggregate score at 6–6.

Sunderland AFC

Being the first year of the play-offs, no one quite knew what was happening. There was no replay or penalties. As a pocket of Newcastle United supporters gleefully celebrated in the Clock Stand paddock, Sunderland were relegated on away goals – simply because the extra-time had been played on Wearside after identical scorelines over 90 minutes on each ground! Had away goals counted in the final, Gillingham would have been promoted after beating Swindon Town 1–0 at home and losing 2–1 away. Instead, a replay took place at Crystal Palace, where they lost 2–0.

However quirkily, Sunderland were relegated. Play-off rules may have been mysterious, but the plain fact was that if the play-offs had not existed they would have gone down after finishing third from bottom. Following the defeat to Gillingham the *Sunderland Echo*'s chief sportswriter Geoff Storey declared: 'What happened to this once proud club at Roker Park yesterday was a disgrace. Sunderland in the Third Division is unthinkable and unforgivable.'

The following month Roker Park staged its first ever rock concert. As David Bowie took to the stage and opened with, 'Hello, Newcastle,' it emphasised that Sunderland had fallen right off the map.

9

MURRAY'S VISION

(1987–2006)
Sunderland started 1987–88 in Division Three. And it was not just on the football field that things were not going Wearside's way. Back in 1984–85 there had been a year-long miners' strike, after which the area's main twin industries of coal-mining and shipbuilding went into rapid decline. December 1988 saw centuries of shipbuilding end with the launch of the last Sunderland-built ship. Appropriately red and white, the *Superflex Kilo* was the final vessel of a shipbuilding tradition that had begun on the Wear in the fourteenth century, and at the time of the club's successful era in the 1930s saw Sunderland as the biggest shipbuilding town in the world in terms of tonnage. Five years and one day after the last launch came the final shift of miners at Wearmouth Colliery. This was the biggest pit in the Durham coalfield and was destined to become Sunderland AFC's future home. In light of what we know now about climate change, ultimately it was a good thing that mining fossil fuels did not continue, but this did not change the fact that in the late eighties and early nineties Sunderland was in disarray, with the future of the town and the team looking anything but bright.

Sunderland were in danger of relegation again when Peter Reid became manager in March 1995. He cheered the place up by being responsible for a remarkable era that took in two promotions and a relegation, followed by some dramatic and scintillating football. This had Sunderland featuring prominently in the upper reaches of the top flight for the first time since the mid-fifties, before his departure was quickly followed by two desperate relegations punctuated by a promotion.

At Sunderland's turn-of-the-millennium peak, the front two of Niall Quinn and Kevin Phillips were as good a double act as existed in the game, but it was another double act that drove the club: manager Reid and chairman Bob Murray. While Reid resurrected the red and whites on the pitch, Murray provided a new pitch on which to play. A visionary figure, Murray moved the club from its home of 99 years at Roker Park to the biggest and best new stadium built in England in the second half of the twentieth century. Murray then added to his legacy by providing the club with what at the time were the best training facilities in the country. Had it not been for Bob Murray, SAFC could have been stuck in a decaying museum piece of a stadium rather than becoming superbly equipped for a new century. The Hillsborough disaster of 1989, which led to the deaths of 97 football fans at an FA Cup semi-final between Liverpool and Nottingham Forest, led to major changes. The subsequent Taylor Report of January 1990 introduced regulations which stated that by August 1994 all stadia in the top two divisions of English football were to be all-seater.

As Third Division Sunderland warmed up for their first ever season at that level with a series of low-key friendlies, including several against local non-league outfits, the thought of moving into a sparkling new 40,000-plus all-seater stadium in just a decade's time would have been dismissed as being as likely as winning the National Lottery, which did not even exist in 1987.

Newly appointed manager Denis Smith and his assistant Viv Busby had come from York City. They knew the division well, having led the Minstermen to promotion there in 1984 and keeping them at that level ever since. Smith prepared Sunderland for life in Division Three with the modest but marvellous acquisitions of defenders John MacPhail and John Kay. Both played every league game as Sunderland won the division, MacPhail scoring more goals in a season than any previous SAFC defender, his sixteen goals including eleven penalties.

MacPhail was third-top scorer after a front two who became known as the G-Force. Recruited from York early in the season, Marco Gabbiadini hit 21 in the league, with Eric Gates just two goals behind his partner. After a difficult couple of seasons under McMenemy, England international Gates was rejuvenated by what seemed an almost telepathic understanding with the young, quick and powerful Gabbiadini. The pair played off each other fabulously. The veteran Gates would receive and hold the ball before laying it into Gabbiadini's path, whereupon the youngster's pace would see him leave defenders trailing in his wake.

A promotion procession saw the instant climb back into Division Two secured at Port Vale and the divisional title sealed at home to Northampton Town, before a final-day party at Rotherham United. Sunderland also played at Wembley during this season, in the Football League Centenary Tournament. Qualifying via a mid-season sequence of results used to organise invitations for the competition, Sunderland were one of sixteen clubs from the entire league to take part. In games of just twenty minutes each way, Sunderland's trip to the twin towers was short-lived, as they were immediately eliminated on penalties after a goalless draw with Wigan Athletic. Losing on penalties at Wembley was to become a recurring theme.

Smith's Sunderland settled into Division Two, gradually getting to grips with the step up in quality after failing to win any of their opening six league games and finding themselves in the bottom three. With Gabbiadini still scoring regularly, the side began to dream of a second successive promotion when they climbed into the play-off places shortly after the turn of the year, but a final position of eleventh following a six-game unbeaten run to end the campaign was perfectly satisfactory.

Real satisfaction came a year later when a second promotion in three seasons was achieved. It was the oddest of promotions.

Sunderland AFC

Having been relegated by a quirk of regulations concerning away goals in 1987, in 1990 Sunderland found themselves promoted despite losing the play-off final. Sunderland finished sixth, level on points with the two teams above them. Paired with Newcastle United in the play-offs, Sunderland went into the second leg at St James' minus the suspended Paul Hardyman. The left-back had been sent off in the dying seconds of the initial goalless draw after following up too aggressively when his last-minute penalty was saved.

The second leg became one of the most famous matches in Sunderland's modern history, as the G-Force blew the Tynesiders away. Having put Sunderland ahead early on, Gates classically linked with Gabbiadini, in what were meant to be the closing minutes, to put the younger striker through on goal. 'Marco Goalo' made no mistake and it was 2–0. Shortly afterwards, hundreds of Newcastle supporters poured onto the pitch from the Gallowgate End. They were intent on having the match abandoned. A similar tactic had worked at St James' in 1974, when their side were 3–1 down to Nottingham Forest in the FA Cup and United fans came onto the pitch – at a time when Sunderland were the holders. After a chaotic hold-up Newcastle had come back to win that match, only for the FA to order it to be replayed. Newcastle eventually progressed to the final on that occasion, but there was to be no reprieve from home defeat here, as renowned referee George Courtney took the players off the pitch but made it clear to them that the game would be completed that night even if he had to have the ground cleared and it took until after midnight. After a nineteen-minute delay the players returned to the pitch to complete proceedings in an eerie atmosphere, as the home crowd knew the game was up.

Victory took the Wearsiders into the final against Swindon Town. Rumours were rife that the Wiltshire side were to be punished for financial irregularities. At Wembley, Swindon outclassed Sunderland, being by far the better side. However, they only won 1–0 thanks to a deflected goal when Alan

McLoughlin's shot went in off Gary Bennett, on a day when Sunderland's goalkeeper Tony Norman performed heroically.

Bob Murray knew that regardless of the outcome of the match at Wembley, Swindon would not be promoted due to their off-field offences, although he kept what he had been told by Football League chairman Bill Fox strictly to himself. With Newcastle United chairman Gordon McKeag well connected in football's corridors of power, it had been known within St James' Park that the winners of the Sunderland–Newcastle semi-final were to be promoted even if they lost the final, should the Wembley opponents be the Wiltshire side. Swindon had already won the away leg of their own semi-final at Blackburn Rovers and completed the job with another win in the second leg on the same evening that Sunderland were in action at Newcastle. Found guilty of 35 cases of illegal payments over a four-year period (and 36 charges in total), Swindon were not only denied promotion but were initially demoted to the division below, before the second part of that punishment was cancelled on appeal. On 13 June, some seventeen days after the defeat at Wembley, came news that Sunderland were to be promoted in Swindon's place.

'You're in the wrong division,' sang Norwich supporters on the opening day of the campaign as Sunderland lost 3–2 at Carrow Road. As in 1976–77, Sunderland's stay in the top flight, where they had once seemed a permanent fixture, lasted only a single season. Peter Davenport was acquired at the start of the campaign to replace the veteran Gates and maintain service to Gabbiadini. Similarly, Kevin Ball was brought in for the ageing MacPhail, but other than replacing two old players there was no team strengthening for a side who three seasons earlier had been two tiers lower. Unsurprisingly, the team did not have the quality to survive, although they made a gallant effort to do so. Despite only twice managing to go three league games without defeat, the Lads were still in with a chance of survival on the final day at Manchester City, where a travelling support of some 14,000 gave City their biggest gate of the season. Ultimately, a 3–2 loss mirrored the campaign's opening day, but with two of City's goals scored by Niall Quinn for a home side managed by Peter Reid, Sunderland had a glimpse into their own future as well as making a lasting impression on two men who would become major figures at SAFC.

Reid would arrive in the Roker management office just under four years later. In the intervening period Sunderland's early 1990s did not match the late 1980s for yo-yoing between the divisions, but it could easily have done so. Having been relegated, Sunderland struggled to avoid returning to Division Three. In 1992 they finished eighteenth, five points above the drop zone. The following season provided an even closer shave. Losing the last two games of the season, escape from relegation was due to other teams not being able to take advantage of Sunderland's ineptitude, as they finished just a point higher than Brentford, who went down.

Sacked in December 1991, Denis Smith was replaced by coach Malcolm Crosby, one of his staff he had brought from York. Given the title of caretaker-manager, Crosby revived memories of Bob Stokoe by leading his team on a remarkable run in the FA Cup. Tony Norman added to his excellent reputation with a remarkable save from West Ham's Tim Breacker in a fifth-round replay win in London, before pulling off a series of important blocks in a quarter-final replay against Chelsea. As that match entered its ninetieth minute, Gordon Armstrong scored one of the finest headers in the club's history to take a tiring Sunderland into the semi-finals. Meeting a Brian Atkinson corner-kick at the edge of the box at the Roker End, Armstrong powered his effort into the same goal that Ron Guthrie and Dave Watson had headed goals at the same stage in 1973. It was a golden moment for Armstrong, an always consistent performer who in 1989–90 had set a record by making the most appearances in a season (59) by anyone in the club's history.

Four days before Vic Halom stood in the general election for the Liberal Democrats in Sunderland North (coming third), Sunderland played in the FA Cup semi-final for the first time since

Halom scored at the same stage in 1973. On the same ground as that where Halom had scored against Arsenal – Hillsborough, astonishingly, a mere three years after the disaster – Sunderland won again. This time John Byrne was the hero, with the only goal of the game against Norwich City, Atkinson once again supplying the cross. Before kick-off the Sunderland supporters on the kop end had provided a spine-tingling rendition of the Liverpool anthem 'You'll Never walk Alone', sung in tribute to the supporters who had died in tragic circumstances at the previous Hillsborough semi-final. After Sunderland's semi-final, only the 1997 FA Cup semi-final replay between Middlesbrough and Chesterfield would be staged there.

Liverpool were Sunderland's cup final opponents. They were not the sort of unstoppable Anfield side who had dominated the 1980s, but they were a far better team than Sunderland. As in 1973, Sunderland were a Second Division club, but whereas in 1973 they eventually finished sixth after being near the bottom of the table when Bob Stokoe took over, in 1992 they were still near the bottom at the end of the campaign. Liverpool had finished sixth in the top flight. Their manager Graeme Souness was recovering from triple bypass surgery on his heart and had only left hospital 48 hours before the final. He was not well enough to lead his team out, and he watched the game accompanied by club doctor Mark Reid. It was the first time the richly decorated Souness had been to an FA Cup final, either as a player or manager.

Poor old Souness's heart probably skipped a beat when at 0–0 a great chance fell to Byrne, who was bidding to become only the thirteenth player in history to score in every round of the cup. Sunderland owed so much to Byrne for reaching the final, but the Irish international was unable to accept a glorious opportunity and Sunderland went on to lose to second-half goals from Michael Thomas and Ian Rush, the latter registering a record fifth FA Cup final Wembley goal.

The Sunderland players that day actually received winners' medals, as the Duke of Kent accidentally handed them out to the

Wearsiders. Most were swapped with the victorious Merseysiders on the pitch before the Reds' lap of honour. Byrne, however, was so upset with his missed chance that he immediately returned to the dressing room rather than staying out on the pitch. 'I've got a winner's medal here and I'm going home before anyone finds out!' he quipped before handing it over. Had John been able to take that chance, maybe, just maybe, Crosby's side could have emulated Stokoe's.

Football is always full of ifs and buts. As in 1985 when Sunderland were without a key defender due to the suspension of skipper Shaun Elliott, in 1992 right-back John Kay was missing through injury. As in 1985 there was a controversial team choice. In 1985 Colin West was left out. Had he played he may well have taken the penalty missed by Clive Walker. In 1992 left-back Paul Hardyman was named on the bench and was only brought on after Sunderland went two goals behind. Liverpool's man of the match was winger Steve McManaman. Playing only his second game after a knee operation, he had been kept fairly quiet by stand-in right-back Gary Owers in the first half, but shredded Sunderland once he moved to Liverpool's right wing after half-time. Who knows if Hardyman might have restrained him? Gabbiadini had been sold earlier in the season, and his replacement, Don Goodman, was cup-tied, meaning constant rotation of Byrne's strike partner, with Peter Davenport coming in for cup-ties.

While Sunderland had done excellently to reach the cup final, once the dust settled it had to be recognised that in the league it had been an enormously disappointing season. Bob Murray had seen Malcolm Crosby as a short-term caretaker-manager, but had been forced to relent and give Crosby the job when he achieved the feat of taking the club to the cup final – although the one-year contract handed out indicated that the South Shields-born coach was not seen as the long-term solution.

Eleven days after the Wembley showpiece, city status was conferred on Sunderland. At this point Murray even contemplated changing the club's name to Sunderland City. He had more important matters to attend to, though. A little over a quarter of a century earlier Roker Park had been seen as one of the nation's finest stadia, a venue worthy of a World Cup quarter-final. In 1992, a decade after the vast reduction of the Roker End, the ground was increasingly a dilapidated venue.

Roker Park was nowhere near able to cope with the Taylor Report's requirements, and the club certainly did not have the money to convert the stadium into an all-seater arena. The vast majority of supporters at Sunderland stood. There were seats in the Main Stand and Clock Stand that ran along the length of the pitch, but both had standing accommodation at the front, in what were known as the paddocks. Both the Fulwell End and Roker End were all-standing, with the Roker End not even being covered. In November 1990 Bob Murray announced that supporters would be consulted with regard to their views on the club seeking a new ground. A referendum was duly held in 1992.

Sunderland needed a new home. Buying a house for anyone is a major financial undertaking. To fund a new football stadium requires an astronomical amount of money – and Sunderland had very little, if any, hence the state of the team. Regardless of the cup run, they had only been good enough to finish seventh from bottom of Division Two. Vice-chairman Graeme Wood was tasked with exploring the potential of several sites to house a new stadium.

Meanwhile, moves were afoot in the game to revolutionise the sport with a breakaway from the Football League, just a few years after its centenary tournament, which Sunderland had taken part in. Two days before Sunderland dismally lost at Southend United in a league game on 22 February 1992, every member of Division One had formally resigned from the Football League. By 27 May the Premier League came into being as a limited company supported by BSkyB, the broadcaster who would pump endless riches into the top clubs but also make many changes, such as increasingly moving the dates and times of games to accommodate live television.

The split was far from a shock. Six months before Murray became Sunderland chairman in 1986, First Division chairmen had delivered an ultimatum to the Football League, insisting that their desire for a 'super league' would come about. Not only was Murray not chairman at this point, but neither were Sunderland in the First Division. They weren't part of the decision-making at fundamental stages, although having been in the top flight in the penultimate season prior to the break-up of the Football League, the 1990–91 season, Murray was very involved at a key time.

Top English clubs between 1985 and 1990 were denied the extra money they normally made from participation in European competitions, due to the ban on English participation following the Heysel disaster in 1985. Domestic attendances during this era were falling. Dilapidated stadia combined with horrendous hooliganism made football an unpleasant experience for too much of the time. The leading clubs wanted change, but Sunderland were far from a leading club at this time, regardless of their Wembley appearance.

Murray fought to keep the Football League intact, but despite support from some quarters, the most powerful clubs of the time were set on their new path. While it is Sky who have revolutionised the way football is presented and analysed on television, it was ITV who were the main movers in the game's biggest structural change. In the mid-eighties Greg Dyke, a future Manchester United director and chairman of both the FA and Brentford, was chief executive of London Weekend Television and chairman of ITV Sport. He wanted to show the so-called big five of Manchester United, Liverpool, Everton, Arsenal and Tottenham Hotspur's matches on ITV and tried to buy their TV rights separately from the other seventeen clubs who made up the First Division. To try to ward off this attack, the Football League struck a four-year TV deal that allowed the clubs in the top flight to hold on to three-quarters of the money, whereas previously half of it had been spread throughout the lower reaches of the league.

Rivalry between the Football Association and the Football League had long been a factor within the sport, and during this period the Football League was looking to develop a more holistic approach to the game centring around itself. Consequently, the FA was a willing partner when, led by Arsenal's David Dein, the big-five clubs sought an alternative that became the FA Premier League and gave them much more power, and with it much more money. Football has changed dramatically since the creation of the Premier League. Money going to money has made the strongest clubs stronger. In the first twenty-five years of the Premier League six clubs won the league, with Manchester United and Chelsea swallowing up eighteen of the titles. In contrast, the twenty-five years before the creation of the Premier League saw eight clubs crowned champions, with only Liverpool taking more than three titles. Moreover, in the decade before the split, fourteen clubs finished in the top four, whereas by the second decade after the split this had reduced to just eight clubs (down from ten in the opening decade of the Premier League), with Manchester United, Chelsea and Arsenal taking twenty-four of the available thirty top-three places across the second Premier League decade.

A situation that allows the rich to become richer and removes the dream of success for the also-rans cannot be good for the long-term health of the game, regardless of Sky's expert marketing of even relatively run-of-the-mill fixtures. As the gravy train of the Premier League pulled out of the station, Sunderland were left on the platform and likely to be there for a long time.

The 1992–93 season kicked off with just over 11,000 seeing a Glenn Hoddle goal sink Sunderland at Swindon Town. On the same afternoon the Premier League kicked off, although with gates ranging from 12,681 at Coventry to 28,070 at Sheffield United (where Manchester United were the visitors and future Sunderland forward Brian Deane scored the competition's first goal), it had a long way to go to reach the dominance it now asserts. The highest attendance in the country that day was in the Football League, to see Southend United. This match was at Newcastle, who in their first full season under Kevin Keegan got their opening goal through Sunderland's cup-final captain of that year, Paul Bracewell. He had crossed from Wear to Tyne, lured by a longer contract than Sunderland were offering.

As Keegan's Magpies took off to catch that Premier League gravy train by winning Division One, Sunderland struggled to stay in it. Crosby survived as manager until January, when he was jettisoned with his team in seventeenth place and out of the FA Cup after an uncharacteristic error by keeper Tony Norman at Sheffield Wednesday. In Crosby's place came Terry Butcher, the former England centre-half and Coventry manager whom Crosby had brought onto the playing staff at the start of the season, as SAFC's first, and to date only, player-manager.

After losing his first game 1–0 at home to Swindon, a sequence of five consecutive clean sheets implied that Butcher had sorted out at least one half of the team, but come the end of the season Sunderland were four places lower than when Butcher's predecessor was given the chop. The two relegations in three seasons experienced between 1985 and 1987 could easily have been repeated. Only fortuitous results elsewhere on the final day saved Sunderland from a horrendous return to the Third Division. A 3–1 last-day defeat at fellow strugglers Notts County was one of the poorest Sunderland displays on record.

While the future of the team looked bleak, the future home of the club was being explored, and not without ambition. A new 'Wembley of the North' was proposed in Washington, out of town but still within the boundaries of Sunderland and adjacent to the Nissan car plant. While such possibilities were considered, the club were granted dispensation to continue with standing on all four sides of Roker Park until three years after the Taylor Report's deadline of 1994. Hemmed in by houses, Roker Park was situated on a site of eight acres. Sunderland's plan was for a 118.92-acre site with a proposed 48,000 capacity stadium featuring twin towers reminiscent of those at the original Wembley Stadium. Included in the plans were spaces for 12,000 vehicles, a 12,000-capacity indoor arena, a bowling alley, health club and cinema. These plans hit a roadblock in March 1993 when Nissan made a formal objection. They feared that matchday traffic would hinder their model of 'just in time' arrival of materials/supplies and the subsequent delivery of new vehicles to ferry ports.

After the near-miss of relegation, in the summer of 1993 the board provided Butcher with more money to spend on the team than any previous manager, only for most of his new signings to be injured in a road accident a week before the start of the season. Newly signed midfielder Derek Ferguson was driving. He took up the story in his autobiography *Big Brother*: 'I was driving the four of us to the hotel. Bottom line? I hammered it from the minute we left the car park ... When I look back the other boys must have been terrified at how fast I was going ... I've slammed the brakes on but too late to avoid hitting the other car.' Speaking of Ian Rodgerson, Phil Gray and Andy Melville, Ferguson continued: 'Then I look round and realise Ian's screaming in agony and holding his shoulder. I look to my left and Phil's got blood pouring from a cut eye. I look in the rear-view and Andy's just sitting there, staring in shock.'

A week later a 5–0 first-day defeat at Derby County became Sunderland's heaviest opening-day loss. While Ferguson and Melville played, Gray would miss the first four games and Rodgerson would not be able to make his debut until November. Two games later the man who signed him was sacked, with coach Mick Buxton taking over. A seventh successive defeat in Buxton's first match dropped Sunderland into the relegation places, but Buxton was an experienced and methodical manager who lifted the team to a final placing of twelfth, fifteen points clear of the drop and only six shy of the play-off places. A 4–1 defeat at Middlesbrough in October, when still under Butcher, had seen the side sport squad numbers on their shirts for the first time.

Nine months after Nissan's objection to the proposed new stadium, Wearmouth pit closed. The final shift at the colliery took place on 10 December 1993 ahead of a weekend when Sunderland's game at Grimsby Town was abandoned after only six minutes due to a water-logged pitch. The pit closure created the possibility of a new home for the football club, one that would be closer to the city centre than Roker Park. Plans for the club's new base enabled the regeneration of a piece of land that already had a long and proud history. The Tyne and Wear Development Corporation (TWDC) backed the club's ambition to make the site their new home, and by February 1995 – the month that future vice-chairman John Fickling came onto the board – the TWDC reported on a club-commissioned feasibility review of the finance-raising opportunities for a new stadium on the site. While Murray would provide the vision and impetus for the new ground, Fickling would become the hands-on problem-solver once construction got underway.

Originally given planning permission for the stadium to have a capacity of 30,000, Murray managed to get that extended to 42,000. Just three seasons after its 1997 opening, the North (Vaux) Stand was extended to lift the capacity to over 48,000. The ground is constructed in such a way that it is a simple task to also extend the original East and South stands in the same way. This would give the stadium an ultimate capacity of 66,000, should the club be restored to its former glories on the pitch and require it. 'I'm hopeful that one day it will go to 66,000. The same can be done to the rest of the stands as we did to the North Stand,' Murray told me for the book *SoL 20*, which commemorated the first two decades at the ground.

The board focused on the million and one tasks needed to obtain the funding for the new stadium and the practicalities of its construction by design and build contractor Ballast Wiltshier, after work done by chartered surveyors Drivers Jonas

Murray's Vision

and the Miller Partnership. Meanwhile, the team were failing to look like they might be able to reach the still new FA Carling Premiership, for which the stadium at least looked like being well-equipped. Starting 1994–95 with six draws and two wins, Buxton's side could not build on that solid start in a season when only two teams went up and four were relegated from the Premiership, as the new top flight reduced its size to twenty clubs, thereby making it even more difficult for Sunderland and other clubs to reach the top level and be capable of staying there.

Buxton's time in charge came to an end in late March after a dreadful 2–0 defeat at Barnsley. It was a fourth loss in a row and a sixth in seven league fixtures. Supporters saw new £600,000 centre-forward Brett Angell claim a 'goal', only for the match officials to rule that he had not got a touch to a throw in. Angell was not the only debutant. The other, Dominic Matteo, never played for the club again. On loan from Liverpool, Matteo had not been registered in time and had played when ineligible.

In the very early years of the club Sunderland had been docked the first points they ever earned in the league when Ted Doig was fielded without being properly registered, while before the club were admitted to the Football League they had been thrown out of the FA Cup in 1887–88 as punishment for playing three men who were deemed to be professionals. This was after they had been ordered to replay an earlier round after defeating Morpeth Harriers as punishment for not having registered Peter Ford in time. In the light of such historical precedents Sunderland were perhaps fortunate to escape a more serious punishment for the fiasco involving Matteo.

Already in dire straits whereby if the two teams below them won their games in hand Sunderland would drop into the bottom three, this was not a time to risk a points deduction. Thankfully, Sunderland were relieved to only be given a £2,500 fine.

Peter Reid replaced Buxton. Reid met deputy-chairman Graham Wood in Sheffield, after being sounded out by journalist Paul Hetherington to see if the former England international would be interested in the job. He had been out of work for two years, and arrived with a swagger, soon transmitting his self-belief to the team and the fans. Tasked with seven games to rescue the situation, Reidy achieved his target with two games to spare. Given the job permanently after keeping the team up, Reid would, incredibly, win Endsleigh League Division One in his first full season to take Sunderland into the FA Carling Premiership for the first time.

Reid turned to his former Everton midfield partner Paul Bracewell to come back to the club as player/assistant manager. He paired Bracewell in the centre of the park with captain Kevin Ball. Ball's conversion from centre-back to central midfielder was perhaps the most successful positional change at the club since Dave Watson switched from centre-forward to centre-half almost quarter of a century earlier. Within a few weeks of the new season Reid brought in David Kelly as the club's first million-pound player in a deal structured so that Wolves would receive an extra £100,000 on top of an agreed £900,000 if Sunderland were promoted. The problem was that Reid agreed the deal before informing the board, but Fickling and Murray funded the transfer, the lifetime supporters doing what they could to help the manager build a team while they looked to build a stadium.

Craig Russell had scored the first goal of Reid's reign to provide a 1–0 win over Sheffield United. The 'Jarrow Arrow' came up with another 1–0 winner in the sixth league game of the season, against Southend United, to lift Sunderland from a worrying start, which had seen them in nineteenth spot. By then the first round of the Coca-Cola (League) Cup had been dramatically negotiated. Having drawn a first leg at Deepdale, Reid's side were 2–0 down at home to bottom-tier Preston North End at half-time in the second leg. Reid became renowned for his ability to strip the paint off the dressing-room walls when he went on a rant, and never was this more the case than at half-time in this game. He reportedly threatened the players that without an improvement many of them would find that they'd played their final game for the club. Against a defence that included future Sunderland manager David Moyes, Sunderland scored twice in the first three minutes of the second half and went on to win with a late goal from Lee Howey's second of the match.

The side built momentum with an eleven-game unbeaten run in the league, starting with Craig Russell's winner against Southend. A few days before the last game of that sequence in November came news that the club had been given planning permission for a stadium with a 30,000 capacity on the site of Wearmouth Colliery. At long last the club were on the up, although not everything went to plan. Signed just under a month after the meeting with Preston, David Kelly scored in his second and third games, but they would be the only goals of the season for the player who had top-scored for Newcastle United with 28 goals when they won the First Division four seasons earlier. Restricted by injury, Kelly played in only ten league games, but Wolves still received their extra £100,000, as Sunderland won the league with an attack that was outscored by all but two teams in the top half of the table. In contrast, the defence was by far the tightest in the league.

Reid had shown how bold his approach could be when goalkeeper Alec Chamberlain was dropped after keeping nine clean sheets in the opening twenty-three league games. In his place came on-loan teenager Shay Given, who kept twelve clean sheets in seventeen games before injury necessitated the return of the dependable Chamberlain. Given went on to play over 450 times for Newcastle United and win over a century of caps for the Republic of Ireland.

Reid had worked wonders since coming in. Fans came up with the song 'Cheer Up Peter Reid' (to the tune of the Monkees hit 'Daydream Believer'), which Simply Red and White took to number 41 in the charts in the week of Given's last game in April 1996, and the side were promoted in time for what would be the 99th and final season at Roker Park in 1996–97. Two days before the first Premiership adventure kicked off with a goalless draw at home to Leicester City, a time capsule containing club memorabilia was buried under the site of what would become the Stadium of Light. Later the same month steelwork started to rise at the club's new home.

Reid's team strengthening, to try to assemble a side capable of keeping Sunderland in the Premiership for when the new stadium opened, included the record buy at £1.3 million of Niall Quinn. He had played for Reid at Manchester City and had scored twice for Reid's side against the Lads in their last match at the top level back in 1991. Quinn would also score twice in SAFC's first ever Premiership win, a 4–1 triumph in the opening away game at Nottingham Forest, when Michael Gray grabbed his home town's first goal in the new competition, with another local lad in Richard Ord also getting on the scoresheet. Along with dynamic midfielder Alex Rae from Millwall, Reid's other big signing was experienced goalkeeper Tony Coton from Manchester United, another player who had played for Reid at City. As with the big purchase of Kelly the previous year, Reid's marquee signings were afflicted by injury. Rae started only thirteen league games (although he was regularly on the bench), Quinn missed six months of the season due to a knee injury and Coton never played again after breaking a leg at Southampton on his twelfth appearance.

'You never really know, of course, but I believe if those two had stayed fit we would have stayed up – hey, I think if Tony Coton had stayed fit we would have stayed up!' Reid reflected in 2018 to Graeme Anderson for a book we did together with Lance Hardy, called *Managers*. Sunderland did indeed go down, although they did well to accrue 40 points, which is often sufficient to stay up. Relegation came on the last day in a defeat at Selhurst Park to Wimbledon, who were groundsharing with Crystal Palace at the time. As in the 1977 relegation at Everton, once again relegation rivals Coventry City kicked off their final game late, this time at Tottenham, where they had been held up in traffic.

A week earlier Allan Johnston, a talented winger brought in from Rennes, had claimed the last competitive goal ever scored at Roker Park as Everton were defeated 3–0. There would be one more first-team match at Roker Park, John Mullin notching the final first-team goal in a Farewell to Roker match against Liverpool. The Merseysiders had been invited to close the ground, as they had opened it in 1898, Mullin's goal mirroring the 1–0 scoreline of almost a century earlier. The game was preceded by a parade of former players and was followed by a ceremony where player of the century Charlie Hurley dug up the centre-spot, to be relaid at the new stadium.

From December onwards, the 1996–97 season was filmed in an open-access documentary series called *Premier Passions*. Screened on BBC One in February and March 1998, the series showed the inner workings of the club, not least the premier passion of Reid and his assistant Bobby Saxton, the latter a coach players loved due to his enthusiasm, humour and knowledge; he had that ability to make players want to play for him. Saxton remained a big help to Reid in some of the club's successful years to come.

In the month before filming commenced on *Premier Passions*, the club floated on the Stock Exchange. The *Independent* of 15 November 1996 reported that the £10–12 million raised would be used to repay £6 million-worth of loans taken out to help build the new stadium, with some money possibly being directed to Peter Reid's transfer kitty. Reid himself had reportedly paid £300,000 for a 5 per cent stake in the club that was said would be worth £2–2.5 million.

Money – though buttons in comparison – was also raised from an auction of items from Roker Park, everything from seats from the stands to seed-tray sized patches of the pitch going under the hammer of Henry Butcher auctioneers in June of 1997. The auction itself took place in the Fulwell End, with much frenzied bidding for items such as signs from the stadium. The chair from the manager's office attracted a bidding war, which, once settled, created some amusement from all but the winning bidder when the auctioneer next said: 'The next item is for the other chair from the manager's office, the one the manager actually sits in.'

While the fixtures and fittings were sold off from the grand old ground of Roker Park – which was eventually bulldozed and replaced by a housing estate where former player Nigel Saddington and long-term managers' secretary Moira Whitmore bought houses – work continued apace to build the club's new home. Twenty-four hours before the scheduled opening game with Ajax of Amsterdam (whose new Amsterdam ArenA had been constructed by the same firm of builders), the name of the new stadium remained a mystery, although a sponsored name was widely anticipated. Leading up to midnight on the night before Ajax were due – and with work still taking place within the stadium – Bob Murray and John Fickling announced the name to invited press and VIPs in the stadium's sports bar. In the pre-amble to revealing the name, as Murray alluded to light, a whispered rumour circulated within the room that it was going to be named after the battery firm and be the 'Ever Ready Stadium'. Given that Newcastle United fans had long nicknamed Roker Park as Joker Park, it was immediately sussed that they would refer to the ground as the Never Ready Stadium, just to make it easy for them. When the stadium's real name was revealed it only took a second to fathom out what its Tyneside nickname would be. Another nice, simple one!

The name the Stadium of Light met with an underwhelming reaction. Fans who had gathered outside awaiting the announcement had to be soothed by the chief executive, who went on to explain the reasons for the name. Often wrongly assumed to be named after Benfica's home of the same name – which takes its nickname from the area of Lisbon known as Luz, meaning light, its real name being Estádio do Sport Lisboa e Benfica – the Sunderland Stadium of Light owes its name largely to the miners who worked at the colliery the stadium replaced. They depended on their miners' lamps to illuminate the way forward, and the safety lamp used by the miners was invented in the Durham coalfield by Sir Humphrey Davy. Moreover, the inventor of the incandescent electric lamp was Joseph Swan, born not more than a few decent goal-kicks from where the stadium stands. Additionally, as Bob Murray explained in his naming address, footballers are in the limelight, and on the riverside,

Murray's Vision

below the stadium stand lime kilns from the glassmaking heritage of Sunderland. A year after the Stadium of Light opened, just a quarter of a mile downriver from the stadium the National Glass Centre also opened, itself built adjacent to St Peter's Church, where the first stained glass in Great Britain was used. Initially, the name the Stadium of Light was viewed by some as being pretentious, but as it has gained its own history, most people have become fond of the name. In 2024, over a quarter of a century on from its opening, while individual stands have had sponsored names, the stadium itself has yet to take on a commercially sponsored name.

People knew on the opening night that no matter how grand it was – and the Stadium of Light was like being in another world compared to Roker Park – it wasn't big enough. This was because mistakes had been made with the numbering on the new seats, which meant some supporters couldn't find their seat or they discovered that someone was already in it. It turned out that row number 36 had been missed out. These were simple teething troubles, as was a burst pipe in the home dressing room, which John Fickling explained in the book *SoL 20*:

> On the afternoon of the Ajax match we had a leak in a pipe above the home dressing room. Yellow liquid was coming through and I thought, 'Bloody hell, it looks like it's a pipe from one of the loos,' but somebody must have plucked up the courage to test it and it turned out it was lager. I can remember Reidy was over the moon. He said, "******* great! Draught lager in the home dressing room!' That was Reidy all over!

The opening match would kick off shortly after the advertised kick-off time of 8.10pm following a two-hour build-up. With Wembley MC Steve Kemsley keeping the excited crowd informed, the evening kicked off with football juggler Rob Walters performing his tricks while local kids accompanied the Ipi Tombi dancers, who were followed by the Shekinah Gospel Choir. A moment of calm saw the Bishop of Durham, Michael

Turnbull, offer a blessing to the stadium. Pop music then ramped up the atmosphere with up-and-coming bands Orange Orange, FKA Upside Down, Clock, Kavana and Code Red. These were followed by superstars Status Quo arriving by helicopter and performing a short set on a red and white striped stage. Status Quo weren't the only people to arrive at the stadium from the heavens. They were followed by parachutists of the Red Devils, who brought with them the match ball.

The evening had everything – even a half-time kit change as Sunderland modelled their new change strip in the second half – except a goal, as the game finished 0–0. Kevin Ball thought he had claimed the distinction of being the stadium's first scorer, only for referee Jeff Winter to disallow the skipper's effort. It would be Niall Quinn who would go on to net the ground's first goal, and later its first hat-trick. Regardless of not seeing a goal, fans went home after the Ajax match astonished that this splendidly equipped ultra-modern stadium was really the club's new home. Roker Park had deep emotional ties, not least through people knowing that generations of their families and friends had (mainly) stood there since the nineteenth century. Now it was understood that future generations would occupy the Stadium of Light, a venue that had dazzled supporters even before the first night's closing spectacular fireworks display.

The Stadium of Light was barely a quarter of a mile away from Roker Park, but in terms of readiness for the twenty-first century it was a world away. In fact, it was even closer to The Team of All The Talents' Newcastle Road ground, just a few hundred yards away. Now Sunderland had a world-class stadium, the hope and ambition was that one day they would have a team fit to grace the stage they had been given.

Five days before the Ajax game a new signing from Watford had scored his first goal in a 1–0 friendly win at Macclesfield. This relative unknown would go on to break Brian Clough's post-war scoring record for a season and Gary Rowell's post-war goals record, fire Sunderland back into the Premiership and establish himself as the first Englishman to win the adidas Golden Shoe as Europe's top scorer. This was Super Kev himself – Kevin Phillips.

Fittingly, the first competitive fixture at the Stadium of Light was against Manchester City. They had been the opponents in the 1973 game voted the Match of the Century at Roker Park. Just as the 1–0 Farewell to Roker encounter against Liverpool matched the scoreline against the same club in the inaugural match there, City were defeated 3–1, just as they had been in 1973. The opening league match at the new stadium was Sunderland's first home game on a Friday for two decades. As with the meeting with Ajax, the kick-off had to be delayed. The division's highest attendance for almost a decade, 38,827, caused a sixteen-minute delay. Once the game got going, former City striker Quinn took barely sixteen minutes to put Sunderland one up with his historic strike. There was to be drama with late goals from debutant Phillips and home debutant Lee Clark, after Georgiou Kinkladze levelled with the stadium's first penalty, after a City side managed by former Sunderland assistant manager Frank Clark – and featuring future SAFC second in command (to Chris Coleman) Kit Symons and soon-to-arrive winger Nicky Summerbee – had been reduced to ten men with the sending off of Alan Kernaghan.

Although the City game was the only one of the first four that was not lost, Reid's side quickly picked up before a 4–0 defeat at Reading in early October led to ugly post-match scenes, as travelling fans vehemently voiced their displeasure at Reid and co. A midweek League Cup exit at Middlesbrough did not help matters, and there were rumblings of discontent the following Saturday when winless Huddersfield, the bottom of the table team, equalised on the stroke of half-time. After just a few weeks it seemed that the sheen of the new stadium was already wearing thin and, despite the plush new surroundings, the fare on offer was once again disappointing. As in the opening game the team then succeeded in fashioning a 3-1 win, with Lee Clark on the scoresheet.

Amid the cost of the new stadium, Clark's £2.5 million fee from Newcastle United made him Sunderland's record signing. He was soon looking to be worth every penny, as his class and control in midfield stood out. Victory over the Terriers was the first of a sixteen-match unbeaten league run that took Sunderland to fourth place, three points shy of an automatic promotion position, with a game in hand.

Six games into this sequence the Stadium of Light had been officially named by Prince Andrew, Duke of York. The plaque commemorating this was quietly removed in 2022 after his mother, Queen Elizabeth II, stripped him of a range of royal patronages and military affiliations when he was caught up in a furore concerning his alleged sexual liaison with a seventeen-year-old and links with convicted sex offender Jeffrey Epstein.

After missing out on automatic promotion by a single point, Sunderland lost a play-off first-leg match 2-1 to Sheffield United at Bramall Lane. Any fears that, with the crowd being further from the pitch than they were at Roker Park, the atmosphere on big occasions would fail to match the renowned Roker Roar were banished as the Blades were beaten 2-0 in the return leg.

Wembley Stadium has staged many great matches. At the time of writing Sunderland have played at the old or new Wembley a dozen times. Every such occasion has contained its own drama. Twice Sunderland have played at the national stadium in matches that have taken their place in the country's collective conscience of truly great games. The first of these was the 1973 FA Cup final. The second was the play-off final of 1998. Pitted against Charlton Athletic, 120 minutes brought a 4-4 stalemate in a match that saw Sunderland-raised Clive Mendonca score a hat-trick for the Addicks and Sunderland lose key men Kevin Phillips and Lee Clark to injury. Five minutes from the end of the regulation 90, Sunderland had one foot in the Premiership as they led 3–2. It was at this moment that Sunderland's French goalkeeper Lionel Pérez came for a cross he should have left to his defenders, got stranded and allowed Charlton defender Richard Rufus to score his first ever senior goal to take the match into extra-time.

Pérez was unable to stop any of Charlton's seven spot-kicks in the shootout, with Michael Gray having Sunderland's seventh saved by Sasa Ilic. Talking to me on a WhatsApp call from France in 2022, Pérez reflected:

> I was feeling terrible. It was the first time I cried for the game. I was crying because I went for this corner and I punched Chris Makin as the opponent scored with a header to make it 4–4. On the penalties I thought, 'It's my time', and I went well on the first three but I couldn't stop them. After the third one the energy went out of my body and I knew I wasn't going to save them, because the penalties were so well played. It was a terrible feeling.

Later the same year, Michael Gray spoke to me over the phone:

> I can say this now because it's over twenty years ago, but I felt the weight of the whole city on my shoulders. The feeling that I had was awful. The walk from the centre circle was the longest, loneliest walk I've ever had. I've seen my penalty back since and I know it wasn't a brilliant penalty. The goalkeeper chose the right way and made the save and I was the villain and have had to live with that.

Gray was not the villain. He had the bottle to step forward to take a penalty after two hours' worth of booming up and down the flank. Neither did he miss his penalty: the keeper saved it. Gray's redemption was to come the following season when – along with Phillips – he got into the England side while playing in the second tier. Forming a lethal left-flank partnership with winger Allan 'Magic' Johnston, Gray was part of a superb side who registered a record 105 points, more than any club had ever achieved in any division up to that point. This was achieved despite fresh injuries that ruled key men Phillips and Clark out of much of the season.

Reid had replaced Pérez with new Danish goalkeeper Thomas Sørensen during the summer. Sørensen immediately set a new club record of 29 clean sheets in all competitions for the season. Reserve keeper Andy Marriott also kept one on his only appearance of the campaign. Only 3 league games out of 46 were lost, and the team reached the semi-final of the League Cup. On the final day of the season, as the team took their richly deserved lap of honour, Gray approached the main stand and the PA system blasted out Chumbawamba's hit record 'Tubthumping', with its rallying cry to get back up again after being knocked down. Rarely, if ever, has there been a better sentiment to sum up SAFC or the city of Sunderland itself. After being the 1998 Wembley fall guy, Gray's brilliantly successful season was the perfect redemptive arc, part of a wider picture of success best illustrated by other lyrics, this time from the 'Cheer Up Peter Reid' song: 'Oh what can it mean, To a Sunderland supporter, To be top of the League?'

Reid had barely got started – there was better to come – but once again the city that constantly takes knocks suffered another one. March 1999 saw the announcement of the closure of the city's Vaux brewery, a mainstay of Wearside since 1806. Vaux had been Sunderland's shirt sponsors since 1985. Today the link with Vaux lives on at SAFC through the name of the mascot Samson: ironically, since the mascot is aimed at children, the name came from one of Vaux's brands of beer featured on the kits at the time. The link with Vaux is also remembered due to the private road behind the North End of the stadium, which is called Vaux Brewery Way.

The Stadium of Light had been built for Premiership football, only for Sunderland to be relegated from the top flight just as the venue opened. Coming back into the big league on the back of 192 points from the last 88 league games (after losing three of the first four games of the first of those two seasons out of the top-tier) and with a superb new arena to welcome Premiership teams, Sunderland felt more equipped to take on the top flight than at any time since before the 'Mr. Smith' debacle of the late fifties. They had possessed a really good team when promoted in 1964 but had lost their manager and with it their momentum. This time Reid had reinforced with experience and class. New signings included veteran centre-back Steve Bould from Arsenal. He would prove to be a colossus until he got injured halfway through the season. Also coming in was another ex-Arsenal man, Swedish midfielder Stefan Schwarz, who arrived from Valencia for a new club record £3.75 million.

Unfortunately, the team was also weakened. Allan Johnston and exciting home-grown striker Michael Bridges were ostracised by the manager, as they would not sign new contracts. Both would move on without playing for Sunderland again (although Bridges would later return). Sunderland also stepped back into the top level minus midfield dynamo Lee Clark. A dedicated Newcastle United supporter – nothing wrong with that, as he is a Newcastle lad – Clark had gone to the FA Cup final to see the Magpies lose to Manchester United. Persuaded by some Newcastle fans to briefly wear a T-shirt bearing a derogatory slogan directed at his employers, the action ended his time at the club. 'I really liked Clarky and he was one of those who was going to be important to us in the Premier League,' wrote Reid in his autobiography, inevitably called *Cheer Up Peter Reid*, '... he wore a T-shirt bearing the slogan, "Sad Mackem b******s". As soon as pictures of him started to appear in the media it was obvious to everyone at Sunderland, particularly me, that his time with us would have to be brought to an abrupt end. When I next saw him I told him he had to go, it was as simple as that. Our fans wanted him out and there was no way back.'

Without Clark and co., the new look but buoyant Sunderland went to Chelsea for the opening day. In their first match after the fortunate promotion in 1990, Canaries fans had chirped, 'You're in the wrong division' as a narrow defeat was tasted at Norwich. Much was expected this time around, but a hefty 4–0 loss, which could have been much worse, provided a reality check.

Handed a lovely opening home fixture against play-off winners Watford, two goals from Phillips against his former club put three early points on the board. A home draw and away defeat left Sunderland sixteenth after four games, with only one goal that was not a penalty to their name. Next up was a visit to old rivals Newcastle, on what was to be a seismic night in the cyclical nature of the North East's big two. At no point in history have Newcastle United had as many league titles to their name as their Wearside rivals, but there have been times when they have temporarily been the region's top dogs, and the 1990s was such a period. Since the Tynesiders' 1993 promotion, when Sunderland were lucky not to plummet into Division Three, the Magpies had become media darlings due to their exciting brand of football in the Kevin Keegan era. During a storm of biblical proportions, this night in late August 1999 was the evening when the Black Cats became top dogs once again.

Managed by Ruud Gullit, Newcastle were joint bottom of the table and left star strikers Duncan Ferguson and Alan Shearer on the bench for the game. Things appeared to be going to plan for them when they led at half-time, thanks to a goal from Kieron Dyer. But, with Sunderland attacking the end that housed their supporters, little over an hour had been played when Niall Quinn stooped to conquer, expertly directing home a header from a low Nicky Summerbee free-kick. Eleven minutes later Phillips scored one of his classic goals, deftly chipping keeper Tommy Wright to secure a famous and important win. Gullit departed St James' before the week was over.

Boosted by the derby victory Sunderland soared, going on to enjoy their best two years in the top flight for nearly half a century. In the quarter of a century since this win in the rain, the Lads haven't come close to matching the standards set in this period under Reid. Within a month five goals were scored in successive away games, Phillips bagging a hat-trick in a 5-0 win at Derby County, with a largely second-string XI repeating the feat four days later in a League Cup tie 36 miles away from Derby at Walsall. Schwarz then popped up with a winner against Sheffield Wednesday before a 4-0 success at Bradford City had some Sunderland supporters checking their eyesight when they looked at the league table in that night's *Football Echo*. With twenty points from ten games, newly promoted Sunderland were second in the table, a point behind Manchester United. These were heady times at Sunderland, as a week later England played at the Stadium of Light, beating Belgium 2-1 with a team that included Kevin Phillips and a squad that also featured Michael Gray.

Sunderland were still in a UEFA Champions League place when Chelsea came to Wearside two months later. 'Four-nil!' chorused the visiting fans before kick-off, but they were silent long before Sunderland went 4-0 up themselves seven minutes before half-time. This was the apex of Reid's reign. 'Greatest Day in Decades' screamed the *Football Echo's* headline on a day when future SAFC head coach Gus Poyet pulled back a late consolation goal for the Blues. With Phillips and Quinn scoring twice each – one of Super Kev's being used in the title sequence of the following season's national TV highlights programme, then on ITV – the way Sunderland outclassed Gianluca Vialli's side was every bit as convincing as the demolition job the Londoners had performed on the Lads on the opening day.

Home wins over south coast visitors Portsmouth (in an unusual early third round of the FA Cup) and Southampton were followed by a chastening 5-0 Boxing Day defeat at Everton, before the millennium ended with the first visit of Manchester United to the Stadium of Light. Despite missing Phillips through injury, rampant Sunderland were 2-0 up against the league leaders within quarter of an hour. Producing one of the very best displays ever seen by a visiting player at the ground, future Sunderland manager Roy Keane halved the deficit and drove United on before they got a fortunate equaliser four minutes from time. It had been a thrilling match in what was proving to be a pulsating season as Sunderland ended the century in fourth place – the same position they had been in when the century began.

The millennium year began poorly with four defeats, including a controversial FA Cup defeat at Tranmere Rovers, who managed to complete the closing stages of the tie with eleven men despite having a player sent off. Confusion among the match officials saw Rovers bring substitute Stephen Frail on for the closing minutes in place of the dismissed Clint Hill. Frail headed clear the free-kick given for Hill's dismissal before the Sunderland bench made the match officials aware of their error. After a lengthy stoppage while referee Rob Harris took advice, play resumed with the home side reduced to ten men, but only for a few seconds before the referee called time, with the Sunderland fans chanting, 'You don't know what you're doing.' Surprisingly, the FA allowed the result to stand and Sunderland were eliminated in the most unusual circumstances.

This came during an eleven-game winless run in the league, but Sunderland's start had been so good that they dropped no lower than eighth before a positive end to the season brought a final placing of seventh, the highest since 1955 and the third best since the war. With the winning goal against West Ham United in the final home fixture, Phillips had hit 30 Premiership goals. This made him the winner of the adidas Golden Shoe as Europe's top scorer, ahead of Mário Jardel of Porto and Ruud van Nistelrooy, then of PSV Eindhoven. The goals earned Super Kev a place in the England squad in that summer's European Championships, although he never got a game as England dismally failed to progress from their group.

On three of the previous four occasions Sunderland had been promoted to the top flight, the club had suffered immediate relegation. The exception was between 1980 and 1985, when five seasons were managed with a highest placing of thirteenth. When Sunderland followed up their highly creditable seventh position by achieving the same finishing spot again, it was hoped that the five-year stretch would be beaten. Sadly, that was not to be the case, as Sunderland's top-flight tenure this time lasted four years – 2000–01 was to be the last of the good years under Peter Reid.

The season started with a new Stadium of Light record attendance of 47,121 enabled by the extension of the Vaux Stand. This opening match, against Arsenal, saw one of the great debuts when Reid's new Slovakian centre-half Stanislav Varga, recruited from Slovan Bratislava for an initial £650,000, looked like an astonishingly good piece of business. The clean sheet he contributed to was capitalised on by former Gunner Niall Quinn scoring the game's only goal. Unfortunately, second time out – in a match at Manchester City that also marked Bould's final appearance – Varga suffered an injury that kept him out until November. A decent defender who would have two spells at Sunderland, Varga never again reached the heights of his phenomenal debut.

Despite the latest expenditure on the stadium, Murray's board had looked to support Reid in the transfer market as the club aimed to build on the foundations of the previous season. Don Hutchison, who had run the show and scored twice in Sunderland's previous Boxing Day's hammering at Everton, had been signed for £2.5 million. The Gateshead-born midfielder played a couple of away games before he made his home bow as part of an array of over £10 million of new talent in a home match against West Ham. Joining local lad Hutchison were two South Americans, record £4.5 million purchase Emerson Thome from Chelsea and teenager Julio Arca from Argentinos Juniors. Arca would get a debut goal to earn a point and quickly become a cult hero to the fans.

After a slow start, which saw the team seventeenth following the next weekend's defeat at Manchester United, the side clicked into gear and had lost only two Premiership games out of the next nineteen by the time the Red Devils came to Wearside for the return fixture. This run included another superb 2–1 win at Newcastle, where Sørensen sensationally saved a late Shearer penalty. In Manchester United's case they had already lost at

Sunderland in a League Cup tie on the day of the death of the Clown Prince of Soccer Len Shackleton.

As United rolled into town at the end of January, they were well ahead at the top of the table, with Sunderland third, a point behind Arsenal who had played a game more having been in action the previous evening. It was set up to be a fabulous occasion, but turned out to be a controversial one with three red cards, two of them to Sunderland, as United edged a 1–0 win courtesy of an Andy Cole goal that involved a handball missed by referee Graham Poll. The official then sent off Michael Gray for protesting before Cole and the home side's feisty midfielder Alex Rae were dismissed together.

From there the season fell apart. It was a sign of things to come. After the controversial top-of-the-table defeat, the team went almost three months with only one win – a stunning 4–2 victory at Chelsea. Ending the season by winning Southampton's last league game at the Dell, followed by a home win over Charlton, the Lads went into the final fixture at Everton with a chance of qualifying for Europe. Phillips's brace at Goodison earned a point 24 years to the day since the Lads had been relegated on the same ground, but Chelsea's win at relegated Manchester City left Sunderland seventh once again.

The first four seasons at the Stadium of Light had witnessed more than half a century of victories and fewer than ten defeats, but the good times were grinding to an end. Quinn had for so long been the fulcrum of the side, with Super Kev delivering the coup de grâce. But as Quinn aged there was a need to replace the target man. Which was a lot easier said than done. French forward Lilian Laslandes struggled after arriving from Bordeaux and was soon discarded. Without a good supply and now tightly marked after his previous exploits, Phillips found goals harder to come by. Having got thirty in his first Premiership season, there had been fourteen (plus four in the cups) in his second, but just eleven (plus two in the cups) in this third season at this level. Quinn managed six, having miraculously appeared in every league game, fourteen of them as sub, but the third-top scorer had just three. That was USA international Claudio Reyna. His £4.5 million transfer from Rangers had equalled the club's record signing of Emerson Thome.

Reyna was a class act, who, at the end of Sunderland's third season in the top flight, was one of six players from the squad who headed off to play in the 2002 FIFA World Cup, in which he would be selected for the Team of the Tournament. Despite the quality in the squad, Sunderland had struggled in 2001–02, finishing fourth from bottom rather than seventh off top. Fifth at the end of September after Phillips scored his hundredth goal for the club in a 2–0 win at Bolton Wanderers, it seemed as if the season was going to be another serenely enjoyable one, but that was the first league game in which anyone but Phillips or Quinn netted (Jody Craddock getting on the scoresheet). Failing to score in over a third of their Premiership fixtures led to a slow slide down the table. Three games from the end, a season's low of seventeenth was reached, and despite draws in the last two games that proved to be the final resting place for the campaign. Sunderland could have even gone down on the last day if they had lost and Ipswich won. Not noted for winning last-day games, thankfully they did not have to, as Liverpool saw off Ipswich 5–0 to take the pressure off while future Sunderland keeper Mart Poom thwarted the Lads' attempts to win at home to already-relegated Derby County.

By the time the 2002–03 season came round, Peter Reid had been in charge for seven and a half years. The last manager to take charge of the club for longer in one unbroken spell was Bill Murray, who had been appointed before the Second World War. Reid's side had been struggling, and while some of his earlier signings such as Niall Quinn, Kevin Phillips, Thomas Sørensen and Gavin McCann had been outstanding successes, in more recent years there had been too many unsuccessful deals, most notably one for a forward from Honduras called Milton Núñez. Officially five-foot-five tall, he looked a couple of inches smaller than 1973 cup-winning captain Bobby Kerr, who is five-foot-four. Having cost a reported £1.5 million,

Núñez made just a couple of appearances as a substitute. Interviewed in the Honduran newspaper *Diez* in 2017, he claimed that Sunderland signed him by accident, having got him mixed up with another player of the same name! It was rumoured that SAFC later reached an out-of-court agreement with Núñez's agent Pablo Betancourt.

More recently, just as Laslandes had failed to adequately replace the talisman Quinn in the preceding season, record £6.75 million buy Tore André Flo from Rangers at the beginning of the 2002–03 season proved to be an extremely disappointing signing, despite a goalscoring debut in an early season home draw with Manchester United. During his tenure at Sunderland, Reid signed 65 players, regardless of this being a spell when initially Sunderland were in dire financial straits and trying to fund a new stadium.

Peter Reid had been responsible for some of the greatest times in the club's modern history. Sunderland had been a fun place to be while he was in charge. He didn't suffer people who did not want to do things his way, but for a long time his way was a successful way. Reid was sacked at a time when the team were outside the relegation zone with eight points from nine games. While that was disappointing, it was significantly better than what happened next. Only eleven more points were gleaned from the remaining twenty-nine fixtures. Incredibly and embarrassingly, only one of those points was gained after Christmas, and that from a home goalless draw against Blackburn Rovers in early January. The last fifteen league games of the season were all lost, with only two goals scored in the final ten games.

Reid had been replaced by Howard Wilkinson. He had managed Leeds United to the league title in 1992 – the last English manager to lead a team to the title – but like Lawrie McMenemy early in Murray's reign, a previously successful boss found the nadir of his managerial career at Sunderland. Stoke manager Steve Cotterill relinquished his position to come to Sunderland as Wilkinson's assistant, anticipating that he would succeed the veteran boss. He did not get the chance to do that, as the pair were sacked after just twenty-seven games in charge. Only eleven points had been taken from Wilkinson's twenty league games.

For the final nine fixtures of the campaign, Wilkinson was replaced by Mick McCarthy, the former manager of the Republic of Ireland and now Sunderland's third boss in a single season. He was more like Reid in that he was a motivational speaker and in times of trouble tried to apply a back-to-basics approach, but to start with it simply did not work. Sunderland had been relegated seven times before 2002–03, but the relegation of this season was particularly dismal.

Relegation brought over 80 redundancies. Chief executive Hugh Roberts had brought the entire staff together during the season to spell out that there would be significant job losses if the team went down. There were also huge departures from the playing staff. Losing Premiership finances meant losing most of the players who had done well before the recent decline. Kevin Phillips, Thomas Sørensen and Gavin McCann were among those to move on in the summer, while Quinn had retired after one game under Wilkinson. McCarthy accepted and understood all this and planned to build his team around centre-back Jody Craddock.

However, on the evening of the penultimate pre-season friendly, at Hearts, McCarthy was devastated to learn that Craddock was going to have to be sold, as the club continued to struggle financially. Without Craddock, Sunderland were tortured by Hearts centre-forward Mark de Vries, whose physicality Sunderland simply couldn't cope with. Not a good sign heading into the Championship.

With the club on its knees, McCarthy worked miracles to turn the team around, but there was more misery to come before good times started to emerge again. Losing the first two league games of the 2003–04 season meant an incredible seventeen consecutive league games had been lost. This was just one fewer than the all-time worst league run set by Darwen in 1898–99. Sunderland could have equalled that appalling record had they lost at Preston North End. The game was live on Sky and the TV company had brought along members of the current Darwen squad to see their club's record equalled after over a century. However, on a day when Republic of Ireland international midfielder Colin Healy made his debut, the tide turned, as Sunderland won 2–0 to reward the vast army of fans who were still travelling to back them.

Just as in 1977, when after going ten games without a goal the team flipped form with a tremendous run, the 2003 victory at Deepdale lifted a collective weight from the shoulders of the players. Led by new centre-back and skipper Gary Breen, who had served McCarthy well at international level, the team were transformed. Starting at Preston, seven out of nine league games were won, and a goal by Julio Arca in a 4–0 win at Bradford City early in that run was a goal from the gods. The ever-popular Argentinian was playing at left-back. Picking up the ball on the edge of his own penalty area he dribbled his way to the edge of the Bantams box, before sumptuously chipping the keeper for one of the best goals Sunderland had scored in years. Suddenly, Sunderland had a team bursting with confidence, having had none whatsoever after those seventeen losses.

McCarthy has to be given a lot of credit for revitalising the team. They finished third but were robbed in the play-offs when Crystal Palace scored a controversial last-minute goal at the Stadium of Light, which brought the scores level on aggregate. Palace had just been reduced to ten men a few minutes before the equaliser, but they negotiated extra-time successfully to take the tie into a penalty shoot-out. Shaun Derry had the chance to bury the decisive penalty for the Eagles, only for Mart Poom to save and keep Sunderland alive. The drama continued when Jason McAteer failed with his spot-kick, only for Poom to again produce a save, this time from Wayne Routledge. With the scores level Jeff Whitley stepped forward to take one of the most infamous penalties in Sunderland's history. Whitley had been brought in on a free transfer. What he lacked in finesse he made up for in effort, and at least he had the bottle to stand up and take a penalty when he was neither a penalty taker nor a regular scorer. Whitley produced a run up that might have been better suited to a night of ballet at the Empire Theatre over the bridge. Palace keeper Nico Vaesen saved easily, leaving Michael Hughes to slot home the spot-kick that ended Sunderland's hopes of an immediate return to the Premiership they had dropped out of so despairingly.

The season proved to be a case of 'so near yet so far'. McCarthy's men had also reached the semi-finals of the FA Cup, a fifth-round replay at Birmingham City coming in the same month that 1973 cup Messiah Bob Stokoe passed away. Sunderland had only ever participated in a major European competition following the success of Stokoe's Stars. Going into the 2004 semi-final with fellow second-tier side Millwall, there had never been a better chance of another continental adventure. With the other semi-final being contested by Arsenal and Manchester United, who were both virtually guaranteed to finish in the Champions League places in the Premiership, it was nailed on that the victors of the Sunderland–Millwall semi would qualify for Europe even if they lost the final. The meeting with McCarthy's old club Millwall proved to be a scrappy game. The Lads were unlucky to see an early John Oster free-kick come back off the underside of the bar, but they lost to a goal from Australian Tim Cahill. He would go on to become a thorn in Sunderland's side throughout his career, mainly for Everton.

When the dust settled on the season, finishing third and being unlucky in the semi-finals of both the play-offs and the FA Cup meant that for a club relegated in such dire circumstances, the corner had at least been turned. The 2004–05 season could be looked forward to with anticipation rather than trepidation, and although behind the scenes the club were operating on a fraction of the staff they had possessed a year earlier, there was a 'can do' spirit that offered hope for the future. Nonetheless, in July 2004 the club announced that Sunderland Football Club plc was to leave the Stock Exchange, at a time when the club's valuation was reported to be just £3.4 million, a fall of 93 per cent since its flotation eight years earlier.

With the help of his long-serving chief scout Dave Bowman, McCarthy went shopping for bargains. Future captain Dean Whitehead was plucked from Oxford United, Liam Lawrence came from Mansfield Town and Stephen 'Sleeves' Elliott – who McCarthy and Bowman knew from the Republic of Ireland setup – arrived from Manchester City reserves. Wales international Carl Robinson, a crisp-passing midfielder who had been on loan the previous year, was also brought in from Portsmouth. These were soon added to by defender Danny Collins after he impressed in a League Cup tie with Chester City, who had just returned to the Football League. All arrived for initial fees of between £125,000 and £175,000. Centre-back Steve Caldwell also arrived on a free transfer from Newcastle and went on to start more league games than anyone as fifteen more points, combined with a goal difference more than 100 per cent better than the year before, made Sunderland champions.

Caldwell headed the goal that secured promotion. It was one of fourteen scored from corners throughout the campaign, and it came in the third from last fixture, in which Sunderland came from behind to beat Leicester City at the Stadium of Light. Making his debut, eighteen-year-old goalkeeper Ben Alnwick had to pick the ball out of his net after only five minutes, but showed the character to keep his cool and make two great saves (one from David Connolly, who would be leading scorer when Sunderland next won promotion two years later) before the Lads levelled though Marcus Stewart, who top-scored with sixteen league goals that season. Alnwick had been preferred to reserve Michael Ingham, who had endured a tough time in a couple of games, having replaced the injured Norway number one Thomas Myhre. It was a big call, but McCarthy got most of them correct as he took Sunderland up.

Respectful of everyone's contribution, at the end of the campaign the manager undertook a tour of all areas of the club's bases at the academy, stadium and administration centre at Black Cat House to offer his thanks to everyone who had worked for the common good. Then, as now, while for some people behind the scenes at SAFC their employment is 'just a job', many of them are dyed-in-the-wool Sunderland supporters who go above and beyond normal employee commitment because they live and breathe the club.

As the final whistle was blown against Leicester, promotion was not quite secured. The players huddled in the tunnel for a few minutes, awaiting the result from Elland Road, where Sunderland needed third-placed Ipswich to fail to win against Leeds United. News of their draw in Yorkshire started the party, which continued with a classy victory at promotion-chasing West Ham before Stoke were beaten in front of a capacity crowd at the Stadium of Light on the final day. The Championship trophy was presented to Gary Breen, the First Division having been renamed the Championship as part of the Football League's rebranding following sponsorship by Coca-Cola. In 1891–92 Sunderland had been the last winners of the single-tier Football League before becoming the first winners of the First Division a season later. Now, just two years after the most humbling of relegations, Sunderland were back at the top table, having achieved the second-highest number of points – 94 – in the club's history.

Bob Murray had been chairman since August 1986, barring a two-and-a-half-year hiatus between December 1993 and June 1996, when he relinquished the role to John Featherstone as he focused on getting the club a new stadium. While Sunderland-born Featherstone took the chair, having been on the board since 1990, Murray remained by far the biggest shareholder and effectively called the shots. Having taken over the stewardship of the club from Tom Cowie, Murray had protected the club from administration, won the mid-eighties boardroom battle with director Barry Batey, seen the club drop into the Third Division for the first time and in total experienced ten promotions or relegations in his twenty seasons 'in charge'.

But the true legacy of 'Bob the Builder' as the club's longest-serving chairman is the Stadium of Light and Academy of Light. Having stumbled along without decent training facilities since stopping training at the Northumbria Centre in Washington, in 2003 Sunderland had opened the fantastically well-equipped Academy of Light. Murray's vision in providing the club with state-of-the-art facilities around the turn of the millennium ensured that the club were well prepared for the century ahead.

Some might scoff that not enough money was spent on the team during Murray's tenure, but self-made millionaire Murray was exactly that – a millionaire, not a billionaire of the sort that in more recent years has become common in football-club ownership. Bob Murray and his long-term vice-chairman John Fickling were lifelong Sunderland supporters, but they did not have bottomless pockets, and as his two decades as the club's leader neared its end, Murray realised that it was time to hand over control of the club to someone else.

Attempts were made to attract an American buyer. Club delegations met with several interested parties in the USA, but ultimately to no avail. Bob did not want to simply sell the club to the highest bidder. Had he done that he could have lined his pockets, but his desire was to pass the baton on to someone who could be trusted to properly act as the custodian of the club.

That person would be Niall Quinn. As a brilliant centre-forward, Quinn had been the focal point of the turn-of-the-millennium team under Peter Reid that made the early seasons at the Stadium of Light such a joy. Niall was approaching veteran stage when he first came to Sunderland, but like so many before him he fell in love with the club. Most notably, he summed up his feelings with the oft repeated quote: 'I learned my trade at Arsenal, became a footballer at Manchester City but Sunderland got under my skin.'

Among many other acts of generosity, Quinn had donated the entire million-pound proceeds of his benefit match, between Sunderland and his international team the Republic of Ireland, to charity in 2002. A most charming and astute man, Quinn had been hugely admired as a player but was to become even more popular when he succeeded Murray as chairman in 2006.

By the time Murray bowed out and Quinn took over, the club had suffered its second shattering relegation in three years. A meagre fifteen points were accrued all season, four fewer than in the disastrous 2002–03 campaign. Incredibly, in a season of nineteen home Barclays Premiership games, there was not a league victory for home supporters to cheer until the twentieth opportunity! The scheduled nineteen home fixtures had brought four draws, fourteen defeats and a game with Fulham that had been abandoned with Sunderland trailing when heavy snow caused what until the end of the 2023–24 season was the only Premier League game in history to be abandoned due to weather conditions. The game had been in April! The re-arranged fixture at the end of the season at long last afforded the die-hards the chance to celebrate a victory, with a 2–1 scoreline. The only other visiting teams to have left Wearside defeated all season were non-league Northwich Victoria in the FA Cup and Cheltenham in the League Cup, extra-time having been needed to see off the League Two outfit.

Away from home, just eight points were gleaned all season. One of those came on the night that inevitable relegation was made mathematically certain at Manchester United. The pre-match media talk had been focused not on whether Manchester United would win, but on how many they would win by as the title chasers sought to boost their goal difference. With former captain Kevin Ball now in charge as caretaker-manager following the sacking of McCarthy, Sunderland battled to an unexpected goalless draw, with much-criticised goalkeeper Kelvin Davis having a fine match.

Davis had endured a season as horrendous as Iain Hesford in 1986–87, but like Hesford did not lack guts or character. Taken out of the firing line after a 4–1 autumn home reverse to Portsmouth, the easiest thing for the keeper would have been to quietly accept a place on the substitutes' bench, take his money and keep a low profile. Instead, he wanted to play, regained his place and did his best. The plain fact evidenced by the league table is that he was not good enough at Sunderland. That was the case for the players who played regularly. The likes of Dean Whitehead, Steve Caldwell, Danny Collins and new signing Nyron 'Nugsy' Nosworthy – brought in on a free transfer from Gillingham – gave every last drop of effort. They could just have done with more quality around them. New £1.8 million centre-forward Jon Stead ran himself into the ground but managed a single goal in 30 Premiership outings, and that coming 1,706 minutes into his Sunderland career. Despite defeat after defeat, the team were never beaten by more than three goals. The towel was never thrown in, so there were no six- or seven-goal batterings.

Being relegated with a then Premier League record low of only fifteen points was a really tough time for supporters. Added to the second half of the previous Premiership season, it meant that just 16 points had been taken from 57 games, with 47 of those lost. Despite the desperately bad results of the final season of his stewardship, Bob Murray unquestionably left the club in a much stronger position then when he took over, especially with regard to its infrastructure, but now it was time for a fresh start.

Niall Quinn had approached Murray when the club were struggling to see if he could help in some way. Murray's vision was still in evidence when he suggested to Quinn that he should actually take the club over. Always one to think big and accept a challenge, Quinn proceeded to do just that.

10

NIALL'S TAXIS

(2006–2011)
Niall Quinn had earned massive respect and popularity as a player. In the excellent years around the time of the opening of the Stadium of Light he had been the queen bee that the rest of the team buzzed around, most of all Kevin Phillips, who supplied the sting, plundering goal after goal from Niall's knockdowns. As the new chairman of the club, Quinn was every bit as central to the club's ambitions as he had been on the pitch. A man of natural charm and charisma, Niall was viewed by many as being all heart, but off the pitch Niall knew how to use his head as much as he did when he was a totemic centre-forward.

Having accepted the challenge of not just helping, but taking over the club that had got under his skin, the Dubliner assembled a group of financial backers from the then booming Celtic Tiger. At this point the Irish economy had been thriving for over a decade. In the two decades to 2007 there was an astonishing 229 per cent increase in Ireland's GDP. The make-up of this group, who were given the name of the Drumaville Consortium, seemed to change frequently, as Niall spent hour after hour negotiating with potential Irish backers who had sporting interests, in many cases through the horse-racing world that Quinn was well known in.

Quinn astutely also brought Wearside businessman and lifelong Sunderland fan John Hays – founder of the Hays Travel firm – onto the board as vice-chairman. A solid character, Hays was an equivalent off-the-field partner for Quinn to what Super Kev had been on the pitch. The pair dovetailed effectively, and backed by the wealth and ambition of the Drumaville Consortium, the club looked to be on the up. After the financial difficulties of the latter years under Bob Murray, SAFC now looked set to be able to maximise the potential of the fabulous stadium and training facilities 'Bob the Builder' Murray had provided the club with.

As the summer of 2006 progressed Quinn resembled not so much a footballer or a football club chairman, but someone from the floor of the Stock Exchange. It seemed as if he was never without a mobile phone clasped to each ear as he juggled the backers who were being assembled to form the consortium as the new season got ever closer.

As the team headed for pre-season training at the modest surroundings of Bath University, coaching duo Kevin Richardson and Tim Carter were put in interim charge of preparing the team. Midway through the week's preparations before the first match under the new regime, Quinn visited the training camp to raise spirits. Everyone could see he was trying to move heaven and earth to build the understanding of his backers, attract a new manager of calibre and bolster a squad that had just been relegated with a record low number of points.

During the training camp the club's most popular player, Julio Arca, asked for my advice. The skilful Argentinian had stayed after the 2003 relegation, but now, after another dismal campaign, he had decided it was time to move on, as at the age of 25 he was approaching his peak years. Amidst interest from fierce local rivals Newcastle United and also near-neighbours Middlesbrough, Julio wanted to know if it would upset the fans if he joined Boro. He had already accepted that a switch to Tyneside was out of the question if he didn't want to harm the rapport he had built with supporters who had warmed to him from the moment he arrived from the southern hemisphere as a teenager. Julio sounded me out as a long-standing supporter and member of staff. I told him I'd love him to stay, but understood why he needed to move to progress his career, and that I felt people would be unlikely to be annoyed with him if he chose to go to Middlesbrough, especially after he had already shown loyalty to Sunderland by staying after the 2003 relegation.

Arca's final outing for SAFC came in the first match under the new ownership, before he departed for Teesside, where again he gave great service. That first game saw Liam Lawrence score the opening goal as a 3–0 win was registered against then non-league Forest Green Rovers. Sunderland old boy Gary Owers was their manager, and he made his side wear their change kit, as at the time Forest Green's home strip was black and white stripes. 'I didn't want to offend the fans,' explained Owers. 'I'd given up playing by then. The biggest regret I ever had was I never got the chance to play against Sunderland, so I brought myself on for the last ten minutes and I wasn't going to play against Sunderland in black and white stripes.'

That kind of love for the club from players, be they local lads like Owers or from other countries such as Arca, or indeed Quinn, illustrated that whatever the problems faced at any given moment, there is always a groundswell of goodwill for the club, not just from the fanbase, but from many, if by no means all, of those who have had the honour of wearing the famous stripes.

As pre-season progressed and Quinn looked to create excitement and impetus, he struggled to bring in the high-profile manager he and his backers craved. The predominantly Irish owners wanted an Irishman installed in the hotseat, but Quinn could get neither Martin O'Neill nor Roy Keane to accept the post. Not yet, anyway. Instead he found his man in the mirror and appointed himself ahead of the fourth and final pre-season friendly at Carlisle, bringing in the highly regarded Bobby Saxton as his number two. 'Sacko' had been a coach hugely popular with the players during Peter Reid's reign when Quinn led the line.

In appointing himself manager Quinn became the first person to play for, manage and be chairman of the club, although he made it quite clear that his time as manager was to be short-term and he would replace himself as soon as possible. The need for that quickly became clear, as the season started extremely badly, with the boost hoped for from a new start rapidly being lost as supporters – wearied from those exceptionally depressing relegations of 2003 and 2006 – saw what appeared to be a false dawn.

After losing the first four league games, the last of these a depressing 3–1 defeat at Southend United where Sunderland's last-minute goal hardly even merited the description of being a consolation, the next match was a League Cup tie at Bury. Going into the game at Gigg Lane, Sunderland were rock bottom of the Championship. The only side in the four divisions with a poorer record were Bury themselves. They were propping up the entire Football League. Like Sunderland, they had no points from four fixtures and their goal difference was even worse than the Lads'.

One of Quinn's new faces had offered a glimmer of hope at Southend. Spanish midfielder Arnau Riera had once captained a Barcelona B team that included Lionel Messi. Reira had come off the bench for the last 35 minutes to debut at Roots Hall, where he impressed with his confidence and assured passing. Encouraged, and requiring something fresh, Quinn put him in the starting line-up at Gigg Lane. Having delivered his team talk as manager, Quinn saw the match kick off and then made his way to the directors' box, from where he intended to watch the game and leave the touchline instructions to Bobby Saxton. As he took his seat Quinn saw Arnau heading for the dug-out and wondered if the midfielder had taken a knock. He had to be told by head of media Louise Wanless that, in fact, Arnau had been sent off. Just four minutes had gone, after which ten-man Sunderland laboured and eventually lost by two late goals to the league's back-markers, who themselves finished with only ten men.

Five games into the much-heralded new regime and it seemed as disastrous a start as Lawrie McMenemy's first season in 1985–86. Quinn had taken over the club and sold a dream to the backers from Ireland, who were expecting Sunderland to soar back to the big time. Instead, they were bottom of the table and had crashed out of the first cup competition, humiliated by the league's poorest side. Eight years earlier Niall had unceremoniously smashed up the Nationwide Division One signs in the Sunderland dressing room at Bury after he had scored on the night the Lads mathematically secured promotion to the Premier League. Now he stood pitch-side post-match at the same ground and informed the assembled press that he had a world-class figure lined up to come in as manager.

Six days later Roy Keane sat in the stand as Quinn's tenure as manager ended on a high with a home victory over West Bromwich Albion. Keane had not turned up for Quinn's benefit match between Sunderland and the Republic of Ireland just before the 2002 FIFA World Cup three years prior. Before the tournament Keane infamously walked out of his country's squad amidst an acrimonious spat with manager Mick McCarthy.

Extremely unhappy with what he viewed as inadequate training facilities and preparation for the World Cup about to take place in Japan and South Korea, Keane sensationally withdrew from his country's squad while they were warming up on the Pacific island of Saipan. Reportedly, the star midfielder produced a lengthy foul-mouthed rant criticising McCarthy's competence. Niall Quinn was among those to back McCarthy, an action that led to such friction between Quinn and Keane that the prospect of Keane agreeing to take his first steps in management under the chairmanship of Quinn was a coming together that neither the media nor the watching public had realistically contemplated. Keane had described Quinn as a 'coward' and a 'muppet' in the aftermath of that affair, but was now coming to Sunderland to work for Quinn and hopefully do better than McCarthy had managed at the Stadium of Light in the intervening period.

A legend as a player, mainly for Manchester United, Keane was untried in management but was arguably the biggest star name to arrive at Sunderland since Jim Baxter in the 1960s. Keane's first home match pulled in a crowd over 11,000 up on the previous home game. Quinn always denied that he said it would be a 'magic-carpet ride' at Sunderland, but the image was a good one, and by the time of Keane's first match in charge at the Stadium of Light that magic carpet had well and truly taken flight. The 'Roy-volution' had begun on the final night of the transfer window. Six players were brought in, including his old Manchester United colleague Dwight Yorke, tempted back from the sunshine of Australia to become a midfield general as a veteran rather than the nimble goal-getting front man of his prime. All of the signings had previously been teammates of Keane, including centre-half Stan Varga, who returned to SAFC having played alongside the new gaffer at Celtic.

Varga, Ross Wallace, David Connolly, Liam Miller and Graham Kavanagh were all slotted straight into the side for Keane's first match at Derby County. Sunderland trailed to a goal on the stroke of half-time but came back to win. A few days later Miller and Kavanagh were among the scorers as a 3–0 victory was achieved at old enemies Leeds. By the time Leicester City arrived for Keane's first home match, a draw, the investment made by the members of the Drumaville Consortium was looking like a wise one. Sunderland had been 'Roy-juvenated', and the dream sold to the investors by Quinn quickly looked like coming true.

After the initial bounce things calmed down. Starting with that Leicester game only eleven points were gleaned from ten matches, with the team still only nineteenth in mid-November. Keane quickly discarded the players he did not want, including his old international teammate Kenny Cunningham, who had been brought in by Quinn during the summer. Cunningham's central-defensive partner Steve Caldwell was also jettisoned. In their place Keane combined January acquisition Jonny Evans, on loan from Manchester United, and erstwhile right-back

Nyron Nosworthy. The duo formed a perfect blend. 'Nugsy' Nosworthy was a strong and powerful stopper, while Evans was a maestro with the ball at his feet. They were not as good a partnership as Jeff Clarke and Shaun Elliott from the 1980 promotion team, but they were reminiscent of them and that was good enough.

Evans debuted in the same game as winger Carlos Edwards. Brought in from Luton Town, Edwards would be a revelation, a wide-right player with a penchant for scoring screamers. The new signings kept coming, as the Drumaville Consortium sanctioned many a move. Not all of these paid off, but the club now was in top gear. Quinn was the best communicator in the club's history, a pied piper of a leader. On the pitch the players were working their socks off for Keane, who possessed his own special aura, while the fans, so long suffering through the bad times, were lapping up the change of direction and enjoying coming to the match again.

One of the longest chants in memory (of 'Keano' to the tune of 'Hey Jude') serenaded a 4–2 January win at Sheffield Wednesday, but the manager was furious that his side had let up and allowed the Owls two late goals that had turned a 3–0 lead into a tight scoreline before Edwards added a fourth. A return to South Yorkshire two months later saw Keane go without Anthony Stokes, Marton Fulop and Toby Hysen, who were late for the bus to Barnsley, where this time a clean sheet was part of the victory. Keane's men had not lost in between and would not do so until mid-May, by which time the team who had lost their first four league games were top of the league.

Success was secured on a day Sunderland were not playing, as promotion contenders Derby County lost to Crystal Palace at Selhurst Park, a ground where Sunderland had been relegated (against Wimbledon) in 1997. In all but mathematical terms promotion had been sealed on the previous Friday night, when in a pulsating game full of drama, a Burnley side managed by former Sunderland assistant Steve Cotterill had been beaten 3–2. As Carlos Edwards pulled the trigger on his late blockbuster winner, the TV pictures turned to Quinn in the directors' box. Niall had scored many an important goal in his career, for his clubs and country, but as Edwards's pile-driver almost burst the net at the Kronenbourg North Stand, Niall rose and you could see the weight of expectation that he had taken onto his broad shoulders fall away like water tumbling over the edge of High Force. Next to him, the sheer delight of his wife Gillian made clear that she knew just how much emotional effort he had invested in turning the club around.

The biggest ship ever built on the Wear was the 292-metre, 160,000-tonne *Naess Crusader*, but even that was not as big as the good ship Sunderland, the club which for many years had a ship on the badge, a homage to Sunderland once being the biggest ship-building town on the planet. Quinn and Keane, those unlikely bedfellows after the Saipan incident in 2002, had combined to provide SAFC with one of its truly great modern moments.

On the night before the last game of the season at Luton, I went for a curry with Niall and some club staff in Northampton. Spirits were high, not least when the chairman ordered 50 poppadoms before ceremoniously karate-chopping them and then instantly becoming ever-so apologetic to the waiters. It wasn't just that night's curry that was hot, the team were blistering. Luton were already relegated and many of their season-ticket holders had sold their seats to Sunderland supporters eager to join the party. So much so that as player of the century Charlie Hurley (a resident of nearby Hertfordshire) surveyed the scene, Kenilworth Road was a sea of red and white as Sunderland romped home 5–0. As news filtered through from Deepdale, where Steve Bruce's Birmingham City had lost to Preston North End, it transpired that Sunderland were not just promoted – they were champions.

Keane did not want an open-top celebratory bus ride. He made it clear that promotion was not something for a club of Sunderland's stature to be shouting from the rooftops. Instead, a private celebration was held at Seaham Hall, where skipper Dean Whitehead was presented with the Championship trophy.

Supporters may not have had a bus parade to enjoy, but over a hundred of them had a taxi ride back after a win at Cardiff at the end of March. Fans were in high spirits after the victory as they queued for an easyJet flight back from Bristol airport. Those spirits were heightened further when fans realised Quinn and a handful of club staff were about to board the same flight. Once on board the airline staff took exception to a couple of supporters who were loud but not abusive and threw them off the flight. At this point Niall, followed by his staff, got off in solidarity with the fans, at which point the rest of the fans followed Quinn – the Pied Piper – off the plane.

Faced with over a hundred Sunderland fans stranded in Bristol, phone calls were hurriedly made to every bus company a phone number could be found for. With no buses instantly available, a fleet of airport taxis was commandeered. Negotiations with the taxi company agreed a price of £500 per taxi to transport fans back from the South West to the North East. As Quinn, with help from one or two others, emptied the ATMs of cash, stashes of £500 were stuffed into my hands. It was my job to get fans into groups of four, bundle them into taxis and set them off. The drivers were mostly Iranian and had no idea where Sunderland was, or how far. I was in the final taxi with Niall and a couple of club officials. When we eventually reached Newcastle airport, where we had left Niall's car, the taxi driver refused to stop for a rest and a coffee, setting off immediately for Bristol. We could only hope he got there safely.

Ambition was not in short supply as SAFC prepared for their return to the Premier League. Whipping boys in their last two top-flight campaigns, this time around Sunderland were to be more competitive. For the first time since the Bank of England Club-era acquisition of Trevor Ford in 1950, Sunderland set a transfer record, paying a British record fee for a goalkeeper when buying Craig Gordon from Hearts for £7 million, with another £2 million committed depending upon appearances. Big fees were also paid for attacker Kieran Richardson from Manchester United, former Newcastle striker Michael Chopra from Cardiff City, midfielder Dickson Etuhu from Norwich City, and defenders Danny Higginbotham from Stoke City, Greg Halford from Reading, Paul McShane from West Bromwich Albion and Russell Anderson from Aberdeen. Soon after, a further £6 million was spent on centre-forward Kenwyne Jones from Southampton. Veterans Andy Cole and Ian Harte also arrived, as did promising young forward Roy O'Donovan from Cork City, a deal lined up while Sunderland spent pre-season in Ireland playing Bohemians, Cork City and Galway United.

With Charlie Hurley travelling as club ambassador – and overwhelmed to be travelling on charter flights, as the tour transport was provided by Irish airline Aer Arann – Sunderland made a full-blooded charm offensive on the Irish footballing public as they aimed to muscle in on the nation's interest in the Premier League. Increasingly monikered Sund-Ireland, the red and whites marketed themselves aggressively, for instance having a stall complete with the Championship trophy at the Galway races and getting the club magazine *Legion of Light* stocked in shops throughout the country.

Five of the new boys made their debuts on the opening day of the season. Entering added time in the first game, it looked to be a rerun of the first home match after promotion in 1990, when a goalless draw with Tottenham Hotspur was played out. Suddenly, substitute Chopra popped up with a last-minute winner to complement Gordon's clean sheet. Having not won a home game until the final home fixture of the season last time at this level, the Lads had got off to a winning start and the feel-good factor continued. The late goal was to be one of eight Sunderland scored after the 88th minute throughout the season, all but one of them in wins or draws. They were important goals, as, despite the investment in the squad – which continued with the January signings of Andy Reid, Phil Bardsley, Rade Prica and the return of Jonny Evans on a second loan – the team found it hard to stay out of the bottom three.

They dipped into the drop zone after a horrific 7–1 loss at Everton in November, by which time the only other league victory had come against Reading in a match which marked a commemoration of the death of 1973 cup final goal-scorer Ian Porterfield. Having not managed to put back-to-back Premier League wins together all season, maximum points were suddenly taken from three games in the spring. Despite losing four of their final five fixtures, Sunderland survived, finishing fifteenth, three points above the dreaded drop zone.

More investment was put into the team for 2008–09, but with three points fewer than in the previous season, Sunderland finished a place lower, staying up in dramatic circumstances after coach Ricky Sbragia had replaced Roy Keane. The manager left in late November 2008 after a 4–1 home loss to Bolton Wanderers, on a day when Craig Gordon was pressed into action despite allegedly not being fit. It was the goalkeeper's only league appearance between mid-October and April. Defeat to Bolton dropped Sunderland into the bottom three, just four league games having been won out of the first fifteen despite the sizeable purchase of a host of players, including: Steed Malbranque, Teemu Tainio and Pascal Chimbonda from Spurs, El Hadji Diouf from Bolton, David Healy from Fulham plus Anton Ferdinand and George McCartney from West Ham, while Djibril Cissé had come in on loan from Liverpool. Ironically, the undisclosed fee paid to the Hammers to bring McCartney back to the club meant that the record fee for a product of the Sunderland youth system had been paid by … Sunderland!

It was not just in the playing squad that new faces were arriving. With the previously buoyant Irish economy now struggling, chairman Quinn sought new investment. In September 2008 Ellis Short was revealed to have taken a reported 30 per cent stake in the club, thereby becoming the majority shareholder. An American billionaire with Irish roots, Short became very enthusiastic about the club, got very excited when the team won and seemingly upset when they lost. Apparently, he was unhappy about the amount of time the manager did – or did not – spend at the club.

I interviewed Keane ahead of every home game for his programme notes. It's probable that I did more one-on-one interviews with him than anyone ever has. He was good to work with, punctual and polite, though he would fix you with a steely glare and challenge you to maintain direct eye contact – which I did. Apart from discovering a shared love of Bob Dylan, I came to realise that Keane was fascinated by Brian Clough, who had been his first manager in English football at Nottingham Forest. Knowing Clough's managerial mentor had been Alan Brown, Keane sometimes asked me what 'the Brown Bomber' had been like. I hadn't known Brown personally, I was a young supporter when he was in charge, but I had come to know many of his players well, so I was able to offer some background.

Keane's approach to management took some leaves out of Clough's playbook. At the beginning of the week (unless there was a midweek game) the manager often would not spend much time at the training ground. He would insist he was still doing the job via the phone and watching games. Training would be left to his lieutenants, chiefly Tony Loughlan, who had been an apprentice at Forest when Keane was there. Loughlan had been plucked from looking after young teams at Leicester City's academy to come and be first-team coach. Keane would arrive in the lead-up to the game, seeing that as a way of pepping up the players as they looked to peak for the week on matchday.

Short had upped his initial 30 per cent stake in the club to 100 per cent by the end of the 2008–09 season, buying up the shares of supporters with tiny holdings in the process. The first person to be accurately described as the club's 'owner', as he possessed all of the club, the American apparently didn't appreciate his employee Keane not being seen to put in the hours, and with results not yet matching the transfer investment, a parting of the ways became inevitable.

Sunderland did reach an FA Cup final in 2009 – the FA Women's Cup final. After beating Chelsea in the semi-final at the Stadium of Light, captained by Steph Bannon, they lost 2–1 in the final to Arsenal at Derby County's Pride Park. The origins of the women's team can be traced to 1989, when they were a five-a-side team called the Kestrels. After several name changes and a progression to eleven a side, they became part of Sunderland AFC in 2001. Rather like the men's team they developed a reputation for producing home-grown talent. By 2020 eight of the England women's team had played for Sunderland, including Jill Scott, Steph Houghton, Beth Mead and Lucy Bronze, with Bronze playing in the 2023 FIFA Women's World Cup final and being named in the Ballon d'Or Féminin top ten on three occasions (as of 2023). Some of those top players left to further their careers after Sunderland were controversially rejected from attempts to join the inaugural FA Women's Super League in 2010. Despite having just finished fourth in the National Premier Division a year after being cup-finalists, the women's team were rejected on commercial and marketing grounds rather than sporting achievements. Nonetheless, Sunderland's women's side went on to win the FA Women's Premier League Cup in 2012. In 2022 they changed their name from Sunderland Ladies to Sunderland Women.

Had Keane stayed maybe the men's team would have fallen away and continued to struggle. Maybe they would have come good, as they did the previous season. Undoubtedly Roy Keane was box-office material. Had he stayed longer, the potential for him and Sunderland to succeed was enormous.

With Keane gone in December 2008, Quinn replaced him internally with Ricky Sbragia. The Scot was in his second spell at the club. A highly regarded youth coach during the 1990s, Sbragia had been brought back after working at Manchester United and Bolton Wanderers. Always seeing himself as a coach rather than a manager, Sbragia was in stark contrast to Keane in terms of his persona. Beginning at Old Trafford, where Manchester United had dropped just two points all season, Sbragia tightened the defence and was unlucky to lose 1–0 to a last-minute goal from defender Nemanja Vidić. Following that up with 4–0 and 4–1 wins, Sbragia's new-manager bounce bumped the team up the table, but there would be just three more league wins all season. In the final analysis Sunderland narrowly stayed up despite taking only a single point from their last five fixtures. On the final afternoon, a home defeat to Chelsea was played in a surreal atmosphere, as news from elsewhere made it apparent that not only were Sunderland staying up, but they would be the region's only Premier League members, as both Middlesbrough and Newcastle were going down, along with West Bromwich Albion. Moments after the final whistle of the campaign Sbragia stood down, having fulfilled his brief to keep Sunderland up.

For the third time in a row the new manager was a former Manchester United man. This time it was Steve Bruce, who initially brushed off murmurings about his background as a Newcastle United supporter by looking out of the windows at Black Cat House towards the statue of former Magpie Bob Stokoe, pointing out that Stokoe had become a hero in red and white, and that he (Bruce) relished the challenge.

Backed by Short's money and Quinn's support, Bruce had the same willingness to think big as Keane had shown. He worked hard to secure the record signing of Darren Bent from Spurs and also brought in Teessider Lee Cattermole, who had played for him at Wigan Athletic. Bruce partnered Cattermole in midfield with Albania captain Lorik Cana, acquired from Olympique Marseille, while future England striker Fraizer Campbell was also bought from Manchester United.

Bent was a revelation. Only Kevin Phillips in his European Golden Shoe-winning season has ever scored more Premier League goals for Sunderland in a single campaign than the 24 Bent bundled in during 2009–10. Bent rarely seemed to catch shots perfectly, often appearing to scuff them, but it didn't stop him scoring. Perhaps it was his unique ability? During his second season, a goal for England against Switzerland in Basel made Bent the first Sunderland player to score for England since Len Shackleton in 1954.

Bent's goals helped Sunderland get off to a really good start in Bruce's opening season. Cana and Cattermole were a ruggedly effective midfield base until Cattermole was injured in a 1–0 home win over Liverpool where Bent netted with the help of a deflection off an errant beachball! From mid-August until late November, Sunderland commanded a place in the top eight. Another Bent winner against Arsenal in November had fans looking up for the first time since the golden days of Peter Reid, only for a mid-season slump of fourteen league games without a win to temper optimism. Due to the good start the team were still no lower than fourteenth at the culmination of this run, which was emphatically ended by a Bent hat-trick in a 4–0 victory over Bolton. A final position of thirteenth, a cool fourteen points clear of relegation, augured well for further progress under Bruce.

Only Didier Drogba and Wayne Rooney, of Chelsea and Manchester United respectively (the top two sides by a long way that season), outscored Bent, who had firmly established himself as Sunderland's main man in a squad that had been further strengthened by the arrival of towering centre-back Michael Turner and the vastly experienced Dutch midfielder Bolo Zenden.

That strengthening looked to be building when, during the summer of 2010, Cristian Riveros became the first current Sunderland player to score at the World Cup finals. Paraguay midfielder Riveros had not actually played for Sunderland yet, but his signing had been announced before he found the back of the net against Slovakia in South Africa. What's more, the assist for Riveros' goal came from Paulo da Silva, who was already with Sunderland.

With Ghana World Cup star Asamoah Gyan among a host of other red and white recruits, Ellis Short's continued investment in the playing staff meant that optimism abounded for the

2010–11 season. Riveros' only goal for Sunderland would be on his fifth and final league start. It came on the last day of the season, when a 3–0 win over bottom-of-the-pile West Ham gave Sunderland a top-ten finish, as they inched into the top half of the table on goal difference.

The season had started well, despite the unexpected departure of captain Cana. At Christmas Sunderland were sixth and along with leaders Manchester United the only club unbeaten at home. There had been a shock 5–1 defeat at Newcastle soon followed by a superb 3–0 win at Chelsea, with the team mostly looking pretty solid. Sunderland were still sixth when Newcastle came to the Stadium of Light in January.

Bent was strangely subdued in the derby, in which Gyan grabbed a last-minute equaliser to deny Newcastle a season double and keep Sunderland in a healthy sixth place. Only two days on from the game, Bent was sold to Aston Villa, where he never found the same form as in the North East. Although a brace from Kieran Richardson provided a win at Blackpool next time out, a horrendous run of just one point accrued from the next nine outings replaced the chase for a European spot (Sunderland had been one point off a Champions League place after the win at Blackpool, albeit having played more games than their rivals) with the awkwardness of looking over their shoulder at the relegation zone. After a 2–0 defeat at Birmingham City – where the goals came from Seb Larsson and Craig Gardner, both of whom Sunderland would sign in the summer – the Lads had tumbled to fifteenth place, just five points off the drop with five games to go and the team in freefall.

Jordan Henderson would go on to become one of the most decorated Sunderland-born players, being awarded an MBE in 2021. The midfielder missed just one league match all season – being an unused sub in the penultimate game of the long winless run. He had made his England debut during the season and popped up with his only brace for the club, in an important 4–2 win over Bruce's old club Wigan, to kickstart a run of three wins from those last five games and ultimately a place just inside the top half of the table. Henderson was just a few days short of his twenty-first birthday when he was sold to Liverpool for £16 million; he was one of half-a-dozen players to depart after the final fixture.

Despite the long, worryingly bad run in the spring, Sunderland looked to regroup over the summer. Funded by Short, the signings kept coming, the aforementioned duo from Birmingham City being joined by experienced Manchester United pair John O'Shea and Wes Brown, along with £8 million wonderboy Connor Wickham from Ipswich, midfielder David Vaughan from Blackpool and Ji-Dong-won, a forward from South Korea, plus Nicklas Bendtner, an Arsenal striker who soon arrived on a season-long loan.

Larsson lashed home a superb volley at Anfield to earn a terrific point on the opening day against a Liverpool side for whom Henderson was debuting, but it was not a sign of things to come. After eight league games Sunderland were above the bottom three only on goal difference. Asamoah Gyan had left to go to Al Ain in the United Arab Emirates (initially on loan) after the European transfer window was closed, while defender Titus Bramble had a sexual-assault allegation hanging over him. Bramble was later found not guilty by a jury, but the case gave great concern to the good name of the club at the time, and of course concern for the woman involved. There had been a previous example of players involved in a sex scandal in 2006, when the quartet of Liam Lawrence, Ben Alnwick, Chris Brown and Martin Woods were reported to be involved. Sadly, there would be worse to come in the future.

On the pitch in 2011 results continued to be poor. By the end of November, Bruce was under serious pressure as he looked to gain three points from the visit of bottom-of-the-table Wigan. At that stage of the season a draw would have been a disappointing but not disastrous result, but a draw was no good for Steve. His side had taken an early lead but been pegged back by a penalty from future Sunderland midfielder Jordi Gómez. Looking for all three points, Bruce took defenders off to bring on more attack-minded players, only to come unstuck when the normally reliable

Brown made a last-minute error that resulted in a calamitous winner by the visitors' Franco Di Santo. Torrents of abuse rained down on the Sunderland manager, worse than anything since the McMenemy days.

Bruce did not deserve that. He has subsequently annoyed some supporters with comments about people not giving him a chance because he was of black and white stock, but while manager of Sunderland he was totally committed to the red and white cause. I worked with him and know that to be true. On the worst of days, when he took Sunderland to St James' for what proved to be a horrible 5–1 loss, he chose to turn up in a Sunderland tracksuit rather than a suit and tie. As things went from bad to worse, he steadfastly stayed in his technical area facing the music, rather than retreating to the dug-out as other managers have done when the heat has become too much.

On the Monday morning after the Wigan defeat he asked me, 'Rob, you've been here a long time, what do I have to do?' Meaning what did he have to do to begin getting the fans back onside. 'Keep your head down, say nothing and win a game,' I advised him. But Bruce never got that chance. He was sacked two days later.

The following Sunday, Bruce's right-hand man Eric Black took charge of a defeat at Wolves. The new manager, Martin O'Neill, was already in the stands and came down to the dressing room to address the players. The personnel in the boardroom were also changing. The largely Irish investors of the Drumaville Consortium had been replaced by Ellis Short, but Niall Quinn was still there, although he was no longer chairman. Short had taken on that role three days before his fifty-first birthday in early October. Bruce had lasted six games before Chairman Short pulled the trigger. Having relinquished the role as chairman, Quinn had taken on the mantle of director of international development. Sunderland were pushing hard to maximise their brand globally, as they looked to build on what by now was a fifth successive season in the Premier League. Shortly after the beginning of 2011, Quinn had installed the MP for South Shields and former foreign secretary David Miliband as non-executive vice chairman, Quinn stating at the time:

> Adding David to our board in a non-executive capacity provides us with someone who possesses a different spectrum in envisaging how the club can grow. As a former Secretary of State for Foreign and Commonwealth Affairs, with worldwide knowledge and links, he can also help us become better known around the world as we look to grow and develop the club on an international stage.

Martin O'Neill was the new man in charge following Bruce and Black's departure. Quinn had tried to attract the boyhood Sunderland fan when the Drumaville Consortium took over. A charismatic manager who had enjoyed terrific success at numerous clubs, including Leicester City and Celtic, O'Neill had been an outstanding midfielder during Brian Clough's European success with Nottingham Forest. O'Neill transformed Sunderland. Twenty-two points from the first ten Premier League games started what was known as the 'Party with Marty'.

There was also an FA Cup win at Peterborough United, where his lieutenant from his previous managerial positions, John Robertson, turned up to spark interest that Robertson might be about to complete O'Neill's backroom team, which included goalkeeping coach Seamus McDonagh – a goalie who had once claimed that the goals at Grimsby were different sizes when he was on loan at Sunderland during Lawrie McMenemy's time in charge.

Robertson never linked up with O'Neill at Sunderland, and it would be another partner that O'Neill would come to miss most. Cup progress continued as the quarter-finals were reached, but three days after a draw at Everton, with Sunderland eighth in the Premier League, Niall Quinn announced his departure. It was midway through the sixth season since the former centre-forward had come back to the club that had got under his skin. Niall had arrived as Sunderland slumped out of the Premier

League with a record low number of points and a disillusioned crowd. Knowing when to get off the stage, Quinn left the club in the upper reaches of the top flight and with an FA Cup quarter-final replay to look forward to. He had revitalised the club and its connection with the fans, but the departure of such a totemic figure – even though he had not been chairman for almost five months – left a void that the club would struggle to fill.

11

SHORT CHANGED

The era of chairman Ellis Short (2011–18)
It had been hard work to replace Niall Quinn as a centre-forward. Lilian Laslandes, Tore Andre Flo and the ever-willing academy product Kevin Kyle were all tried, Kyle being the best of these, although he was never going to have Quinn's quality. If replacing Niall on the pitch had proved difficult, however, filling the void left by his departure from the board proved to be nigh on impossible. Other than a spell when Mark Blackbourne had been director of football operations under Bob Murray, largely looking after the administrative side of the game, Sunderland had not had a director of football or sporting director.

While Quinn was chairman, or at least still on the board, he was there to offer the voice of knowledge and experience, having spent a lifetime in the game and having the contacts to go with it. While Sir Tom Cowie had tried to influence Lawrie McMenemy's team selection – at one point telling him never to pick Alan Kennedy again, although McMenemy ignored him – Bob Murray always relied on the expertise of the managers he had appointed rather than trying to dictate playing matters from the boardroom. Lacking sufficient football knowledge at decision-making level, Short would go on to install a director-of-football model. His choice boiled down to the not unreasonable thinking that as managers spent vast sums of his money in the transfer market only to be sacked if he deemed them a failure, instead of the next manager coming in and demanding a whole host of expensive new players – while the last cohort sat on fat contracts and were difficult to move on – a director of football could bring in the players, then whenever the head coach was replaced the new incumbent could work with the existing playing staff. That was fine in theory but turned out to be not so good in reality when director of football Roberto De Fanti brought in a raft of players, many of whom failed to make the grade in England.

That would not happen until Short sacked Martin O'Neill, who survived for just over a year after Quinn quit. The FA Cup quarter-final replay following Quinn's exit from the club was disappointingly lost to David Moyes' Everton. Eighth in the Premier League at the time, none of the remaining eight games were won as the side slid to a final berth of thirteenth. The first of those last eight games should have been sensationally won. Three–one up with five minutes to play at eventual champions Manchester City, two late goals were conceded to turn three points into one. There was at least a historical consolation to this result. Sunderland were the only team to deny City a home win in the Premier League all season, thereby protecting Sunderland's own record – from 1891–92 – of being the only team to ever achieve a 100 per cent home record in a top-flight season.

One day short of a year after the March 2012 draw at Manchester City, Martin O'Neill was dismissed following a home defeat to Manchester United. The Red Devils had also won at Sunderland on the final day of the previous season. As the final whistle went on that occasion, Sir Alex Ferguson's side thought they were about to be proclaimed champions, only for a very late Sergio Agüero winner for Manchester City against QPR to wrestle the title away from them. In their many victories over Sunderland, United fans had felt entitled to lord it over the Wearsiders, but when Sunderland supporters reacted to the title drama with glee it went down like the heaviest of lead balloons with some of the United hierarchy – regardless of the fact that Sunderland had done more than any club to aid United's title bid by taking more points off City than anyone that season, having also beaten City at home with a sensational last-minute winner by the South Korean Ji Dong-won on New Year's Day. There was traditionally no ill feeling between Sunderland and Manchester United; in fact quite the opposite, as there had been many great and largely controversy-free meetings between the clubs over the years.

The following season, 2012–13 (O'Neill's last) local company Tombola (who were established by Phil Cronin, the son of former SAFC board member Frank Cronin) would be replaced as shirt sponsors by the words 'Invest in Africa'. This was a deal with the oil company Tullow, who had been the founding partner of the so-named initiative that sought to promote investment in the continent. Premier League data claimed that sub-Saharan Africa had over 200 million fans following the English game. Sunderland's courtship of the continent saw them subsequently have South African company Bidvest as shirt sponsors. Their UK subsidiary has a large base in Gateshead, and as well as becoming involved with the catering at the Stadium of Light, they entered into a partnership with the club's 1879 Events Management brand. South Africa, Ghana, Zambia and especially Tanzania were also targeted by the club, with a sports centre in Dar es Salaam (the JMK Youth Park – JMK being the Tanzanian president Jakaya Mrisho Kikwete) the focal point of the club's attempt to make an impact in the country. There was also a partnership with the Asante Kotoko club of Ghana struck in the summer of 2011, while Graham Robinson, SAFC's South African-born head of international football development, did extensive and impressive work on the continent.

Preparing for what he hoped would be his first full season as Sunderland manager, O'Neill wanted big signings. As was so often the case he struggled to get them for the start of the campaign. Free transfer men Carlos Cuellar and Louis Saha were the only opening-day debutants as an excellent goalless draw was achieved at Arsenal. However, by the time of the second game, a League Cup tie with Morecambe, Short had sanctioned the eight-figure purchases of Scotland international centre-forward Steven Fletcher and England international winger Adam Johnson. Fletcher hit the ground running, scoring twice on his Premier League debut and netting in each of his next three appearances.

The last of those goals by Fletcher was in the first win of the season after a run of four draws. Seven points from five games should have equated to a healthier and more confidence-building position than thirteenth, but Sunderland were playing catch-up after the opening home match of the season was postponed due to a water-logged pitch. That fixture against a Reading side who would be relegated was seen as a great opportunity to obtain an early victory. It was something that really frustrated O'Neill, who knew how important it was to create early season momentum. It was also due to be the first fixture in which away fans would be situated in their new location, having been moved from pitch-side in the South Stand to the upper section of the North Stand, then sponsored by Strongbow.

By the time of the re-arranged game with Reading in December, Sunderland were in a relegation position, having only won two of their opening fifteen Premier League matches. Reading were duly despatched 3–0 to belatedly spark that momentum, as five out of eight Premier League fixtures were won to take O'Neill's men to within a point of entering the top half of the table. However, despite the January signings of forward Danny Graham and midfielder Alfred N'Diaye, Sunderland did not win again under O'Neill after a mid-January victory at Wigan Athletic. Eight games without a win dropped Martin's men to sixteenth, only a point above the relegation zone, with the teams immediately below them having a game in hand.

Martin O'Neill was a proven manager with eighteen pieces of silverware or promotions to his name. However, his win percentage of under 32 with Sunderland was the lowest of his managerial career. Many supporters maintained that his sacking was correct because the football, as well as the results, had been disappointing in his last weeks. Others argued that sacking the manager every time the team had a bad run was a recipe for having to constantly start again in a game that tends to reward stability. Ellis Short was in the former camp, and as the owner it was his opinion that counted. A month before sacking O'Neill, Short had appointed Italian agent Roberto De Fanti as a consultant.

What came next was one of the most dramatic and controversial periods in SAFC's modern history. Short appointed Paolo Di Canio as head coach after sacking O'Neill, the Italian becoming the first man from outside Britain and Ireland to take charge of Sunderland's team (not including Terry Butcher, who was born in Singapore but whose family moved back to England while he was still a young child). Di Canio had legendary status as a player at West Ham United and had been the League Managers Association's League Two Manager of the Year when winning promotion with Swindon Town in 2012. He had left the Wiltshire club having won 54 and lost only 23 of his 95 matches in charge of the only club he had managed prior to Sunderland.

Learning of Di Canio's appointment a day before it was announced, I informed the club's head of media Louise Wanless that it would be massively controversial because Di Canio was an avowed fascist. She said she realised that, but a week later at Chelsea, after a narrow defeat in Di Canio's first match, she admitted to her Stamford Bridge counterpart that she'd had no idea how controversial the Italian's appointment would be. It also seemed to surprise some of the club's senior staff. Vice-chairman and high-profile Labour Party politician David Miliband immediately resigned, citing Di Canio's past political statements as his reason for no longer being able to work for the club. Numerous supporters similarly said they would not come to the club until Di Canio was gone, and the Durham Miners' Association (DMA) asked for the return of the symbolically significant miners' banner from Monkwearmouth Colliery, the pit on which the Stadium of Light stands. Having asked permission of the club to speak to the DMA after negotiations had ended negatively, I was able to arrange with their chairman Dave Hopper that the banner would remain at the club, having assured Mr Hopper that I felt Di Canio would not be there for long, and in any case the banner was there in honour of the many people who had worked at the pit and whose descendants were attending the Stadium of Light now and in the future.

The banner remains at the Stadium of Light now. Di Canio lasted for twelve Premier League games and one League Cup tie. There was no shortage of fireworks while he was in charge! In his second match he inspired Sunderland to a sensational 3–0 win over Newcastle at St James' Park. With his side 3–0 up Di Canio had no intention of sitting on the lead; instead, he was an animated figure in the technical area, gesticulating wildly for his team to get forward. With his suit trousers muddied due to his celebratory knee slide when his team scored, it was clear things were going to be anything but dull during his tenure – even if, like a firework, this would be short-lived.

A week later Di Canio was on the pitch at the Stadium of Light conducting an adoring crowd at the final whistle as they chorused 'Paolo Di Canio' after Stéphane Sessègnon had scored the only goal of the game as Everton were beaten. These wins over the Tynesiders and the Toffees were to be the only league victories under Di Canio. Next time out a 6–1 loss at Aston Villa was chastening for a team who went on to collect just two points from their remaining three games. While Sunderland stayed up, they finished a place lower than they had been at the point of O'Neill's dismissal.

The summer of 2013 was once again a time of renewal at Sunderland. Having initially come in as a consultant, De Fanti was appointed as director of football. During the summer an A4 sheet of paper with three or four potential signings in each position was shown to a tiny number of club insiders. When I was shown it by a director I had to admit that I had heard of only a handful of players on the list. So it was that fourteen new players came into the club, all but one of these being identified by De Fanti, the exception being Duncan Watmore from non-league Altrincham, who had come to the attention of academy manager Ged McNamee. Of De Fanti's selections, the

Italian pair Emanuele Giaccherini and Vito Mannone did well, as did another Italian, Fabio Borini, who came on loan from Liverpool. Several of the others failed to make an impression, though. Midfielder Cabral, for instance, only played twice, while defenders Valentin Roberge and Modibo Diakité likewise failed to establish themselves. While that trio had at least arrived on free transfers, a reported £6 million was spent on striker Jozy Altidore, who would score just one goal in forty-two Premier League appearances during his time at Sunderland, although he had netted over thirty times in his previous season with AZ Alkmaar in the Netherlands.

Di Canio declared himself unhappy with the recruitment. He wanted more players with experience of playing in England (Altidore had previously had an unsuccessful stint with Hull, while three other newcomers, including loanees Borini and Ki Sung-yueng, had played in England). Tom Huddlestone, the Spurs and England midfielder, who that summer moved to Hull City for a reported £5.25 million, was the man Di Canio most wanted but had to do without.

Excitement for the season built when Spurs were beaten 3–1 in a weather-affected game in Hong Kong, where Sunderland had been invited to participate in the Barclays Asia Tournament. A 1–0 defeat would be suffered in the final against Manchester City, but no one imagined that later in the season Manchester City would be the opponents in another cup final. Di Canio would be long gone by the time of that Wembley appearance, but he was in charge for the opening game of that League Cup run, when four goals in the last twelve minutes overturned a 2–0 deficit at home to League One MK Dons. That win would be Di Canio's only other victory after his early successes. With just a single point gleaned from the first five league games Di Canio was dismissed after a 3–0 defeat at West Bromwich Albion, where he was met with torrents of abuse from the visiting fans when he strode onto the pitch at the final whistle, signalling for them to keep their chins up.

Kevin Ball stepped in on a caretaker basis again, overseeing progress in the next round of the League Cup against a

Peterborough side coached by another Sunderland promotion-winning captain in Gary Breen. After losing hard-fought home games with Liverpool and Manchester United, the new permanent manager arrived in the shape of Gus Poyet, the Uruguayan who had scored Chelsea's consolation when Peter Reid's Sunderland had beaten the Blues 4–1 in 1999.

Poyet wanted to turn the team into a possession-based side and introduced an ultra-passing game. The style was not to every supporter's taste, as some admitted to being bored watching the ball go from side to side instead of forward. He had some success with it nonetheless, and he had a huge admirer in former captain Lee Cattermole (Di Canio had stripped Cattermole of the captaincy). Like Di Canio, Poyet lost his first game and beat Newcastle second time out. After being thumped 4–0 at Swansea there was delight as goals from Fletcher and Borini lifted Sunderland off the bottom of the table with a 2–1 defeat of the Magpies.

However, Sunderland would not get out of the bottom two until late January – by which time they had reached Wembley after a thrilling penalty shoot-out victory in the second leg of the semi-final away to Manchester United. The feel-good factor from that was followed by back-to-back league victories for the first time in the season, with Sunderland climbing out of the bottom three. Nonetheless, the team were back in the relegation positions by the time of the Wembley showpiece.

Vito Mannone in goal had been the hero of the shoot-out, and he played at Wembley on his birthday. At half-time it looked as if Sunderland might win. Borini had put the Lads ahead with a well-taken early goal. Shortly before half-time he had the chance to double the lead, only to be dispossessed by a magnificent tackle from Vincent Kompany. Poyet's Black Cats were purring until ten minutes into the second half, when two wonder goals within a minute from Yaya Touré and Samir Nasri turned the tables. There was a glorious late chance for Fletcher to level, but after that opportunity went begging Jesús Navas killed the tie in the last minute with a breakaway goal. The final 3–1 scoreline was harsh on the Wearsiders.

A week later there was an opportunity to secure a return to Wembley (for a semi-final) with an FA Cup quarter-final at Hull City. Four decades earlier Bob Stokoe had rested his five-man forward line at Hull ahead of a European Cup Winners' Cup tie at Sporting Lisbon. That rotation failed to work, as the games on Humberside and in Portugal were both lost. On this occasion Poyet made five changes at Steve Bruce's Tigers, bringing in a trio of Argentinians he had wanted the club to acquire in Oscar Ustari, Santiago Vergini and Ignacio Scocco. Although Ustari became the first Sunderland keeper to save a spot-kick in the FA Cup, it was to be a poor performance that ended in a 3–0 defeat. Poyet wanted to concentrate on the league after two long cup runs, but for fans the lure of reaching Wembley again meant that tamely going out of the latter stages of the competition without some of the team's best players was seen as a waste.

Sunderland's only previous League Cup final appearance in 1985 had been followed by a dismal run of results that concluded in relegation. In 2014 it looked as if history was to repeat itself. After a home goalless draw with Crystal Palace in the first league game after the pair of cup defeats, a sequence of five losses left the team in dire straits before a trip to cup conquerors Manchester City, in a fixture re-arranged after the original February date had been postponed due to high winds.

Chasing the title they would go on to secure, City had won 14 of their 15 home games, whereas Sunderland propped up the table. The Lads were seven points from safety with six fixtures to play, including difficult trips to Chelsea and Manchester United, albeit with a couple of games in hand due to their cup exertions. Poyet had already declared that his side required a miracle to stay up even before Fernandinho swept City into a second-minute lead. Sunderland, though, sprang a surprise: Giaccherini came off the bench midway through the second half to create two goals for Connor Wickham, who would prove to be Poyet's miracle worker. A hero in Manchester on his previous visit with his penalty-saving exploits at Old Trafford, Vito Mannone fumbled a shot from Samir Nasri two minutes from time. But while that cost two points, the fact that one had been taken from such a daunting fixture provided players, supporters and indeed Poyet himself with a shot of self-belief.

The next game was no easier, away to Chelsea who had not lost in 77 home league games under Jose Mourinho. As at City, Sunderland fell behind to an early goal, but once again Wickham stepped forward to find the equaliser. Midway through the second half he was replaced by Jozy Altidore. The USA international was left in no doubt as to the shift he was expected to put in, as Lee Cattermole could be heard from the centre circle yelling at Altidore to let him know that nothing less than 100 per cent was required. Rarely a hero in red and white, Altidore played his part, using his nous and experience eight minutes from time when he got across César Azpilicueta to engineer some contact, which resulted in a penalty. Chelsea old boy Borini coolly despatched the spot-kick to give the visitors a sensational three points, as Mourinho tried to restrain his assistant Rui Faria, who was sent to the stands for his protests.

Mirroring the performances of Colin West, another big, young, blond centre-forward in 1981–82, Wickham continued to rise to the challenge of rescuing Sunderland from relegation. Next time out he scored twice in a big win over Cardiff City and then created the only goal of the game for Seb Larsson at defending champions Manchester United. Securing safety with a game to spare after beating West Bromwich Albion, fans produced a banner for the head coach bearing the words 'Miracles Do Happen Gus'. The miracle may have been scuppered, however, had calls for a points deduction during the run-in been acted upon. As it was, Sunderland escaped with just a fine for fielding Ji Dong-won earlier in the campaign, despite not renewing his international clearance in time after he returned from a loan in Germany with FC Augsburg. The situation was reminiscent of the Dominic Matteo case from 1995, but the fact that it was SAFC that originally brought this latest error to the attention of the Premier League showed there had been no intent to deceive or break the rules.

The next four seasons, from 2014–15 to 2017–18, would bring frequent managerial changes and two dramatic but ultimately successful relegation battles, before the club suffered catastrophic back-to-back relegations for the first time in its history as the period under Ellis Short's ownership came to a calamitous end.

Poyet remained in his role for a year and two weeks after the 2014 League Cup final. With Lee Congerton having replaced De Fanti as sporting director, the summer of 2014 saw Sunderland bring in a raft of new faces, including two from champions Manchester City. Giant goalkeeper Costel Pantilimon had played against Sunderland at Wembley, while England international midfielder Jack Rodwell's final game for City had been against Sunderland in the 2–2 league draw. Rodwell cost a reported £10 million but would not live up to his stellar billing. Ultimately, even more was spent on Argentinian Ricky Alvarez. He arrived on loan from Inter Milan but the deal ended up causing untold damage to the club following legal disputes after he got injured.

The Alvarez affair was not the only disaster to afflict SAFC during this period. An even bigger catastrophe concerned England winger Adam Johnson, at the time one of the club's most important players. He was arrested on child sex offences on 2 March 2015 and eventually sentenced to six years imprisonment, having been found guilty of a serious sexual assault on a fifteen-year-old girl. Johnson was also stripped of his twelve England caps and ordered to pay £50,000 towards the fees of the prosecution. Two subsequent appeals were rejected. Johnson served three years in prison before being released. His career and the life of the victim were shattered, and the good name of the club seriously tarnished, not least as he had appeared in 28 games after his arrest. He scored in a draw against Liverpool at Anfield on what proved to be his final appearance almost a year after his arrest, and four days before the start of his trial in February 2016.

Poyet was sacked a fortnight after Johnson's arrest. The Uruguayan had recently seen his side suffer a home defeat by a

Queens Park Rangers side that had previously lost all eleven of its away trips in the Premier League that season. When struggling Aston Villa won 4–0 at Wearside a month later to leapfrog the Lads and leave the Black Cats just a point above the drop zone in mid-March, Short pulled the trigger, with Poyet replaced by the experienced Dutchman Dick Advocaat. He exuded self-belief and was brilliant at transferring this to others. He would invariably introduce me to people and say I was a 'magnificent writer'. I don't think I am, but the point is that he built me up and did the same with the players. People felt that bit more self-confident around him, and it showed when he kept Sunderland up. Even after a poor 4–1 home defeat by Crystal Palace early in his reign, Advocaat insisted he could keep the team up. When asked in a press conference why that was, he simply shrugged his shoulders and said with a smile, 'Because I am here.'

Just as his predecessors Di Canio and Poyet had done, Advocaat began with a defeat followed by a win over Newcastle second time out, in his case thanks to a stunning volley from Jermain Defoe, who had arrived in January 2015, a couple of months before Advocaat's arrival. Following Advocaat's 'Because I am here' comment SAFC didn't lose again until after safety was assured, and that defeat was away to champions Chelsea. The previous Wednesday night, goal-poacher Defoe summed up the grit and defensive organisation Advocaat had instilled by running his socks off to cover his full-backs as a goalless draw was achieved at third-placed Arsenal to secure safety. Interviewed on BBC television afterwards, Advocaat explained: 'The most important thing is that the players believe in you. The good thing for me is that I did something in the past so they know, so I don't talk nonsense – let's say it that way, and they know that and they picked it up.' He had got into their heads and inspired them. In contrast, in two seasons time David Moyes would declare a relegation battle after only two games.

Advocaat, who was in tears after the Arsenal result – along with his highly experienced coach Bert van Lingen – was only intended to be at Sunderland as a stop-gap until the end of the season, but he was persuaded to stay on partially as a result of supporters sending flowers to his wife as a show of appreciation. Not quite coals to Newcastle, but almost tulips to Amsterdam.

Having decided to stay, Advocaat made it crystal clear to the owner that for Sunderland to stop having their annual skirmish with the threat of the drop there needed to be a greater depth of quality in the squad. Netherlands international Jeremain Lens, who had played for Advocaat at PSV Eindhoven, arrived for a big fee, while Younes Kaboul came from Tottenham and Congerton managed a deal with well-staggered payments to acquire Fabio Borini from Liverpool. The sporting director had already pulled off one of the best deals in the club's history earlier in the year when he had facilitated a deal with Toronto FC to send Altidore to Canada and bring Defoe back to Britain. Among the other arrivals for the 2015–16 season was dominant French midfielder Yann M'Vila, on loan from Russian club Rubin Kazan, and Ola Toivonen, a Swedish international forward who had also played for Advocaat at Eindhoven.

Advocaat, though, was not content that sufficient quality had been added to the squad. He departed after just eight Premier League games, the last a match in which Lens scored an exquisite goal but was also dismissed, as Sunderland earned their third point of a season in which they were yet to win a league match.

Incredibly, for the fourth appointment in a row, the new man in charge lost his first fixture and beat Newcastle in his second. A 3–0 victory over the Magpies was the sixth win in a row in the fixture, the best sequence either team have achieved during the long local rivalry. The new man in the Sunderland hotseat was Sam Allardyce, who had made 27 appearances for the club in the early eighties, the last of these in a dramatic last-day survival victory at Anfield in 1981. 'Big Sam' exuded the same sort of self-confidence that Advocaat had, but it took him a little while to lift the team out of the bottom three. With Lee Congerton departing, Allardyce and his contacts produced a fabulous January transfer window, which brought in a group of players who eventually lifted the side to safety.

New centre-back Lamine Koné was a colossus alongside Kaboul and scored twice in a 3–0 win over Everton in the penultimate match to keep Sunderland up and condemn local rivals Newcastle United to relegation. Along with German midfielder Jan Kirchhoff and Tunisian attacking-midfielder Wahbi Khazri, Koné transformed the team, which lost just one of its final eleven games, and that to surprise champions Leicester City. After that Wednesday night match with Everton, Allardyce and Short had a long discussion, and Big Sam apparently made the same sort of points that Advocaat had a year earlier regarding the urgent need for a stronger squad. Given the success of most of Allardyce's acquisitions, the signs looked good if Big Sam was given the licence to strengthen further.

Unfortunately, that summer England performed dismally at Euro 2016, even managing to lose to Iceland – a country with a population of only 100,000 more than the city of Sunderland – and manager Roy Hodgson resigned. Just under a month later Allardyce was announced as his successor, two days after he had overseen the first friendly of the new season at Hartlepool.

Newly appointed chief executive Martin Bain moved quickly. The appointment of Big Sam to the England job had been widely expected, so just a day after his departure Bain turned up at Rotherham, where Sunderland were due to play another friendly, with new boss David Moyes in tow. I had arrangements to meet Bain in the foyer of the Millers' stadium. As he and Moyes arrived, the new manager was keen to go and have a chat with Rotherham boss Alan Stubbs before he met his new players, who were about to play their game under coaches Paul Bracewell and Robbie Stockdale. Stubbs had played for Moyes at Everton, and infamously in his short spell at Sunderland in 2005 had reportedly been seen celebrating a late winner for the Toffees at the Stadium of Light while still on Sunderland's books, shortly before he returned to Goodison Park. Moyes wanting to see Stubbs before his Sunderland players was not a good sign.

So highly regarded in his decade-plus spell in charge of Everton that he became Sir Alex Ferguson's successor at Manchester United,

Moyes had struggled at Old Trafford and in his next job in Spain with Real Sociedad. His time at Sunderland was to become even more of a struggle, not just for him, but for the supporters and the club staff. Whereas Dick Advocaat made everyone around him feel ten feet tall, backroom staff at the club largely felt they were walking on eggshells around Moyes, who was very difficult to please.

Ellis Short bankrolled Moyes' moves in the transfer market more than any Sunderland manager in history, perhaps taking heed of the comments of Allardyce and Advocaat. A record initial fee of a reported £13.6 million was spent on Gabon midfielder Didier Ndong from Lorient – in 2023 described as the worst record signing in Premier League history by *FourFourTwo* magazine – with another £8 million spent on defender Papy Djilobodji from Chelsea. A further £5.5 million went to Moyes' old club Manchester United for their fringe players Donald Love and Paddy McNair, with United also allowing winger Adnan Januzaj to come on loan. Come the January window, £7.5 million was invested in Everton duo Bryan Oviedo and Darron Gibson, while at the start of the campaign Moyes was also allowed to bring in further Everton old boys in Steven Pienaar and Victor Anichebe, as well as Portuguese goalkeeper Mika, plus on loan defenders Javier Manquillo and Jason Denayer from Atlético Madrid and Manchester City. In January Moyes also signed former Evertonian Joleon Lescott. He made two outings, one as a sub when the team were already 4–0 up on a rare day when everything went right at Crystal Palace, with his solitary start coming in a 5–1 defeat at Chelsea after relegation had been mathematically confirmed.

Moyes and Martin Bain largely balanced the books with a lot of outgoings, most notably full-back Patrick van Aanholt to Crystal Palace for a reported £14 million, while they did well to hold on to Koné, for whom Everton had offered £18 million, a sizeable fee in 2016, when £30 million represented the tenth-highest fee paid by any Premier League club in the calendar year. Unfortunately, in allowing Kaboul to leave they lost the guiding hand that had helped Koné in central defence, so despite his lucrative new contract he never hit the heights he had in earning his new deal. The other key decision in the restructuring of the squad under Moyes was the choice of bringing in Ndong instead of the previous season's loanee M'Vila. No doubt he would have commanded higher wages than Ndong, but he had proved he was an accomplished midfielder, something Ndong never did to the same level.

In addition to his many signings, Moyes started with a team that included a strong spine. There was a choice of the dependable Mannone or up and coming Jordan Pickford in goal, Koné and initially Kaboul at the heart of defence, where the manager also had the experienced and versatile John O'Shea; in central midfield there were Lee Cattermole and Jan Kirchhoff, and a top striker in Jermain Defoe. England international Defoe got fifteen Premier League goals in each of his two full seasons at the club. There can be little doubt that Moyes had a squad strong enough to compete.

After holding Borussia Dortmund in the final pre-season friendly, Sunderland were doing well on the opening day of the new campaign away to Manchester City, in what was Pep Guardiola's first match in charge. Recovering from conceding an early goal, Sunderland drew level with under twenty minutes of the game remaining thanks to Defoe. With seven minutes to go Moyes withdrew his main goal threat to try to protect the point, throwing on one of his new signings, Paddy McNair, only for the debutant to score a decisive own goal.

A week later home defeat was tasted against newly promoted Middlesbrough (it would remain the Teessiders only away win of the season). Despite the fine end to the previous campaign, the investment in the squad and the fact that in their most recent match they had gone within three minutes of holding Manchester City on their own patch, when asked after the Boro game what he would say to supporters fearing another relegation fight Moyes answered:

> Well, they would probably be right because that's where they've been every other year for the last four years, so why

would it suddenly change? I think it will be, I don't think you can hide the facts, that will be the case, yes. People will be flat because they are hoping that something is going to drastically change. It can't dramatically change, it can't.

Moyes may well have been realistic, but the message he was sending out to both the footballers and the fanbase stood in stark contrast to the effect of Dick Advocaat's 'Because I am here' statement and the successful scrap his side put up to survive. Wearside was deflated when the team's leader sounded so negative after just two games.

Just two points were taken from the first ten fixtures, inevitably meaning the team were already marooned at the bottom of the table. There was to be no discernible improvement. The club's second-longest run in the top flight ended without so much as a relegation battle, as the fight looked to have been given up long before the mathematical certainty of the drop was confirmed with four games still to play, the team finishing sixteen points adrift of safety.

Dismayed by the reported prospect of not being provided with any of the forthcoming parachute money for relegated clubs with which to invest for a promotion challenge (although apparently he had been promised money from player sales), the manager resigned. Moyes had never appeared happy to be at Sunderland.

At this time Ellis Short was said to be actively seeking to sell the club, with the CEO Martin Bain tasked with finding a buyer. As Sunderland went down, over 40 non-footballing staff lost their jobs, Bain having made it clear that this would be the case even if the team stayed up; staff had been told it was part of 'Martin's vision' for the club. That vision resulted in Sunderland finishing bottom of the Championship in the season after they had finished bottom of the Premier League. In Bain's two seasons in charge Sunderland had doubled the number of times they had finished bottom of any division since first becoming a league club in 1890.

Goalkeepers Jordan Pickford and Vito Mannone were sold during the summer. To August 2024 only four men have kept goal for England more times than Pickford. Only Albert McInroy has ever been capped as a goalkeeper by England while with Sunderland, although Johnny Mapson did play in a wartime international. Jim Montgomery was an unused substitute once, while Pickford sat on the bench three times when still with SAFC. Just 23 at the time of his sale to Everton, Pickford needed to go both for the club's bank balance and his own career. Selling Mannone as well turned out to be extremely costly. Going to Reading for a fee reported to be in the region of £2 million, he was replaced by £500,000 purchase Jason Steele and Dutchman Robbin Ruiter.

Steele conceded five goals on his Stadium of Light bow in a friendly with Celtic and never seemed to recover. He played fewer than twenty games, with Ruiter managing under thirty before returning to the Netherlands. The pair struggled so much that in the January transfer window Northern Ireland international Lee Camp was brought in on loan from Cardiff City. He was to play a dozen games but have an even more torrid time than Steele or Ruiter. For a club with a magnificent tradition of custodians – including Doig, Roose, Butler, McInroy, Thorpe, Mapson, Montgomery, Turner, Norman, Sørensen, Poom, Gordon and Pickford – to have such a shocking time with not one but three goalkeepers in the same season was hugely disappointing but also avoidable. Vito Mannone sat in the Reading team hotel adjacent to the Stadium of Light on the night before his return to Sunderland (as Reading won 3–1 in December) to tell me that he had never wanted to leave the club, but had felt pushed out. Eighty league goals were conceded in that 2017–18 campaign, the most Sunderland had ever let in in a season outside of the top flight.

By the time Camp arrived in January, Sunderland had already sacked manager Simon Grayson, who had been appointed as Moyes' replacement. With the team one place off the bottom of the table and still without a home win going into a midweek home meeting with Bolton Wanderers, the only club beneath them, Sunderland had to come from behind to take a point in a

3–3 draw. Fewer minutes had elapsed after the final whistle than there had been goals in the Halloween-night game before Martin Bain appeared in the tunnel after the horror show to sack Grayson.

Wales had reached the semi-finals of Euro 2016, so, after a couple of games under caretaker Robbie Stockdale, to appoint Chris Coleman who had led them there was a coup for Bain, who rejected suggestions of Ange Postecoglou from former Sunderland striker and Australian football expert Michael Bridges. Postecoglou was managing in Japan at the time, having previously managed Australia, including a game at the Stadium of Light against England in 2016, but because he was relatively unheard of the CEO decided not to pursue the matter. Postecoglou later went on to immense success with Celtic before taking over at Tottenham Hotspur in 2023. He joined a long list of top post-war managers Sunderland missed out on appointing, such as Don Revie, Jock Stein, Brian Clough and Bobby Robson.

Coleman conducted himself with a touch of class and was always very respectful of the club's history and potential, but try as he might he could not get a tune out of the team. He was not helped by the departure of top-scorer Lewis Grabban after just six games under the new gaffer. Grabban had scored a dozen goals in twenty games for the struggling team but was on loan from AFC Bournemouth. The deal was terminated early after he told Sunderland he no longer wished to play for the club. Grabban returned briefly to his parent club in January before swiftly going out on loan again to promotion-chasing Aston Villa, for whom he scored back at the Stadium of Light a couple of months later.

From the turn of the calendar year into 2018, Coleman's side could not escape the bottom three, spending all but one week of it in the bottom two and much of it rooted to the foot of the table. A second ever relegation to the third tier was confirmed in the third-last fixture. The nature of the denouement encapsulated the calamity of the season. At home to a Burton Albion side who would finish second bottom themselves, Sunderland led from before half-time only to concede twice in the last four minutes to lose. The scorer of the 86th minute leveller? Former SAFC striker Darren Bent with the 216th and final club goal of his career. The chaos of the campaign was further exemplified by the fact that at the final whistle, many did not seem to realise that the death knell had sounded on the season. A glance at the table suggested that Sunderland still had the slimmest of chances of avoiding the drop, but the realisation that strugglers Burton and Bolton still had to meet meant that whatever the score of that match, Sunderland could not escape the clutches of League One.

All this was being played out before the intrusive cameras filming the documentary *Sunderland 'Til I Die*. This would be released to a worldwide audience in December 2018 after a premiere at the Sunderland Empire a fortnight earlier. For years afterwards SAFC supporters would be subjected to opposition fans thinking they were being ever-so witty and original by chanting, 'We saw you crying on Netflix.' It had indeed been a time for tears. They were not just the tears of a single season, but for the running down of the club as owner Short had decided to sell.

Having one person own 100 per cent of the club had always been subject to the problem of what would happen when, like a kid who owns the ball in a childhood game, s/he decides they want to take the ball home. Once Short had reached the stage where, after throwing many millions at the club with no great success, he wanted out, Bain had been tasked with making the club financially leaner and finding a buyer. The outcome was that after back-to-back relegations – to League One, 24 months after a decade-long stay in the Premier League – the club was worth much less to potential buyers. But it was only worth much less on the balance sheet. To supporters the club was worth as much as it had ever been. Owners, managers and players come and go, but to supporters the reason the chant and the documentary title is *Sunderland 'Til I Die* is precisely because supporters have red and white blood. Loyalty is not for sale. That loyalty would be sorely tested in the coming four-year stay in League One, but never would it be better illustrated.

12

SUNDERLAND 'TIL I DIE & BEYOND

(2018–2024)

Another game had been played – a defeat at Fulham – since relegation had been confirmed, when news came that Ellis Short had finally found a buyer for the club. This was Stewart Donald, an insurance millionaire who would have to sell his current club, non-league Eastleigh. He was to take over as majority shareholder with former *Daily Telegraph* journalist Charlie Methven, an Eton- and Oxford-educated PR specialist, taking a 6 per cent stake and becoming executive director. Donald subsequently sought to bring in further investment by selling a 20 per cent stake in the club to Uruguayan businessman Juan Sartori in August 2018, leaving him with 74 per cent.

Sunderland, the club of The Team of All The Talents and once known as the Bank of England Club, were destined for the depths of League One, little over a year after enjoying the riches of a decade-long stay in the Premier League combined with a billionaire owner in Ellis Short. One of the problems was that the lower the club sank, the greater the likelihood that the new owner would be someone who would not have the funds to help restore SAFC to former glories. Donald and Methven are keen and knowledgeable football fans, but simply seemed not to have the level of resources needed for the task in hand.

Reportedly, they had previously been outbid in an attempt to take over the club which was said to be closest to their hearts, Oxford United.

The new owners curried favour with many fans by asking them to volunteer to come and replace the faded, once-red seats in the Stadium. This engaged supporters and got the work done in exchange for hot drinks and bacon sandwiches. Fans contributed over 14,000 hours' worth of labour for the club they love, with the project recognised with the Best Fan Engagement accolade at the Football Business Marketing Awards. Donald and PR guru Methven were very accessible to supporters, engaging with traditional and fan-led media, making themselves available in the pre-match fanzone and, in Donald's case, sometimes preferring to sit with supporters at away games rather than taking his place in the directors' box.

According to Sportsmail, a year later, on 23 May 2018, roughly all but £5 million of the £37 million price reportedly paid for Sunderland AFC came from the parachute money coming into the club from the Premier League to help it acclimatise to life outside of the world's richest association football league. The arrangement broke no laws or regulations. To his credit Short had written off around £150 million of club debt. Sportsmail reported: 'According to evidence seen by Sportsmail, allied with a forensic examination of published accounts at Companies House, Donald committed only £5m in the form of a loan. The remaining part of the deal – just shy of £32m – was covered with parachute payment cash.'

In discussion with Sportsmail, Methven accepted that money had not been paid to Short directly, but to Security Benefit Corporation (SBC) in the USA, explaining that this was to 'pay off the last bit of the debt he hadn't paid off'. This money went through Madrox Partners Limited, a new company used by Donald and Methven. Sportsmail further reported that only £24.5 million of the first £56.5 million of parachute money had gone into the working capital of the club. Unsurprisingly, at this point, what was left of the club's behind-the-scenes staff were struggling to cope with the demands placed on them. In addition to redundancies, staff were regularly choosing to leave.

Sunderland had suffered terribly financially during the First World War when the former captain of the club's first ever title winners in 1892, John Auld, had been among those to provide financial guarantees to help the club survive. Similarly, Bob Murray had bailed out the club financially when taking over from Tom Cowie in the mid-eighties. Now, in 2018, the possibility of SAFC going into administration was severe. According to Sportsmail, Short had threatened to pull the plug on the club with the English Football League if the sale to Donald was not given the go-ahead.

As Short sold up, the manager paid the price for relegation. Short's last act was to sack Chris Coleman: news of his departure came just fifteen minutes before the announcement of the Donald and Methven takeover. They insisted they had nothing to do with any decision made before they took charge, but that stretched credulity for some supporters. For the fourth time Robbie Stockdale stepped in as caretaker-manager. Giving debuts to a trio of youngsters on the final day of the 2017–18 campaign, Sunderland produced an unlikely 3–0 win over Wolves, who were already champions but were surprisingly disinterested for a side who needed just a point to register 100 for the season. One of the debutants was Bali Mumba, who came on with three minutes to go and took the armband from skipper John O'Shea, one of seven players to make their final appearance that afternoon. At the age of 16 years and 210 days at the time, Mumba became Sunderland's fourth-youngest player (after Derek Forster, Jimmy Hamilton and Cec Irwin), and technically the youngest ever captain – joking afterwards in the dressing room that he would soon be handing out fines!

With a second successive relegation to cope with, the club were eager to get the remaining high earners off the payroll. That made financial sense. It also largely made footballing sense, as those players had been part of a failing team, although there were some honourable exceptions whose commitment could not be faulted, such as Lee Cattermole, George Honeyman, Lynden Gooch, O'Shea and Paddy McNair. However, with the new owners needing every penny they could muster, Mumba later became part of a generation of talent who were sold as youngsters rather than being developed at Sunderland and becoming more valuable assets either to the team or the balance sheet.

During Donald's reign, Mumba to Norwich for a reported £350,000, striker Joe Hugill to Manchester United for a rumoured £275,000, England under-16 cap Logan Pye also to Manchester United, Luca Stephenson, James McConnell and Luke Hewitson to Liverpool and Sam Greenwood to Arsenal were among a cohort of potential future stars sold off from the ever-productive academy – Greenwood being sold by the Gunners to Leeds for £3 million in 2020. A boyhood fan of the club, he came back to haunt Sunderland on his first return when on loan to Middlesbrough in October 2023, scoring the opening goal as the Teessiders recorded their biggest-ever victory on Wearside.

In May 2018, Donald appointed former Hartlepool player and recently successful St Mirren manager Jack Ross as the man to take the team forward. In troubled times Ross was a noble figurehead to lead the club. He was deservedly popular behind the scenes and made sure things were done properly. Sensing that some clubs might see Sunderland in League One as 'Billy Bigboots', he would, for example, ensure that the players left away changing rooms neat and tidy, in contrast to the total mess teams often leave them in. His team were neat and tidy on the pitch too.

Six players, including future skipper Luke O'Nien, made their debuts on the opening day of the season, with seven more following in the next seven games as the squad was reshaped. Only 3 of the first 44 league games were lost, but there were far too many draws (19) for the liking of lots of fans. In the final analysis, after losing the last two league matches when realistic hopes of an automatic spot were dashed, Sunderland reached the play-offs, in which they edged a two-legged tie with Portsmouth courtesy of a spectacular volley from ex-Pompey man Chris Maguire. They had already been to Wembley a few weeks earlier when Portsmouth had been the victors on penalties in the final of the English Football League (EFL) Trophy. The play-off final proved to be a horrible case of déjà vu. Opponents Charlton had memorably beaten Sunderland on penalties in the second-tier play-off final in 1998, and while they didn't need spot kicks in 2019 they still broke Sunderland hearts with a winning goal deep into added time, after the Lads had been gifted an early lead by a ridiculous own goal from Naby Sarr.

The turning point in the season had come in the January transfer window. Young striker Josh Maja had plundered 15 goals in 24 league appearances but was sold to Bordeaux, a club apparently still owed money over the deal put in place when Wahbi Khazri moved in the opposite direction in 2016. Under the ever-watchful gaze of the *Sunderland 'Til I Die* cameras, Donald splurged £3 million on Will Grigg from Wigan Athletic, despite Ross saying not to pay more than £1 million for him. Had Grigg lived up to his terrace chant and been on fire, notching the goals to take Sunderland back up to the Championship, then he and Donald would have been heroes. Unfortunately for all concerned, Grigg's goals did not replace Maja's. That season there were just four in eighteen league appearances, one of those a penalty.

Ross got the bullet with under a third of the following 2019–20 season gone and his team in sixth place after a loss at Lincoln City. The seven new players he had given debuts to at the start of the season had barely had time to bed in. Sunderland had picked up nineteen points from the opening eleven games (and won away to two Premier League sides in the League Cup), but Donald had set Sunderland a hundred-point target after losing the play-off final. This was fifteen points more than they had managed in his first season in control, and a figure only five clubs had so far reached in this division in the history of the Football League.

After an EFL Trophy match against Grimsby Town, where Grigg grabbed the winner in the only match with Ross's assistant

James Fowler in temporary charge, Sunderland's owners took the decision to appoint Phil Parkinson as manager. Grigg scored again in Parkinson's first home game as Tranmere were trounced 5–0, but by Boxing Day the club had slumped to its lowest-ever position of fifteenth in League One. One of the game's truest giants languishing as the 59th-placed club of the 92: many asked themselves how it had come to this, although over 33,000 loyal souls were there to witness a goalless draw at home to Bolton Wanderers, themselves a once-great club now bottom of the division, but able to keep a clean sheet at Sunderland despite having conceded 27 goals in their 8 previous away league games. Chants of 'We Want Parky Out' reverberated around the Stadium of Light. Parkinson had gone nine games without a victory, his only two wins in fourteen games since taking over coming against strugglers Tranmere and Southend.

Three days later Lynden Gooch lit the blue touchpaper of recovery with a fine strike in a much-improved performance and victory at Doncaster Rovers. By the end of February Sunderland were fourth, just three points off the top with eleven to play. A narrow defeat to an early goal away to promotion-chasing Coventry was followed by a home draw with Gillingham, in which former SAFC academy product Mikael Mandron scored twice for the Gills, one an injury-time equaliser. When this was followed by a poor 2–0 midweek defeat at Bristol Rovers, who had only won once since Christmas, Sunderland dropped out of the play-off places. It was a disastrous time to take just a single point from three games. As COVID-19 struck and the league was initially suspended and subsequently ended, Sunderland were seventh, outside the play-off places on goal difference, a point behind third place and just three adrift of an automatic promotion spot, albeit other teams had games in hand. With eight games to go, six of them against sides placed twelfth or lower, hopes were high that the Lads were capable of escaping from League One.

However, not another ball would be kicked by Sunderland that season. After much prevarication, a points per game solution was settled on by the Football League as they tried to adapt to the COVID nightmare. After no football for a couple of months, on 15 May it was announced that the seasons of League One and Two clubs would not be completed. Lower levels of football had already ceased. Just over a month later, on 17 June, it was revealed that league positions in Leagues One and Two were to be decided on a points per game basis, with League One and Two play-offs to take place in July. In the Premier League and Championship, football was suspended until mid-June before the seasons were completed, but with no supporters allowed to attend and extensive restrictions on officials and media presence.

Not wanting to be turkeys voting for Christmas, a majority of clubs in Leagues One and Two elected to do what was best for them, Coventry City and Rotherham United securing themselves automatic promotion places without the worry of late-season nerves as they approached the finishing line. Peterborough had the same number of points as Sunderland but also missed out, while Wycombe Wanderers benefited from early season form by being elevated into sixth place, despite having lost over half of their previous fourteen league games – including 4–0 defeats against both Sunderland and Peterborough. Wycombe took full advantage of their good fortune, winning promotion when the play-offs resumed after a four-month gap as the world suffered horribly from the global pandemic.

Parkinson was given an unlucky thirteen league games in the following season before he was sacked with his side seventh. At the time they were capable of going third if they won their game in hand, which would see them two points behind Peterborough in the second automatic promotion place. Before Parky was dismissed thirteen goals had been scored in two games of the EFL Trophy. This included an 8–1 win over Aston Villa under-21s. It was the first time Sunderland had scored eight goals since 1956, but being in a competition where the first team were pitted against the under-21 sides of Premier League clubs illustrated how piteously far Sunderland had fallen.

Caretaker-manager Andrew Taylor took control of a night game with Burton Albion before Lee Johnson became the latest man to take on the task of winning promotion. Ninth after losing his opening game just a matter of hours after taking over, Sunderland soon went on a run of seventeen league games with just a single defeat. By the end of this sequence Johnson had also secured a trophy, as Sunderland ended a near half-century wait for a win at Wembley, having failed to win on any of their last eight visits. After the last two of those – the penalty shoot-out and injury-time losses of 2019 – fans had agonised, 'Why is it never us?' When it was finally Sunderland's turn to win at Wembley, those supporters had to watch on TV while Tranmere Rovers were defeated in front of an empty stadium, COVID still keeping grounds empty as Sunderland won the EFL Trophy. It was a cup for clubs in the third and fourth tiers, a competition a club of Sunderland's stature should never have been in and hopefully won't ever be again after winning promotion a year later.

Lynden Gooch became the first player since Ian Porterfield to score a Wembley winner for the Lads. The American international confidently put away a chance created by the mercurial Aidan McGeady. A wonderfully gifted individual, McGeady had been brought back into the fold by Johnson after Parkinson had sidelined the Republic of Ireland international and banished him to a loan at Charlton Athletic the previous season. A month before his superb through-ball to Gooch at Wembley, McGeady had laid four goals on a plate for Charlie Wyke in a game against Doncaster Rovers in which Lee Burge became the first man to save two penalties for Sunderland in a game (excluding shoot-outs) at the Stadium of Light.

After the Wembley win Johnson's team remained third in the table until the last couple of weeks, when they slipped to fourth. Having beaten Lincoln City on penalties in the semi-final of the EFL Trophy, Sunderland had to endure the Imps gaining their revenge over two legs of the play-off semi-finals, these games being the first fixtures fans were allowed into after COVID, albeit in severely limited numbers.

Despite a Wembley trophy, 2020–21 was yet another season of disappointment, but the biggest result had arrived just under a month before the Wembley win. Twenty-four hours after the cup final place was secured, 18 February saw the club receive approval from the EFL for Kyril Louis-Dreyfus to acquire a controlling interest in the club. This followed a Christmas Eve announcement that Louis-Dreyfus had reached an agreement to buy Donald's controlling interest in the club.

The Swiss-born 24-year-old Frenchman took over from Stewart Donald as chairman with immediate effect. Donald, Charlie Methven and Juan Sartori each retained a minority shareholding. 'I am proud to become a custodian of this esteemed institution,' said Dreyfus via a press release, 'but I also recognise the significant responsibility that comes with it. Today marks the start of an exciting new chapter in Sunderland AFC's history and although the current landscape facing football dictates that there are challenges to overcome, I am confident that together we can weather the present storm and put solid foundations in place to bring sustainable and long-term success to the club.'

At the time most fans assumed that the new owner had purchased a majority stake, but in February 2022 it was revealed that Louis-Dreyfus had acquired 41 per cent of the club, a figure which made him the single largest shareholder rather than majority shareholder. Amid some supporter consternation that they had been misled regarding the nature of the takeover, it was explained that Louis-Dreyfus had 'executive control' and 'all major strategic decisions' were made by the board, which no longer included Donald or Methven. At this point Donald still owned 34 per cent, with Methven hanging on to 5 per cent while Sartori had 20 per cent, with Louis Dreyfus having bought 40 per cent of the club's shares from Donald and a further 1 per cent from Methven.

Over the following fifteen months shares continued to shift as Louis-Dreyfus demonstrated his commitment to the club by buying more of it up. Methven sold his remaining shares in

June 2022 as Donald diluted his holding to 19 per cent, with the chairman's portion rising to a significant 51 per cent, while Sartori increased his segment to 30 per cent. The following March, Donald sold a further 7 per cent to Louis-Dreyfus and another 3 per cent to Sartori. Two months later Donald closed his stake in SAFC altogether by selling his remaining 9 per cent so that the ownership of the club was split between Louis-Dreyfus' 64 per cent and Sartori's 36 per cent.

The club's fortunes took a turn for the better once Louis-Dreyfus took over. A trophy at Wembley within a month was followed by an even more important Wembley victory the following year, when promotion was finally achieved. After this the team exceeded all immediate expectations by reaching the play-offs in the Championship at the first time of asking, all while playing increasingly attractive football.

Nonetheless, regular managerial changes continued to be the norm at Sunderland. Lee Johnson did not survive to take the club to promotion. His side topped the table early in his second season and ended the calendar year of 2021 as leaders after a 5–0 demolition of Sheffield Wednesday. Nonetheless, there were a couple of iffy results, highlighted by the discarded Chris Maguire returning to score all three goals in a win for Lincoln City. In so doing Maguire became the first player to score hat-tricks both for and against Sunderland at the Stadium of Light, and he marked his first strike of the evening by fiercely celebrating directly in front of his ex-manager. As January ended, some 6,000 followed Sunderland to Bolton, where three points would return the Lads to the top of the table. A shock was in store, as Wanderers ran riot, stunningly winning 6–0 with Johnson sacked in the aftermath.

Amid strong rumours that Roy Keane might return as manager, coaches Mike Dodds and Michael Proctor oversaw a couple of defeats before Alex Neil was unveiled as the new man in charge. As head coach, Neil was meticulous in his preparation, looking in detail at the strengths and weaknesses of the opposition as he formulated his gameplan. After taking just one point from his first two matches, Neil oversaw a thirteen-game unbeaten run to the end of the regular season as Sunderland qualified for the play-offs for the third time in four seasons, the exception being the COVID-hit points-per-game campaign.

Sunderland had been bridesmaids too often in these play-offs. Having beaten Sheffield Wednesday 5–0 at home in the regular season, Sunderland were only able to beat the Owls 1–0 at home in the first leg of the semi-final. This left the visitors very confident that they would progress to Wembley at Sunderland's expense, due to their excellent home record which had seen them defeat Sunderland 3–0 when Johnson was still in charge. With Jack Clarke – on loan from Tottenham Hotspur – having an outstanding game, Sunderland looked like holding on to their lead, only for Lee Gregory to bring the tie level on aggregate with quarter of an hour to go.

Happy with how his team were playing, Neil refused to call on his substitutes. He was rewarded late on when Patrick Roberts slotted home the equaliser on the night and the winner on aggregate, before the head coach finally turned to his bench in the closing minutes in order to slow the match down.

Whereas the previous year's Wembley joy had been minus the red and white hordes due to COVID restrictions, over 46,000 Sunderland supporters were able to procure tickets for the final this time. Most of them seemed to be in Trafalgar Square and Covent Garden the night before, Kyril Louis-Dreyfus and numerous former players including 1973 hero Micky Horswill among them, as the Sunderland takeover turned the West End red and white.

Despite the Wembley woes of the past, the jinx had been ended a year earlier, and this time there was an enormous amount of optimism ahead of the showdown with Wycombe Wanderers, a club who, to their credit, had punched above their weight. Wycombe were a team that many supporters felt encapsulated all that was bad about League One due to what can politely be termed gamesmanship. Any nerves were settled early on when, in the twelfth minute, Elliot Embleton became the first County Durham-born player to score for Sunderland at Wembley since Raich Carter and Bobby Gurney in the club's first appearance there in the 1937 FA Cup final. With man of the match Alex Pritchard dictating the game, Sunderland rarely looked like conceding, before the result and promotion were tied up late on when superb centre-forward Ross Stewart drilled home his 26th goal of the season. This sent swathes of supporters into a state of delirium at being able to bid a less than fond farewell to a league Sunderland were desperate to clamber out of.

As the final whistle went, the most spine-tingling rendition of 'Can't Help Falling in Love', the old Elvis Presley number that has become the club anthem (albeit commonly known as 'Wise Men Say'), provided a truly magical moment for fans who are Sunderland 'til I Die. The club's vast support were long-overdue some success. In this fourth consecutive season in League One the average gate of upwards of 31,000 was over 8,000 more than any club in the division, more than 4,000 better than anyone in the Championship, and higher than eight clubs in the Premier League.

That night at the club's promotion party Australian defender Bailey Wright led the singing of 'We Are Going Up!' He had been up and away in his first ever helicopter ride to get him to the stadium; he travelled separately from his teammates having been dreadfully sick earlier in the week. Wright was one of those players from outside the area – indeed, about as far away from Sunderland as it is possible to get – who truly understood what the club means to its supporters. Before the start of the season Lee Johnson had asked me to speak to the whole squad and coaching staff about the club and why it commanded such support. It was something Wright remembered when speaking to the *Sydney Morning Herald* at the end of the season:

> We had a historian come in pre-season and tell us why Sunderland means so much to the fans, and what the city had been through when the shipyards got closed, and the mining industry shut down. People lost their jobs, they lost

their incomes, and it was terrible for the city, but they always had their football club. When you understand that, when you play for the club, we then feel that. If we're performing [badly] they certainly let us know. But when we do ... God, did they get behind us!

Despite rumours emanating from Neil's post play-off final press conference that the head coach was less than happy with the amount of money the club might have to spend to prepare for life at a higher level, all seemed to be well between manager and chairman when they had a late-night tête-à-tête at the promotion party. However, Neil would be in charge of Sunderland for just six more competitive games after promotion!

The 2022–23 season started with defender Dan Ballard being the only debutant in Sunderland's season opener. The first goal of the campaign came from Jack Clarke, who was making his first appearance after signing permanently for the club, having previously been on loan. Visitors Coventry collected a late leveller through their Swedish hotshot Viktor Gyökeres. Replacing him for the Sky Blues in a year's time after a big-money move to Sporting Lisbon would be Everton striker Ellis Simms, a player who was on loan at Sunderland from the Toffees at the beginning of the 2022–23 season. He marked his Sunderland debut with a brace in an away win at Bristol City in the Lads' second game and followed up with another on his home debut against QPR, in a match where visitors' keeper Seny Dieng scored an injury-time equaliser as his side rescued a point having been 2–0 down with three minutes to play.

When Sunderland won at Stoke City to go fifth after five league games, the home fans booed their team off and gave plenty of stick to manager and former Newcastle United player Michael O'Neill. Neither Stoke supporters nor those of Sunderland travelling back to the North East would have expected that the next time Sunderland boss Alex Neil took charge of a game it would be as the new gaffer of the team he had just beaten.

After doing so well at Sunderland, Neil's departure to take over at Stoke was met with a mixture of astonishment and anger. There was an argument that Neil left for Stoke because in the long term he would have more opportunity to sign experienced players compared to Sunderland, whose espoused model was to bring in promising youngsters to nurture and develop. It was also commonly believed that Neil had left in order to substantially increase his own salary, something most people would do in any walk of life. Whatever the truth of the matter, a lot of supporters felt as betrayed as they would if their partner cheated on them.

As Sunderland lost 1–0 at home to Norwich City, with Neil's assistant Martin Canning in charge before linking up with him at Stoke, Neil was pictured in the stands at Ewood Park watching Stoke beat Blackburn Rovers while still technically Sunderland's manager, although he had already said his goodbyes to the players. Neil would return later in the season and see his players become only the second visiting team to score five at the Stadium of Light as his side won 5–1. Nonetheless, when Stoke produced that surprise result in March it still left the Potters well below Sunderland, who had gone from strength to strength in his absence.

In comparison to the amount of time it took Sunderland to replace Lee Johnson with Alex Neil, the latter's replacement was quickly installed. The new head coach was Tony Mowbray, a legend with Middlesbrough who had recently left Blackburn Rovers, where he had been in charge for five years and worked alongside Sunderland's highly regarded head of player recruitment Stuart Harvey.

Soon dubbed 'Uncle Tony', Mowbray was in his late-fifties when appointed, old enough to be the grandfather, let alone uncle, of most of his players, as under the leadership of sporting director Kristjaan Speakman the average age of the team was significantly reduced. With teenagers and players in their early twenties being given more opportunities than at any time since

Alan Brown was in charge over half a century earlier, the eleven who completed an FA Cup tie at Premier League Fulham early in 2023 were the youngest side ever fielded by the club – 55 days younger per player than the youngest eleven to have started a game for the club, against Lincoln City on Boxing Day 1959. That record was smashed again the following season in a game at Southampton.

Despite a catalogue of long-term injuries that left Sunderland shorn of strikers for most of the campaign, Mowbray managed his resources cleverly to keep newly promoted Sunderland mostly in the top half of the table. At one point in mid-season they briefly fell to thirteenth, but at no point did an immediate return to the horrors of League One seem a possibility. Wigan and Rotherham, who had come up with the Lads but as automatically promoted clubs, found it a struggle, the Latics going straight back down, while had it not been for a six-point deduction to Reading, the Millers would have finished just a point above the relegation places.

Instead, Sunderland with Jack Clarke, Patrick Roberts and the wonderfully talented on-loan Manchester United man Amad Diallo producing consistently dazzling football, Sunderland kept their eyes on the top six. Qualification for the play-offs came after a thrilling 3–0 last-day win at Preston, combined with Mowbray's old club Blackburn winning a thriller at Millwall to pave the way for the Black Cats.

Paired with Luton Town in the play-offs, the first leg was won 2–1 in a febrile atmosphere. The second leg at the tight Hatters home of Kenilworth Road saw Sunderland succumb to two headers on a night when injuries caught up with the side. Long-since used to playing without a recognised centre-forward, the absence of so many defenders proved to be the team's undoing. With midfielders Patrick Roberts and Lynden Gooch at full-back and right-back, Trai Hume at centre-back alongside midfielder turned centre-back Luke O'Nien, Luton's route-one aerial bombardment paid dividends, but it had been a fabulous season of exciting progress.

'I knew Sunderland was a massive football club. Until you come through the door, you don't realise how passionate the people who follow the football club are and how much it means to their lives,' commented Mowbray afterwards. 'We hope we've given them some good days this year. Of course we need to get better, be more consistent and win more matches for them next season. It wasn't to be tonight and they'll be disappointed, of course, but I'm proud of the team, proud of the young players, proud of the supporters, proud of the city. We can only grow from this point. If we get it right in the summer, if we recruit well and if we manage to keep more players more fit next year, this squad is good enough to compete again at the top end.'

Tony Mowbray's words at the end of the 2022–23 season rang true. The former Celtic manager's comments were typical of what so many other managers, head coaches and players say once they are at Sunderland. For example, Jack Ross, one of Mowbray's predecessors in the job, noted shortly after he arrived: 'I knew it was a big club, but now that I've been down for a month I didn't appreciate how big in terms of the stadium, support, training ground, everything.'

It might still come as a surprise to some how big a club Sunderland are, but it is no surprise to anyone from the North East. The history of the club intertwined with the passion of its vast support means it remains a giant of football regardless of its relative lack of recent success, compared to its early years in the Football League.

Sunderland's best years were in Victorian times, just before both world wars, and fleetingly in 1973. That is all now ancient history, but blood cells only come in red and white and the love Sunderland supporters have for their club runs through their blood, passed down in many cases from generation to generation. If you are lucky enough to be brought up as a Sunderland supporter you know that you support the most special of clubs. It is the club of The Team of All The Talents, the club of Charlie Buchan, Raich Carter, Bobby Gurney, Len Shackleton, Charlie Hurley, Jim Montgomery, Kevin Phillips, Niall Quinn and the modern generation of exciting young footballers. Even more importantly it is the club of the supporters. No player loved the supporters more than Player of the Century Charlie Hurley. His death shortly before the end of the 2023–24 season brought an enormous outpouring of sheer love for the player always known as 'The King.' The reaction to Hurley's passing away perfectly illustrated that regardless of the ups and downs of the side on the pitch, the connection between the club and its fanbase has the deepest of roots.

Perhaps The King's final gift to his adoring public was to take the first steps in healing a disconnect that had occurred between the club and its supporters. Late at night on the Monday after a draw at Hurley's old club Millwall in December came the shock announcement that head coach Tony Mowbray and his assistant Mark Venus had left the club. Although the team were on a poor run of just two wins from nine games, at the time they sat in ninth place, just three points outside the play-off places. Although the last couple of games had brought below-par performances, mostly Sunderland were dominating games, playing attractive football but suffering from not taking chances and being vulnerable when defending set pieces, particularly corners. The inability of forwards to find the back of the net was the biggest concern. Incredibly, when Mowbray was dispensed a goal was still yet to be scored by a striker that season, the last one having been netted by the on-loan Joe Gelhardt eight months earlier. Four forwards recruited in the summer – Luis Hemir Semedo, Eliezer Mayenda, Nazariy Rusyn and on-loan Chelsea man Mason Burstow – had all been given opportunities without yet producing the goods, and by the end of a disappointing season had managed a meagre three goals between them.

Reaction to the club's decision to make a change was mixed. Some supporters were pleased about it, feeling that Mowbray had taken the team as far as he could and his habit of making multiple substitutions sometimes disrupted the fluency of his side. Less than a fortnight earlier Mowbray had celebrated his sixtieth birthday. He was born on the day John F. Kennedy was assassinated, and Tony's sudden departure hit many supporters with a similar shock to that caused by the killing of JFK – and that is not intended to make light in any way of a tragic moment in world history. For many followers of Sunderland, Tony Mowbray had produced a very youthful side who played with flair and without fear. But for injuries, particularly to Ross Stewart and a plethora of central defenders, there is every chance that he would have won promotion from the play-offs earlier in the calendar year. Whether Sunderland could have survived in the Premier League is a moot point, not least in the light of how promoted Burnley, Sheffield United and Luton Town struggled.

Having pulled the trigger on Mowbray, the club had made a bold decision. Sporting director Kristjaan Speakman stated:

> All at SAFC have thoroughly enjoyed working with Tony and he is quite rightly held in high regard by our players and staff, and our supporters. After arriving at an uncertain time, he helped guide us to the Sky Bet Championship Play-Offs and played an important role in developing our team. This was a difficult decision to make, but we remain loyal to our ambition and our strategy, and felt that now was the right moment to take this step.

The same club announcement quoted chairman Kyril Louis-Dreyfus:

> I would like to place on record my gratitude to Tony for his hard work and commitment to Sunderland, a place where he will always be welcome. As custodians of our great club, we believe in our long-term strategy that we hope will ensure sustainability and success for SAFC. Central to that approach is a relentless demand for a high performance culture to be implemented throughout the Club and the development of a strong playing identity that you, our loyal supporters, can all be proud of.

Fans wondered, would this roll of the dice fall the way they wanted and be a red and white success or might it be a step into the darkness of deterioration? As mentioned in the opening paragraph of this book, drama and intrigue are emblematic of the story of Sunderland AFC. The sudden departure of Mowbray and Venus came the day after the draw for the third round of the FA Cup paired Sunderland with rivals Newcastle United in the competition for the first time since 1956. That cup draw was enough to send the North East wild with excitement, but the changing of the head coach knocked even that story off the headlines.

At Millwall the previous Saturday, when Sunderland came back to take a point with a late penalty, Mowbray had spoken about his team's lack of threat from forwards and alluded to what he felt was his lack of control over policy: 'We don't look like scoring – I think it's because we have inexperienced strikers who aren't really ready at this moment to play for our team, but they have to play and we are playing them. We are trying to develop them and get them up to speed to be able to be a striker in the Championship.' Asked whether he might revert to the successful system he had utilised in the spring when playing without a recognised striker due to injuries, he replied:

> It's not really my decision, the club wants to develop young players and for them to be given an opportunity. That's what I do, I give them a chance. My gut inside me tells me that we need to change, because I want to win. That's the truth, I'm trying to develop young players to create value in them, give them good careers. Sometimes they're not quite ready but that's OK, they'll get game time, they'll get on the pitch to experience the Championship. I signed up for that, I bought into it. I am doing it, picking them, playing them. I'm comfortable with it but there you are at 55 minutes ... and I want to win. We still aren't having shots, so I go with players I think can turn it around. As a club we want to be bold and the young players have to be on the pitch to show they can do it, that's what we're doing.

That boldness in terms of approach to the team and the running of the club saw former Rangers manager Michael Beale appointed as head coach two weeks later, following a brief spell with Mike Dodds in temporary team control, a role he had fulfilled alongside Michael Proctor in between the departure of Lee Johnson and appointment of Alex Neil early in 2022.

Furore accompanied the unpopular appointment of Beale, the ex-Rangers manager who had endured a strained relationship with the media and supporters at Ibrox. He became the first Londoner to take charge of Sunderland. The negative reaction to Beale was soon exacerbated by supporter fury over Newcastle being given 6,000 tickets for the FA Cup tie at the Stadium of Light. This was due to competition rules, but giving over the whole of the Carling (North) Stand following consultation with the local authorities around how the match was to be policed, with many season-ticket holders being moved from their regular seats as a result, was extremely unpopular.

When news leaked out before the game that the Black Cats Bar had been redecorated with NUFC branding it was the last straw for many disillusioned fans. Former goal-scoring hero Marco Gabbiadini noted on local radio that the action was, 'Unbelievable! It's our place … it's embarrassing. This will be mentioned in 50 years' time,' while radio commentator Nick Barnes added, 'In the twenty years I've covered the football club I've never known such anger or had so many messages.' Acknowledging that 'a serious error of judgement was made in relation to the Black Cats Bar', a club statement quickly apologised to the fans as the rival signage was swiftly removed.

Beale survived for twelve games before he was sacked. Only Niall Quinn had been appointed as manager or head coach and lasted for fewer games – and chairman Quinn had removed himself to make way for Roy Keane in 2006. Beale's sixth and final defeat in his dozen games in charge ended at Birmingham City, by now managed by Tony Mowbray, while his most costly loss had been a disappointingly tame 0–3 defeat in the cup meeting with Newcastle United.

Having overseen two good wins from three games in between the departure of Mowbray and the arrival of Beale, Mike Dodds was entrusted with the role of head coach on an interim basis to the end of the season. This spell provided Dodds with one more game than Beale had been given, but this period delivered fewer wins. This run included a freak 1–5 home defeat to a Blackburn Rovers side who had gone ten games without a win, a home loss to Millwall, who had lost their previous two away trips to teams that would go down, and defeat in Watford's final home fixture after the Hornets had not won a league game at Vicarage Road since November.

While there had been some bright moments and continued development of young talent, such as sixteen-year-old Chris Rigg, overall it had been a season of anti-climax. A final position of sixteenth, having been ninth when Mowbray cleared his desk, meant that the campaign had petered out dismally. Despite having by far the highest support in the division, Sunderland lost more games on their own turf than any other team, with the only goal scored in the final six home matches coming in that 1–5 reverse to Blackburn. There had never been any realistic danger of relegation but there was a lingering feeling that so much more could have been achieved. As prices for 2024–25 were announced they were accompanied by news of notable upgrades to various aspects of the stadium and matchday experience. As welcome as these improvements were, what supporters craved most deeply was an improvement on the pitch, a return to the attractive winning football witnessed not too long ago.

That will come. Success will return to SAFC. The cyclical nature of football means that at some point the Sunderland giant will stir again and a new generation of supporters will have new names to toast and celebrate, as people in decades past have had their own heroes. The question is not if that will happen, but when.

Outside the main entrance of the Stadium of Light, the most prominent statue is not of a player, manager or chairman, but of a family: a woman, a man and two children. What makes

Sunderland so special is the people of Wearside. It is a place so often downtrodden and underrated, but a place whose people are full of pride in its heritage. There is pride in the people who once made it the biggest shipbuilding town in the world, pride in its glassmaking, pride in it being the home of the Venerable Bede, the person known as 'The Father of English History', and pride in the coal-mining traditions, not least of those who worked at Monkwearmouth Colliery, the site upon which the Stadium of Light now stands. When the Stadium of Light recreates the world-famous Roker Roar, the supporters are doing what generations of their ancestors have done before: lifting their team in red and white on to greater heights. That is truly very special indeed.

BIBLIOGRAPHY

Managers, Tales from the Red and Whites, Vol 3, Graeme Anderson, Lance Hardy, Rob Mason (Tales From, 2018)
Hotbed of Soccer, Arthur Appleton (The Sportsman's Book Club, 1961)
Sunderland and the Cup, Arthur Appleton (Frank Graham, 1973)
A Lifetime in Football, Charles Buchan (The Sportsman's Book Club, 1956)
Footballer's Progress, Raich Carter, edited by Edward Larchberry (Sporting Handbooks, 1950)
Ha'way the Lads, Edited by Christopher Carrell and Richard Padwick (Ceolfrith Press, 1974)
The Rise of The Leaguers, James Catton (The Sporting Chronicle, 1897)
This Is Your Life Harry Clark, Jonny Clark (Private family publication, 2014)
The Ballymena Boy, Norman Clarke (Self-published by Norman Clarke, 1997)
Sunderland: Building a City, Gillian Cookson (Phillimore 2010)
I Lead the Attack, Trevor Ford (Stanley Paul, 1957)
Hardaker of the League, Alan Hardaker *(Pelham, 1977)*

Gentleman George: The Autobiography of George Hardwick, George Hardwick (Juniper Publishing, 1998)

Stokoe, Sunderland and '73: The Story of the Greatest FA Cup Final Shock of All Time, Lance Hardy (Orion Books, 2009)

Big Brother, Derek Ferguson with Bill Leckie (Mainstream, 2006)

Sunderland, Industrial Giant: Recollections of Working Life, Marie Gardiner (The History Press 2017)

Association Football and the Men Who Made It, Alfred Gibson and William Pickford (Caxton Publishing, 1906)

Football's Black Pioneers: The Stories of the First Black Players to Represent the 92 League Clubs, Bill Hern and David Gleave (Conker, 2020)

The Football Grounds of England and Wales, Simon Inglis (Willow Books, 1983)

Soccer in the Dock, Simon Inglis (Willow Books 1985)

Pioneers of the North, Paul Joannou and Alan Candlish (Breedon Books, 2009)

Jimmy Thorpe, John S. Kelters (Jarrow & Hebburn Local History Society, 2016)

Shack: The Life, Times and Legacy of Len Shackleton, E.T. Laing (Penthesilea Books, 2016)

Peter Lorimer: Leeds and Scotland Hero, Peter Lorimer and Phil Rostron (Mainstream, 2005)

Sunderland's Number Ones, Rob Mason (Northdown Publishing, 1999)

Sunderland: The Complete Record, Rob Mason, Mike Gibson and Barry Jackson (Breedon Books, 2005)

Match of My Life: Sunderland, Rob Mason (Know the Score, 2006)

Sunderland. Greatest Games, Rob Mason (Know the Score 2010)

Sunderland: The Complete Record, Vol 2, Rob Mason, Mike Gibson and Barry Jackson (DB Publishing 2012)

Bibliography

SoL20: Twenty Years at the Stadium of Light, Rob Mason (Twocan 2017)
Sunderland: The Absolute Record, Rob Mason, Mike Gibson and Barry Jackson (Twocan 2020)
Sunderland: The Absolute Record, Volume Two, The Players, Rob Mason (Twocan 2022)
What If? Turning Points in the History of Sunderland AFC, Rob Mason (Pitch Publishing, 2023)
I'd Do It All Again, Sir Bob Murray (Vision Sports Publishing, 2023)
Fighting for Football: From Woolwich Arsenal to the Western Front – The Story of Football's First Rebel, George Myerson (Aurum Press, 2009)
Who Needs Cantona When We've Got ... Dickie Ord!, Andrew Smithson and Richard Ord (Twocan, 2012)
Trevor Ford: The Authorised Biography, Neil Palmer (Amberley Publishing, 2016)
The Impossible Dream, Ian Porterfield with John Gibson (AK Publications, 1973)
Tommy McInally: Celtic's Bad Bhoy?, David Potter (Black and White Publishing, 2009)
Cheer Up Peter Reid: My Autobiography, Peter Reid (Trinity Mirror Sports Media, 2017)
Sir Tom Cowie: A True Entrepreneur, Denise Robertson (University of Sunderland Press, 2004)
The Clown Prince of Soccer, Len Shackleton, Edited by David R. Jack (Nicholas Kay Ltd, 1955)
Tottenham Hotspur: The Official Illustrated History 1882–1996, Phil Soar (Hamlyn/The Book People, 1996)
Shack's Guide to Soccer, Len Shackleton, in collaboration with David R. Jack (Nicholas Kay Ltd, 1956)
Lost in France: The Remarkable Life and Death of Leigh Richmond Roose, Football's First Playboy, Spencer Vignes (Stadia, 2007)

Double International, Willie Watson (The Sportsman's Book Club, 1964)
Short Changed: The Highs and Lows of SAFC During 20 Years at the SoL, Chris Weatherspoon (ALS Publications, 2017)
Scotland's Lost Clubs, Jeff Webb (Pitch Publishing, 2021)
Football Under the Skin: A Historical Glimpse at soccer in Tyne and Wear 1879–1988, edited by Alisdair R. Wilson (Tyne and Wear Museums Service 1988)
Inverting the Pyramid, The History of Football Tactics, Jonathan Wilson (Orion, 2008)

Other sources
Athletic News Football Annual, 1896
Daily Mail (Sportsmail), 23 May 2018
Diez (Honduran newspaper), 2017
The Field, 21 March 1877
Hansard
The Independent
Newcastle Evening Chronicle
Nottingham Football Post
Brendan O'Donnell, great grandson of James Allan, family research
Sunderland AFC match programmes
Sunderland Echo and *Sports Echo*
Sunderland Herald
Yorkshire Post

The Formation of Sunderland [Rugby] FC, Keith Gregson, World Rugby Museum, 15/2/2021
Palatine97.org Freemasonry in Sunderland since 1757, Wayne Rumley
Mightyleeds.co.uk

ACKNOWLEDGEMENTS

Over the decades of writing about Sunderland I have surrounded myself with a large number of expert friends, several of whom I have co-authored books with in the past. For this volume I am especially indebted to Mike Gibson and Andrew Smithson, who have read each chapter of the book and offered me their observations, and often additional information. Increasingly, I have felt like a dodgy centre-back lucky to have both Jimmy Montgomery and Johnny Mapson behind them as they tip my mistakes over the bar. I must stress, however, that any errors which remain are entirely my own responsibility.

Barry Jackson and Niall MacSweeney have also been very generous with their time in support of this book. Barry is always a font of knowledge when it comes to quirky statistics, while his vast collection of post-war *Football Echo*s are immensely useful, as the relevant pages will always be speedily scanned and sent by Barry when I request some information from them. As a long-term member of the Association of Soccer Statisticians, Niall is my go-to person whenever I need to know something about the wider game.

I also have to thank Newcastle United's official historian and esteemed author Paul Joannou, who is invariably helpful when I get in touch about any of the many things that historically link the two great clubs of Tyne and Wear. Ferryhill historian Geoff

Wall was also a great help in looking at the very early links between Sunderland and Ferryhill.

Now chairman of the Senior Supporters' Association at Sunderland, Malcolm Bramley was once secretary to former Sunderland players Brian Clough at Derby County and Len Ashurst at Gillingham. Before that Malcolm was assistant secretary at Sunderland, having worked his way through the ranks in the early sixties. A first-hand witness to much that went on behind the scenes at Roker Park during that era, Malcolm's willingness to help has been important. This is equally true of Keith Gregson, historian at Ashbrooke, the home of rugby and cricket in Sunderland and also one of SAFC's early grounds. Keith's contribution is much appreciated, as is that of Mike Huggins, the president of the European Congress of Sports Historians, North East author Marie Gardiner, journalist James Hunter – the longest-serving journalist to cover all Sunderland games – and Brendan O'Donnell, the great grandson of club founder James Allan.

My wife Barbara has to listen to my endless phone calls with former players, managers and directors, as well as finding that my idea of a day out for her to accompany me on is, for example, to travel to Ayr to find the birthplace of Sunderland AFC founder James Allan and then trek around various Ayrshire villages exploring where Allan and some of the club's early players grew up.

My thanks are also due to my agent Melanie Michael Greer, and to Ellen Conlon, Steve Burdett and the rest of the team from Icon Books, who asked me to produce what I hope is the most thorough history of SAFC that you will find.

ABOUT THE AUTHOR

Rob Mason was born in Sunderland before the club had ever been relegated. He was first taken to Roker Park in 1966 to see games in the FA Youth Cup before he started to see the first team later that season, his first senior game being Sunderland's 7–1 win in the FA Cup against Peterborough United shortly before his ninth birthday. Since then he has seen Sunderland well over 2,000 times on over 150 grounds in 14 countries. In 1986 he began to write for the match programme and has done so ever since. During two decades of working full time at the club when editing the publication, Sunderland won more Programme of the Year awards than any other club. He has also written over 50 books on Sunderland AFC and become an honorary member of the Former Players' Association. As SAFC's official historian he set up the Blue Plaques Trail, marking all of the club's former grounds; proposed and drove the project to bestow the Freedom of the City on the 1973 FA Cup-winning team; and created the Sunderland AFC Hall of Fame.

INDEX

5th Kirkcudbright Rifle Volunteers 39

Abbs Field 37, 40
Academy of Light 238
Accrington 43, 58, 73
Adamson, Jimmy 167, 183, 185, 186
Advocaat, Dick 272-3, 274, 275, 277
Ajax 218, 220
Alcock, Charles William 12-13, 22, 53
Alcock, John Forster 12
Allan, Adam 115
Allan, James 9, 10, 11-12, 13-14, 15, 16, 18, 19, 24, 26, 27, 28, 30, 38, 41, 42, 46-7, 49, 50, 51, 52, 53-4, 55-6, 60, 101-2
Allan, Tom 100
Allardyce, Sam 189, 273-4
Alnwick, Ben 236, 257
Altidore, Jozy 267, 270, 273
Alvarez, Ricky 271
Anderson, John 18, 19
Anderson, Russell 250
Anderson, Stan 148, 150, 154
Angell, Brett 213
Anichebe, Victor 275
Arca, Julio 110, 229, 234, 242-3
Armstrong, Gordon 204
Arnott, Kevin 183, 184, 187, 188
Arsenal (Royal/Woolwich) 74, 84, 110, 112, 113-14, 122, 124, 127, 135, 137, 145, 150, 169, 174, 192, 205, 229, 255, 263, 272
Ashurst, Len 64, 142, 147-8, 152, 154, 173-4, 182, 193, 195

Ashville Ground 47
Aston Villa 58, 59, 66, 71-2, 75, 76, 77, 78-9, 83, 91, 94, 103-4, 105, 107, 109, 110, 120, 153, 181, 190, 191, 266, 272, 287
Atkins, Ian 191
Atkinson, Brian 204, 205
Auld, Johnny 68, 83, 95, 108-9, 283

Bach, Phil 87, 91
Bain, Martin 274, 275, 277, 279, 280
Ball, Kevin 203, 214, 220, 239, 267-8
Ballard, Dan 293
'Bank of England Club' 110, 132, 159
Bannon, Steph 253
Barbour, Alex 50
Bardsley, Phil 250
Barnsley 197, 247
Barrie, Alexander 106
Barron, Matthew 18
Bartley, Jack 117
Batey, Barry 194, 237
Baxter, Jim 159-60, 161, 246
Beatles, the 128-9
Bedford, Harry 111
Bell, Paddy 115
Bell, W.H. 76
Bendtner, Nicklas 257
Bennett, Gary 185, 193, 197, 203
Bent, Darren 254-5, 280
Best, Bobby 108
Bewick, Maurice 181
Bingham, Billy 136

Index

Birmingham City 119, 130–1, 139, 145–6, 189, 235, 256
Birmingham St George's 58
Birtley 37
Bishop Auckland Church Institute 44
Bishopwearmouth Mutual Improvement Association Football Club 20–1
Blackbourne, Mark 261
Blackburn Olympic 35, 44, 45
Blackburn Rovers 35, 44, 48, 57, 58–9, 66, 70–1, 74, 87, 88, 105, 117, 126, 195, 232
Black Cats nickname 30–1
Black, Eric 258
Blackpool 118, 138, 145, 256
Blue Bell (pub) 37
Blue House Field 14, 17, 27–8, 29, 37, 47
Bohemians 250
Bolton Wanderers 49, 57, 59, 66, 73, 74, 78, 105, 111, 231, 251, 255, 278–9, 286, 290
Borini, Fabio 267, 268, 270, 273
Borussia Dortmund 276
Bould, Steve 225, 229
Bowie, David 198
Bowman, Dave 236
Bowyer, Ian 189
Bracewell, Paul 192, 210, 214, 274
Bradford City 105, 197, 227, 234
Bramble, Titus 257
Bramley, Malcolm 142, 152
Brand, Ralph 159
Brand, Bob 48, 50, 54
Breconridge, John 50, 51
Breen, Gary 234, 237, 268
Brentford 149
Bridges, Michael 225, 279
Bridgett, Arthur 97, 99, 102
Brighton and Hove Albion 167, 189
Bristol City 149, 166, 182, 183–4, 293
Bristol Rovers 286
Broadis, Ivor 136
Bronze, Lucy 253
Brown, Alan 145, 147, 148, 149–50, 156, 159, 161, 162–4, 252
Brown, Chris 257
Brown, Wes 257–8
Bruce, Steve 254, 257–8
Buchan, Charlie 78, 101, 107, 109, 110, 111, 112–13, 114, 117, 129, 140
Buckley, Mick 190
Burbanks, Eddie 125, 132

Burge, Lee 288
Burnley 59, 62, 66, 74, 79, 103, 107, 145, 167, 247–8
Burnopfield 27, 28
Burns, Robert 13
Burton Albion 279–80
Bury 93, 130, 152, 244–5
Busby, Viv 200
Butcher, Terry 210, 211, 265
Butler, Joe 103
Buxton, Mick 211, 213
Byrne, John 205–6

Cabral 267
Caldwell, Steve 236, 240, 246
Calvert, James Taylor 81
Canning, Martin 294
Cambuslang 44, 48, 65
Camp, Lee 278
Campbell, Fraizer 254
Campbell, Johnny 44, 58, 62, 63, 66, 69, 71, 72, 73, 74–5, 77–8, 79, 82–3, 84
Campbell, Robert 82, 83, 86, 90, 91
Cana, Lorik 254, 255, 256
Candlish, John 11
Cardiff City 170, 186, 249, 270
Carlisle United 165–6, 179, 243
Carter, Raich 119, 120–1, 122, 123, 125–6, 126, 128, 131, 135, 292
Carter, Tim 242
Castle Eden 33, 37, 38
Castletown 38
Catalonia Select XI 122
Cattermole, Lee 254, 255, 268, 270, 276, 284
Caws, Frank 14
Celtic 66, 179, 278
centenary 187–8
Chalmers, Jimmy 87, 106
Charlton Athletic 222–3, 230, 285
Chamberlain, Alec 215
Chappel, Walter 14, 16, 18, 19, 26, 27
Charity Shield win 124, 125
Charles Buchan's Football Monthly 129
'Charlie's Angels' 184
Chatham 107
Chelsea 102–3, 123, 138, 152–3, 194, 204, 225–6, 227, 230, 254, 256, 265, 270, 272, 275
Cheltenham Town 239
Chester City 236
Chesterfield 133

Chimbonda, Pascal 251
Chisholm, Gordon 194
Chisholm, Ken 137, 144
Chopra, Michael 250
Chopwell Colliery 128
Cissé, Djibril 251
Clark, Frank 221
Clark, Lee 221, 222, 224, 225
Clarke, Jack 291, 293, 295
Clarke, Jeff 247
Clegg, Charles 96
Clough, Brian 142, 151–2, 153, 158–9, 162, 166, 190, 195, 252
Coates, John 14, 18, 26, 27, 28
Cochrane, Johnny 116, 117, 118, 119, 121, 127
Cole, Andy 250
Coleman, Chris 279, 283
Coleman, Keith 169
Coleman, 'Tim' 100
Collings, Keith 144, 152, 173
Collings, Syd 144, 158, 161
Collins, Danny 236, 240
Common, Alf 64, 96
Congerton, Lee 271, 273
Connolly, David 236, 246
Connor, Jimmy 119, 120, 126
Cook, John 53
Corinthians 48, 49, 94
Cork City 250
Corner, David 194
Coton, Tony 216
Cotterill, Steve 232–3, 247
Coventry City 183, 286, 293
COVID-19 pandemic 286–7, 288, 291
Cowan, James 137
Cowie, Tom 152, 192, 193, 195, 196–7, 237, 261, 283
Craddock, Jody 231, 233
Cresswell, Warney 110
Cringan, Billy 109
Crook Town 109
Crosby, Malcolm 204, 206, 210
Crossan, Johnny 154, 155–6
Crow, George 127, 142, 143, 158
Crystal Palace 182, 234, 269, 272, 275
Cuellar, Carlos 263
Cummins, Stan 187, 188, 189–90
Cunningham, Kenny 246

Daniel, Ray 137
Dale, Fred 96, 97
Darlington 33, 39, 41, 42, 128

Darlington St Augustine's 44
Darwen 67, 71
da Silva, Paulo 255
Davenport, Peter 203, 206
Davis, Bert 119
Davis, Dicky 135, 136
Davis, Kelvin 239–40
Davison, Arnie 44, 50
De Fanti, Roberto 262, 265, 266, 271
Defoe, Jermain 272, 273, 276
Denayer, Jason 275
Derby County 66, 74, 77, 120, 131, 132, 135, 179–80, 211, 227, 231, 246
Derby Junction 45
Diakité, Modibo 267
Diallo, Amad 295
Di Canio, Paolo 265–6, 267, 268
Dibble, Andy 195–6
Dillon, John 151
Diouf, El Hadji 251
Ditchburn, Bill 142, 143–4
Ditchburn, Jack 143–4
Djilobodji, Papy 275
Docherty, Mick 189
Dodds, Mike 290
Doig, Ted (Ned) 64–5, 66, 69, 80, 86–7, 88, 93, 95, 213
Dolly Field 30, 31, 32
Donald, Stewart 281–2, 283, 284, 285, 289–90
Doncaster Rovers 286, 288
Dove, Peter 18
Doxford, Theodore 97
Drewry, Arthur 142
Druids 49
Drumaville Consortium 241, 242, 246, 247, 258, 259
Dundee 136
Dunlop, Billy 78
Dunn, Joshua 31
Duns, Len 130, 133
Durban, Alan 190, 191, 192–3
Durham Challenge Cup wins 32, 33–4, 42, 44, 47, 82
Durham Miners' Association (DMA) 265–6
Dyke, Greg 208

Eden, Billy 118
Edinburgh St Bernard's 43, 45, 94
Edinburgh University 41
Edwards, Carlos 247–8

Index

Elephant Tea Rooms 14
Elizabeth, Queen 125
Elliot, William 14, 18, 19, 26, 27
Elliott, Billy 137, 148, 165–6, 186, 187
Elliott, Shaun 183, 184, 194, 206, 247
Elliott, Stephen 236
Embleton, Elliot 291–2
England XI 188
England, Ernie 115
English Football League (EFL) Trophy win 288
Etuhu, Dickson 250
Evans, Ian 'Taff' 182
Evans, Jonny 246–7, 251
Evans, Laurie 143
Everton 57, 66, 67, 79, 126, 148, 154, 184, 191, 216, 227, 229, 230, 251, 262, 266, 274
Exeter City 119

FA Cup wins 62, 89, 118, 121, 124–5, 148, 162, 163, 168–79, 222
FA Women's Cup 253
FA Women's Premier League Cup win 253
FA Youth Cup wins 159
Faces, the 175
Fairfield 77
Featherstone, John 237
Fenton, R. 53
Ferdinand, Anton 251
Ferguson, Charlie 184
Ferguson, Derek 211
Ferguson, Matthew 93
Ferryhill 17–19, 29
Fickling, John 212, 214, 218, 219, 238
FIFA World Cup 121, 136, 150, 161, 173, 231, 245, 255
First World War 24, 98, 101, 106, 107–9, 283
Fleming, Charlie 137
Fletcher, Steven 264, 268
Flo, Tore André 232, 261
Fogarty, Amby 149
Football League Centenary Tournament 201, 207
Football League championship wins 61, 70, 71, 74, 79, 89, 92–3, 103, 105, 122–3
Ford, Peter 45, 213
Ford, Trevor 136, 137, 159, 249
Forest Green Rovers 243
Forster, Derek 156–7, 283

Forster, George 28
Fort Lauderdale Strikers 188
Fowler, James 285–6
Fraser, Willie 137
'Friendly Cup' 194–5
Fulham 164, 239, 295
Fulop, Marton, 247

Gabbiadini, Marco 201, 202, 203, 206
Gallacher, Patsy 120, 126
Galway United 250
Gainsborough Trinity 97
Gardner, Craig 256
Gates, Eric 196, 201, 202, 203
Gateshead 130
Gaudie, Norman 108
Gayle, Howard 185
Giaccherini, Emanuele 267, 269
Gibbons, Joseph Lake 18, 26–7
Gibson, Darron 275
Gibson, Will 51, 53, 84
Gilhooley, Michael 110, 112
Gillespie, James 58, 84, 85
Gillingham 197–8, 286
Given, Shay 215
Gladwin, Charlie 103
Glasgow Thistle 72
goal nets 21, 68–9
Gómez, Jordi 257
Gooch, Lynden 284, 286, 288, 295
Goodchild, Johnny 148
Goodman, Don 206
Gordon, Craig 249–50, 251
Gow, Donald 84
Grabban, Lewis 279
Graham, Danny 264
Grainger, Colin 128–9, 139, 147, 148, 149
Grand Hotel 67
Gray, Michael 216, 223–4, 227, 230
Gray, Phil 211
Grayson, Simon 278–9
Grayston, John 15–17, 18, 20, 33, 37, 57, 60, 102
Great Lever 35, 36–7
Greenwood, Sam 284
Gregoire, Roly 185
Grigg, Will 285
Grimsby Town 130, 285–6
Groves Field 30
Gurney, Bobby 71, 78, 101, 113, 114, 115, 118, 120, 121, 123, 125, 126, 292

313

Guthrie, Ron 163, 169, 174, 181, 204
Gyan, Asamoah 255, 256, 257

Halford, Greg 250
Hall, Alec 126
Hall, J.F. 21–2
Halliday, Dave 113–14, 116, 117, 121, 145
Halom, Vic 163, 169, 172–3, 174, 176, 180, 182, 204–5
Hamilton, Jimmy 283
Hamsterley Rangers 33
Hannah, David 66
Hannah, Jimmy 71, 78, 84, 125
Hardaker, Alan 141
Hardwick, George 158
Hardyman, Paul 202, 206
Harrow School 12
Harte, Ian 250
Hartley, James 50
Hartley, John 50
Hartnell, Sammy 106
Harvey, Martin 149, 154
Harvey, Stuart 294
Harvie (Harvey), John 57, 66, 69, 74, 82, 84
Hastings, Alex 119
Hastings, Andrew 45–6
Hawes, Arthur 110
Hawley, John 187
Hays, John 242
Healy, Colin 234
Healy, David 251
Heart of Midlothian 40, 79–80, 233
Hedley, Jack 137
Hellawell, Mike 161
Hemy, Thomas Marie Madawaska 76–7, 117, 141
Henderson, James 81
Henderson, John Potts 81, 82, 86
Henderson, Jordan 256–7
Hendon Board School 15–16, 24
Hendon Teachers' Football Club 23–4
Herd, George 151, 154, 177, 183
Hesford, Iain 197, 239
Hewitson, Luke 284
Heysel Stadium disaster 194, 208
Higginbotham, Danny 250
Hillsborough disaster 200, 205
Hindle, Reverend Robinson 35–6, 54–5, 59, 60
Hinnigan, Joe 187, 188

Hobson Wanderers 33
Hogg, Billy 99
Holden, Bill 138–9
Holden, Mel 183–4
Holley, George 99, 103–4
Holton, Jim 183
Honeyman, George 284
Hood, Harry 161
Hopper, Dave 265–6
Horswill, Micky 170–1, 181, 291
Houghton, Steph 253
Howey, Lee 215
Huddersfield Town 111–12, 126, 129–30, 138, 221–2
Huddlestone, Tom 267
Hudgell, Arthur 134
Huggins, Jack 106, 108
Hughes, Billy 167, 171, 172, 174, 175, 179, 180, 182, 183
Hugill, Joe 284
Hull City 269
Hume, Trai 295
Hunter, James 41
Hurley, Charlie 145, 147, 150, 154, 156, 157, 159–60, 168–9, 187, 217, 248, 250
Hutchison, Don 110, 229
Hylsop, Tommy 78
Hysen, Toby 247

illegal payments 95, 139–44
Ingham, Michael 236
Invest in Africa 263
Ipswich Town 149, 190, 192, 195
Irwin, Cec 147, 154, 283

Januzaj, Adnan 275
Jardine, James 19
Jarrow 33
Ji Dong-won 257, 263, 270
Jobling, Thomas 52
Johnson, Adam 264, 271
Johnson, Lee 288, 290, 292, 294
Johnston, Allan 216, 223, 225
Johnston, Harry 77
Jones, Harry 41
Jones, Jack 157
Jones, Kenwyne 250
Joyce 34

Kaboul, Younes 273, 274, 275, 276
Kavanagh, Graham 246

Index

Kay, John 201, 206
Keane, Roy 162, 227, 243, 245–6, 247, 248, 251, 252, 253, 290
Kelly, Bob 114
Kelly, David 214, 215, 216
Kennedy, Alan 81, 261
Kerr, Andy 154
Kerr, Bobby 167, 177, 181, 182, 183, 186
Kestrels 253
Khazri, Wahbi 274, 285
Kichenbrand, Don 148, 149
Kinnell, George 159
Kirchhoff, Jan 274, 276
Kirkley, Bill 64
Ki Sung-yueng 267
Knighton, Ken 187, 188, 189
Koné, Lamina 274, 275–6
Kyle, Bob 96–7, 98, 102, 109, 110, 111, 114, 115
Kyle, Kevin 261

Larsson, Seb 256, 257, 270
Laslandes, Lilian 230, 232, 261
Lawrence, Liam 236, 243, 257
League Cup final 268
Lee, Bob 182
Leeds United 128, 152, 154, 175, 176–8, 197, 246
Leicester City 156, 193, 215–16, 236–7, 246, 274
Leitch, Archibald 117, 124
Lennon, John 129
Lens, Jeremain 273
Leonard, Jimmy 'Hookey' 118
Lescott, Joleon 275
Leslie, Jimmy 87, 90
Lincoln City 147, 285, 288, 290, 295
Linthouse 40
Liverpool 83, 87, 90, 92, 97, 111, 118, 150, 162, 180, 189–90, 205, 217, 254, 257, 268, 271, 273
Lord, Jack 43
Loughlan, Tony 252
Louis-Dreyfus, Kyril 289–90, 291
Love, Donald 275
Low, Harry 103, 109
Lowrey, Paddy 159
Luton Town 138, 149, 163, 173–4, 181, 182, 248, 295

Macclesfield Town 220
MacFarlane, Ian 183

Mackie, Alex 91, 92, 95, 96, 97
MacPhail, John 201, 203
Madrid Select XI 122
Madrox Partners Limited 282
Maguire, Chris 284–5, 290
Maja, Josh 285
Makin, Chris 223
Malbranque, Steed 251
Malone, Dick 163, 177, 182, 183
Manchester City 103, 122, 126, 135, 138, 170–3, 203–4, 221, 229, 262–3, 267, 268, 269–70, 276
Manchester United 101, 131, 133, 145, 146, 155, 162, 182–3, 192, 227–8, 229–30, 232, 239, 254, 262–3, 268, 270
Mannone, Vito 267, 268, 269, 276, 277–8
Manquillo, Javier 275
Mapson, Johnny 123–4, 128, 133, 278
Marangoni, Claudio 187
Marr, James 34, 44, 53, 59, 60
Marriott, Andy 224
Marshall, Bobby 114
Martin, Bill 142, 143
Martin, Harry 102, 104
Matteo, Dominic 213, 270
maximum wage 95, 139–44
McAllister, Sandy 106
McAteer, Jason 234
McCann, Gavin 231, 233
McCarthy, Mick 233, 234, 236, 239, 245
McCartney, George 251
McCoist, Ally 190, 191
McColl, Ian 159, 160–1
McCombie, Andy 95, 96
McConnell, James 284
McCready, Andrew 77, 78
McCutcheon, J., 18
McDonagh, Seamus 259
McDonald, Jock 34, 37
McDonald, Joe 137
McDowall, Les 138
McGeady, Aiden 288
McGregor, William 58
McInally, Tommy 116, 134
McInroy, Albert 111, 115, 117, 178, 278
McLaughlin, Sandy 157
McMenemy, Laurie 162–3, 195, 196, 232, 245, 261
McMillan, James 24, 33–4, 41, 53, 60
McNab, Jim 147, 154

McNair, Paddy 275, 276, 284
McNamee, Ged 266
McNeill, Bob 77
McPheat, Willie 150, 151, 152, 177
McShane, Paul 250
Mead, Beth 253
Melody Maker 129
Melville, Andy 211
Merrington, Dave 186
Methven, Charlie 281-2, 283, 289-90
Middlesbrough 45, 47, 62, 94, 95, 100, 103, 109, 115, 127, 170, 211-12, 221, 276, 284
Middleton, Matt 123
Mika 275
Miliband, David 258-9, 265
Milkwell Burn 33
Millar, Jamie 66, 68, 71, 78, 88, 93
Miller, Liam 246
Mills, Ian 142
Millwall 125, 235
Milton, Albert 106
MK Dons 267
Monaghan, George 45-6, 47, 53
Montgomery, Jim 64, 81, 152, 154, 155, 159, 163, 168, 171, 173-4, 178, 182-3, 278
Mordue, Jackie 99
Morecambe 263
Morgan, Hugh 84
Morpeth Harriers 45, 47, 48, 64, 213
Mowbray Park 10, 11
Mowbray, Tony 294, 295, 296
Moyes, David 272, 274-7
Mulhall, George 154, 162, 177
Mullin, John 90, 217
Mumba, Bali 283, 284
Murray, Bill 115, 127, 128, 143, 231
Murray, Bob 81, 196-7, 200, 203, 206-7, 208, 212, 214, 218, 229, 237-8, 239, 240, 242, 262, 283
Murray, John 66
M'Vila, Yann 273, 276
Myhre, Thomas 236

N'Diaye, Alfred 264
Ndong, Didier 275, 276
Neil, Alex 290-1, 293-4
New Brompton 135
Newcastle East End 28, 35, 40
Newcastle Road 40, 41, 42, 67, 81-2, 87, 88-9, 220

Newcastle United 77-8, 90-1, 92, 93-4, 97, 99, 100, 102, 103, 108, 112, 137, 138-9, 143, 186, 187, 202, 226, 256, 257, 266, 268, 272, 273
Newcastle West End 28, 43, 44, 45, 47, 69-70
Newton Heath 74, 84
Norman, Tony 203, 204, 210
North Eastern 29, 30
Norfolk Hotel 11
Northampton Town 201
Northumberland and Durham FA 28-9
Northumbria Centre 238
Norwich Victoria 239
Norwich City 150, 153, 194, 203, 205, 226, 294
Nosworthy, Nyron 240, 246-7
Nottingham Forest 67, 88, 146, 216
Nottingham Rangers 43
Notts County 58, 59, 67-9, 70, 73, 84, 101, 168, 179, 193, 210
Notts Mellors 45
Núñez, Milton 231-2

Oakley, Arthur H. 142
O'Donovan, Roy 250
O'Hare, John 159, 161
Oliver, John 'Dowk' 58
Oliver, William 43
O'Neill, Martin 243, 259, 262, 263, 264-5
O'Nien, Luke 284, 295
Ord, Richard 216
Orient (Clapton/Leyton) 103, 152, 178, 179
O'Shea, John 257, 276, 283, 284
Oster, John 235
Oviedo, Bryan 275
Ovingham 27
Owers, Gary 206, 243
Oxford United 163, 173, 180

Palatine Hotel 108
Pantilimon, Costel 271
Parke, John 157, 160
Parker, Charlie 113, 117
Parkinson, Phil 286, 287
Partick Thistle 44
Paterson, Jock 110
Peacock, Andrew 50-1, 53
Peacock, Willie (Wallie) 50-1, 53
Pérez, Lionel 223, 224

Index

Peterborough 267–8
Philip, George 109
Phillips, Kevin 71, 184, 200, 220–1, 222, 223, 224, 226, 227, 228, 230, 231, 233, 241, 254
Pickering, Nick 191
Pickford, Jordan 276, 277–8
Pienaar, Steven 275
Pitt, Ritchie 162, 169, 175, 178, 181
Poom, Mart 231, 234
Porteous, Tom 58, 67
Porterfield, Ian 175, 178, 179, 181–2, 251, 288
Port Glasgow Athletic 38, 40
Portsmouth 143, 146, 167, 181, 227, 239, 284–5
Port Vale 201
Potts, Alderman 47, 65–6
Poyet, Gus 227, 268, 269, 271–2
Premier League formation 207–9
Premier Passions 217
Preston North End 48, 57, 62–3, 66–7, 70, 78, 90, 125, 135, 155, 167, 214–15, 233–4, 295
Prica, Rade 250
Pritchard, Alex 292
Proctor, Mark 197, 290
Professional Footballers' Association (PFA) 140
promotion
  to second tier 201, 290–3
  to top tier 154–6, 182, 188, 201–3, 214, 215, 224–5, 236–7, 245, 247–8
Purdon, Ted 137–8
Pye, Logan 284

Queen's Hotel 73, 97–8
Queens Park Rangers 163, 271–2, 293
Quinn, Niall 28, 56, 200, 204, 216, 220, 221, 226, 227, 229, 230, 231, 232, 233, 238–9, 240, 241–2, 243–5, 246, 247, 248, 249, 251, 253, 254, 258–60, 261, 262

Racing Club de Paris 120
Rae, Alex 216, 230
Raine, Walter 108
Ramsey, Stan 114
Rangers (Glasgow) 40, 42, 74
Rangers (Newcastle) 28
Reading 168–9, 221, 251, 264

Redcar 38, 41
Reid, Peter 199–200, 204, 213–15, 216, 217, 224, 225, 227, 229, 231–2
Reid, Andy 250
relegation
  to second tier 144, 145–6, 162, 185, 194, 203–4, 216, 233, 239
  to third tier 197–8, 279–80
Renton 44, 57, 62
Revie, Don 139, 148, 157, 177, 195
Reyna, Claudio 231
Richard, Cliff 129
Richardson, Joe 45–6
Richardson, Kevin 242
Richardson, Kieran 250, 256
Riera, Arnau 244
Ritchie, Tom 189
Ritson, Stan 143, 181
Riveros, Cristian 255, 256
Roberge, Valentin 267
Roberts (1880s) 28
Roberts, Hugh 233
Roberts, Patrick 291, 295
Robinson, Carl 236
Robinson, Graham 262
Robinson, Jackie 133
Robson, Bobby 187, 195
Robson, Bryan 'Pop' 193
Robson, Ned 110
Rodgerson, Ian 211
Rodwell, Jack 271
Roker 30
Roker Park 77, 86, 87, 89–90, 91, 93, 94, 97, 99, 102, 106, 109, 112, 117, 119, 121, 122, 124, 128, 129, 136, 138, 150, 155, 161, 171, 172, 191–2, 200, 207, 210–11, 215, 216–18, 220
Roose, Leigh Richmond 98, 100, 106, 134
Ross, Jack 284, 285
Rotherham United 148, 149, 201, 274
Rowell, Gary 184, 186, 192, 194
Rowlandson, Thomas 106
Ruiter, Robbin 278
Russell, Craig 214, 215

Saddington, Nigel 218
SAFC Limited 81
Saha, Louis 263
St Bede's 37
St James' Park 28, 94, 128

317

St John's (Middlesbrough) 40
Samson 224
Sartori, Juan 281, 289, 290
Saunders, Percy 129
Saxton, Bobby 195, 217, 243, 244
Sbragia, Ricky 251, 253-4
Scocco, Ignacio 269
Scott, Bill 158-9
Scott, Jill 253
Scott, Jock 66, 125
Scottish League XI 76
Scunthorpe United 149
Schwartz, Stefan 225, 227
Second World War 126, 127-30
Security Benefit Corporation (SBC) 282
Sedgefield 29
Sessègnon, Stéphane 266
Sewell, John 14, 18, 26, 27, 28
Sgt. Peppers Lonely Hearts Club Band (The Beatles) 128
Shackleton, Len 120, 134-5, 136, 137, 145, 157, 159, 230, 254
Shankhouse Black Watch 41, 42, 47
Sharkey, Nick 78, 149, 153, 154, 160-1
Shaw, John 106
Shearlaw, Adam 18, 19
Sheffield FC 9, 39, 41, 45
Sheffield Park Grange 45
(Sheffield) Wednesday 49, 59, 60, 89, 92, 94, 136, 147, 161, 170, 210, 227, 247, 290, 291
Sheffield United 87-8, 96, 110, 111, 119, 128, 148, 186, 196, 214, 222
Sheriff of London Shield 48, 94
Short, Ellis 251-2, 254, 255, 257, 258, 261-2, 263-4, 265, 272, 273, 274, 275, 277, 280, 281, 282, 283
Siddall, Barry 182, 186
Simms, Ellis 293
Singleton, Robert 14, 18, 19, 26, 28, 55, 60
Smart, Joe 41
Smith, Denis 200-1, 204
'Smith, Mr.' 139, 140, 141-2
Smith, Reuben 43
Smyrna Chapel 11
Sørensen, Thomas 224, 229, 231, 233
Southampton 133, 137, 191, 193, 227, 230, 295
Southend United 207, 214, 215, 244, 286
South Shields 109, 127-8

Spain, Jacob 42
Spain/Spanish XI 121-2
Speakman, Kristjaan 294
Spence, John 63, 66
Spennymoor 33
Sporting Lisbon 180-1, 269
Spuhler, Johnny 130
Stadium of Light 77, 89, 90, 200, 212-13, 215-16, 218-20, 221, 224-5, 227, 229, 238, 264, 265-6, 279
Stanley Star 30
Status Quo 220
Stead, Jon 240
Steele, Jason 278
Stein, Jock 157
Stelling, Jack 135
Stephenson, Luca 284
Stewart, Marcus 236
Stewart, Rod 175
Stewart, Ross 292
Stobart, George 28
Stockdale, Robbie 274, 279, 283
stock exchange
 flotation 217
 leaving 235
Stoke (City) 59, 65-6, 119, 183, 189, 196, 237, 293-4
Stokes, Anthony 247
Stokoe, Bob 163, 165, 166, 167, 168, 169, 172, 174, 175, 176, 177, 178, 180, 182, 197, 205, 235, 254, 269
Stubbins, Albert 128
Stubbs, Alan 274
Suggett, Colin 159, 162
Summerbee, Nicky 221, 226
Sunderland Albion 9, 47, 48, 49-55, 60, 64, 67-8, 72
Sunderland and District Teachers' Association 15, 16, 19, 20, 24
Sunderland Rovers 14, 20-1, 47
Sunderland Rugby Club 12, 76
Sunderland 'Til I Die 62, 280
Swansea Town/City 150, 268
Swindon Town 103, 202-3, 209
Symons, Kit 221

Tainio, Teemu 251
Taylor, Andrew 288
Taylor, Ernie 148
Taylor, F.W. 31, 76, 97, 113
Taylor, John Thomas 18
Taylor Report 200, 207

Index

'Team of All The Talents' 58, 61–85, 121, 132
Test Matches 83–4, 90
Thome, Emerson 110, 229, 231
Thompson, Charles Edward 81
Thompson, Robert 44, 81
Thomson, Charlie (1910s) 100–1, 104, 109, 119
Thomson, Charlie (1930s) 119
Thorpe, Jimmy 119, 123
Tinsley, Walter 104, 105
Todd, Colin 159
Todd, Sinclair 95, 97
Toivonen, Ola 273
Tottenham Hotspur 126, 138, 150–1, 194, 250
Towers, Tony 170, 171, 181, 185
Tranmere Rovers 228, 286, 288
Tueart, Dennis 162, 163, 169, 171, 172, 175, 179, 180, 181
Turnbull, Colonel 76
Turnbull, Ronnie 134
Turner, Chris 187, 194, 195
Turner, Michael 255
Tyne 30
Tyne and Wear Development Corporation (TWDC) 212
Tyzack, Sam 53, 57, 60

Usher, Brian 154
Ustari 269

van Aanholt, Patrick 275
Vancouver Royal Canadians 160
van Lingen, Bert 272
Varga, Stanislav 229, 246
Vasas 180
Vaughan, David 257
Vaux brewery 224
Venison, Barry 191
Vergini, Santiago 269

Wakeham, Peter 148, 155
Walker, Clive 194, 206
Wallace, Ross 246
Wallace, William Thwaites 24, 25, 34, 46, 50, 51–2, 53, 54, 108
Walsall 152, 227
Wanless, Louise 244, 265
Watford 226
Watmore, Duncan 266
Watson, Alexander 91

Watson, Dave 163, 165–6, 168, 169, 174, 180, 181, 204, 214
Watson, Edward Guy 18, 19, 27
Watson, Jimmy 95
Watson, Tom 57, 60, 75, 80–81, 82, 83, 90, 92, 95, 108
Watson, Willie 133, 135, 136
Wear Bridge 117–18
Wearmouth (Monkwearmouth) Colliery 199, 212, 215, 265
Wearside League XI 93
Weddle, Derek 143
West Bromwich Albion 58, 65, 73, 112, 139, 245, 267, 270
West, Colin 191, 206, 270
West Ham United 188, 204, 228, 229, 237, 256
Whitburn Cricket Club 29
Whitburn Street (Monkwearmouth) Workmen's Hall 42, 47
Whitehead, Dean 236, 240, 248
Whitelum, Cliff 130, 133
Whitley, Jeff 234–5
Whitmore, Moira 218
Wickham, Connor 257, 269, 270
Wigan Athletic 201, 256, 257–8, 264
Wilkinson, Howard 232–3
Williams, Billy 115
Wilson, Hugh 74, 78, 88, 91
Wilson, Samuel 81, 117
Wimbledon 216
Withe, Peter 196
Wolesey (pub) 31
Wolverhampton Wanderers 63, 70, 124, 126, 128, 136, 137–8, 258, 283
Wood, Graham 207, 213
Woods, Martin 257
Woodward, Frank 18
Wrexham 183, 186
Wright, Arthur 157
Wright, Bailey 292–3
Wycombe Wanderers 291–2
Wyke, Charlie 288
Wylde, Rodger 197

Yeovil Town 135
Yorke, Dwight 246
Yorston, Benny 119
Young, David 163, 169

Zenden, Bolo 255